GREAT
WRITING 5

From Great Essays to Research

THIRD EDITION

KEITH S. FOLSE
UNIVERSITY OF CENTRAL FLORIDA

TISON PUGH
UNIVERSITY OF CENTRAL FLORIDA

Australia • Canada • Mexico • Singapore • Spain • United Kingdom • United States

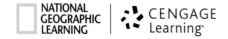

Great Writing 5:
From Great Essays to Research
Third Edition
Keith S. Folse, Tison Pugh

Publisher: Sherrise Roehr

Executive Editor: Laura Le Dréan

Assistant Editor: Vanessa Richards

Director of Global Marketing: Ian Martin

Product Marketing Managers:
Anders Bylund, Lindsey Miller

Director of Content and Media Production:
Michael Burggren

Production Manager: Daisy Sosa

Senior Print Buyer: Mary Beth Hennebury

Cover Design:
Christopher Roy and Michael Rosenquest

Cover Image: Ken Canning/Getty Images

Interior Design: Aysling Design

Composition: PreMediaGlobal, Inc.

U.S. Edition

ISBN-13: 978-1-285-19496-7

International Student Edition

ISBN-13: 978-1-285-75063-7

National Geographic Learning / Cengage Learning
20 Channel Center Street
Boston, MA 02210
USA

Cengage Learning is a leading provider of customized learning solutions with office locations around the globe, including Singapore, the United Kingdom, Australia, Mexico, Brazil, and Japan. Locate your local office at:
International.cengage.com/region

Cengage Learning products are represented in Canada by Nelson Education, Ltd.

Visit NGL online at **NGL.Cengage.com**

Visit our corporate website at **cengage.com**

Printed in the United States of America
3 4 5 6 7 19 18 17 16

Contents

Scope and Sequence

Unit	Writing	Grammar for Writing	Building Better Vocabulary	Original Student Writing
1 p. 2 **WHAT IS AN ESSAY?**	• How Is an Essay Organized? • Common Essay Forms • Example Essays • How Do You Write an Introduction? • What Is the Role of the Thesis Statement? • What Is in the Body of an Essay? • Connectors and Transition Words • What Does the Conclusion of an Essay Do?		• Practicing Three Kinds of Vocabulary from Context: Synonyms, Antonyms, and Collocations	**Original Student Writing:** Write an essay practicing the steps. **Photo Topic:** Write about the accomplishments you hope to achieve in your life. **Timed Writing Topic:** Write about a famous person you would like to meet.
2 p. 32 **UNDERSTANDING THE WRITING PROCESS: THE SEVEN STEPS**	• The Writing Process • Step 1: Choose a Topic • Step 2: Brainstorm • Step 3: Outline • Step 4: Write the First Draft • Step 5: Get Feedback from a Peer • Step 6: Revise the First Draft • Example Essay • Step 7: Proofread the Final Draft		• Practicing Three Kinds of Vocabulary from Context: Synonyms, Antonyms, and Collocations	**Original Student Writing:** Write an essay practicing the steps. **Photo Topic:** Write about an adventure you have had. **Timed Writing Topic:** Write your opinion about whether all students should study a foreign language.
3 p. 52 **PARAPHRASING, SUMMARIZING, SYNTHESIZING, AND CITING SOURCES**	• Using Information from Sources • Methods of Citing Sources in Your Paper • Avoiding Plagiarism • Paraphrasing, Summarizing, Synthesizing			**Original Student Writing:** Write an essay using two original sources. **Photo Topic:** Write about three international foods. **Timed Writing Topic:** Write about why teaching kindergarten is a difficult job.

Overview

About the *Great Writing* Series

Framed by engaging **National Geographic** images, the new edition of the *Great Writing* series helps students write better sentences, paragraphs, and essays. The new *Foundations* level meets the needs of low-level learners through practice in basic grammar, vocabulary, and spelling, while all levels feature clear explanations, student writing models, and meaningful practice opportunities. The new edition of the *Great Writing* series is perfect for beginning to advanced learners, helping them develop and master academic writing skills.

Great Writing: Foundations focuses on basic sentence construction, emphasizing grammar, vocabulary, spelling, and composition.

Great Writing 1 focuses on sentences as they appear in paragraphs.

Great Writing 2 teaches paragraph development.

Great Writing 3 transitions from paragraphs to essays.

Great Writing 4 focuses on essays.

Great Writing 5 practices more advanced essays, including research papers.

The earliest ESL composition textbooks were merely extensions of ESL grammar classes. The activities in these books did not practice English composition as much as ESL grammar points. Later books, on the other hand, tended to focus too much on the composing process. We feel that this focus ignores the important fact that the real goal for English learners is both to produce a presentable product and to understand the composing process. From our experience with ESL, foreign language, and native-speaking English writers, we believe that the *Great Writing* series allows English learners to achieve this goal.

Great Writing 5: From Great Essays to Research provides guided instruction and extensive practical exercises and activities in essay writing at the advanced level, including 18 essays and a research paper with cited and documented sources. At this advanced level, we assume that students can write good paragraphs and that what they need is instruction in, modeling of, and guidance with writing essays. The instruction in this book covers the essay format, introductions with a strong thesis statement, body paragraphs with relevant supporting details, and solid concluding paragraphs. A strong emphasis is placed on using sources in essays, including paraphrasing, summarizing, and synthesizing that new material, as well as citing relevant sources both in the essays and in the end reference lists. This book contains a wide variety of exercises that offer practice in both working with the writing process and developing an appropriate final written product.

The heart of this book lies in the concept that students will learn to become better writers by learning to become better editors of their own essays and of their peers' essays. Just as professional writers have editors to help them hone their prose, student writers also need helpful guidance throughout the writing process—from brainstorming, outlining, and drafting to the final product.

This book is designed for advanced students. Depending on the class level and the amount of writing that is done outside of class hours, there is enough material for 60 to 80 classroom hours. Provided that enough writing is done outside of the classroom, the number of hours can be as few as 40.

Organization

Great Writing 5 contains eight units. Units 1–3 explain how to write an advanced essay, including the citation of sources. Units 4–7 focus on four specific rhetorical modes—process, comparison, cause-effect, and argument. Unit 8 concludes the book with instruction in how to write a research paper.

Unit 1 explains the basic features of all essays. Unit 2 explains a proven seven-step process for writing an essay. Unit 3 teaches students the valuable writing skills of paraphrasing, summarizing, and synthesizing, as well as how to incorporate and cite sources in their papers. These three units form the basis for all essay writing in this book.

Units 4–7 practice writing process, comparison, cause-effect, and argument essays. While it is not necessary to cover these units in numerical order, doing so will allow for recycling of vocabulary and grammar points.

Unit 8 teaches how to write a research paper. This unit starts with identifying a suitable topic, explains the use and citing of sources, and ends with an annotated example research paper.

The *Brief Writer's Handbook with Activities* and the *Appendix* contain additional practice material to support both the process and the mechanics of writing.

Contents of a Unit

Although each unit has specific writing objectives (listed at the beginning of the unit), the following features appear in every unit:

Example Essays

Because we believe that writing and reading are inextricably related, the 19 example essays model a rhetorical mode and/or provide editing activities. All models are preceded by schema-building questions and are followed by questions about organization, syntactic structures, or other composition features. Reflecting the academic nature of this book, all essays have two to five citations in the text and a reference list at the end.

Grammar for Writing

Since good writing requires a working knowledge of the mechanics of English, *Great Writing 5* includes clear charts or detailed instruction that relates directly to the writing assignments. In addition, numerous activities give students the opportunity to practice and refine their grammar and writing knowledge and skills.

Vocabulary

New, potentially unfamiliar vocabulary words are glossed in the margins of each essay. These words can provide students with a list of vocabulary to add to a separate vocabulary notebook. In this advanced composition book, the essays use about 60 percent of the 570 words of the Academic Word List (see pages 230–231 for a complete list).

Building Better Vocabulary

After each essay, a special vocabulary activity practices three kinds of vocabulary from context: synonyms, antonyms, and collocations. An extensive knowledge of synonyms and antonyms is necessary for paraphrasing original material as well as for producing cohesive writing. Learning specific word combinations, or collocations, will improve student writing greatly. This allows students to build connections to more words and thus to grow their vocabulary more quickly. It is helpful to encourage students to use these new words in their Original Student Writing assignment and to add them to their vocabulary notebook.

Activities

The new third edition contains numerous activities, suggestions for additional essay writing assignments, and supplemental activities in the *Brief Writer's Handbook with Activities*. These writing, grammar, and vocabulary activities gradually build the skills students need to write well-crafted essays and provide learners with more input in English composition and paragraph organization and cohesion. To this end, the activities in this book deal with elements that affect the quality of a written product, including grammar, organization, and logic. Although in this text there is information about both process and product in essay writing, it should be noted that the focus is slightly more on the final written product.

Writer's Notes

Great Writing 5 features writing advice that helps writers to better understand language use and composition formatting.

Building Better Sentences

In Units 4–7, students are asked to turn to the *Appendix* and work on building better sentences. Each practice is intentionally short and includes only three problems. In each problem, there are two to six short sentences that the students must combine into a single sentence that expresses all the ideas in a logical and grammatically correct manner. This task is excellent for group work.

Original Student Writing

Each unit includes an activity that requires students to practice some form of writing. Original Student Writing includes writing prompts and a set of directions to encourage students to follow the writing process and refer back to the lessons taught in the unit.

Additional Writing Topics gives students the opportunity to continue practicing their writing skills. The first topic always links back to the opening photograph and writing prompt. The teacher can decide whether all students will write about the same topic or whether each student is free to choose any of the topics listed.

Peer Editing

At the end of each unit, a peer editing activity offers students the opportunity to provide written comments to one another with the goal of improving their essays. Peer editing sheets for each unit can be found at NGL.Cengage.com/GW5. They provide the guidance and structure necessary for students at this level to perform this task successfully. There is also a sample peer editing sheet in Unit 2 on pages 42–43. We recommend that students spend 15 to 20 minutes reading a classmate's essay and writing comments using the questions on the peer editing sheet.

Timed Writing

One way to improve students' comfort level with the task of writing under a deadline, such as during a test, is to provide them with numerous writing opportunities that are timed. The final activity in Units 1–7 features a timed-writing prompt geared toward the grammar and sentence structures presented in that unit. Students are given five minutes to read the prompt and make a quick writing plan, followed by 40 minutes of actual writing. Instructors may use this activity at any time during the lesson.

What's New in This Edition and Series?

- Engaging photographs from *National Geographic* connect learning to the greater world.

- New and updated essays act as springboards and models for writing.

- Updated Grammar for Writing sections clearly present grammar and help students learn the structures for writing.

- Streamlined instruction and practice activities offer step-by-step guidelines to focus writers on both the writing process and product.

- Extensive use of words from the Academic Word List in all essays and vocabulary activities encourages students to expand their word knowledge.

- The *Brief Writer's Handbook with Activities* now includes a Useful Vocabulary for Better Writing section to help writers choose appropriate language for the different rhetorical modes.

- An all-new level, *Great Writing: Foundations* introduces students to the basics of grammar, spelling, and vocabulary.

- New units in *Great Writing 5: From Great Essays to Research* prepare writers for college-level research papers with instruction in citing sources, paraphrasing, summarizing, and synthesizing.

- A new Online Workbook encourages learners to further practice grammar, vocabulary, and editing skills. Students can also write paragraphs or essays, and submit them to the instructor electronically.

- An updated Presentation Tool allows instructors to use the book in an interactive whiteboard setting and demonstrate the editing process.

- An eBook provides another option to use *Great Writing* in a traditional or blended learning environment.

Ancillary Components

In addition to the *Great Writing 5: From Great Essays to Research* Student Book, the following components help both the instructor and the students expand their teaching and learning.

- **Online Workbook:** Includes a wealth of vocabulary, grammar, writing, and editing practice with immediate feedback.

- **Presentation Tool CD-Rom:** Offers instructors the ability to lead whole-class presentations and demonstrate the editing process.

- **Assessment CD-ROM with ExamView®:** Allows instructors to create and customize tests.

- **Teacher Companion Site at NGL.Cengage.com/GW5:** Provides teachers with answer keys, peer editing sheets, and teacher's notes.

- **Student Companion Site at NGL.Cengage.com/GW5:** Provides students with peer editing sheets, glossary, and interactive flashcards.

- **eBook:** Offers an interactive option.

Framed by engaging **National Geographic** images, the new edition of the *Great Writing* series helps students write better sentences, paragraphs, and essays. *Great Writing 5* now also prepares students to write research papers with clear explanations, student writing models, and meaningful practice opportunities. With an all-new level, *Great Writing Foundations*, the *Great Writing* series is the perfect six-level writing solution for all learners from beginning to advanced.

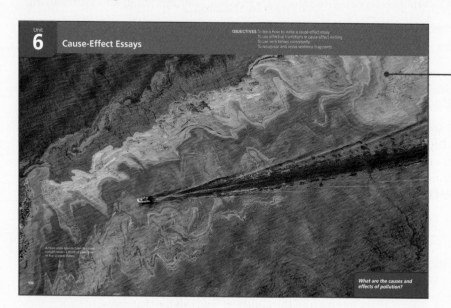

Inspiring **National Geographic** images provide an engaging foundation for student writing.

Structured activities help students practice writing, grammar, and editing.

19 Example Essays focus on specific writing skills and rhetorical modes.

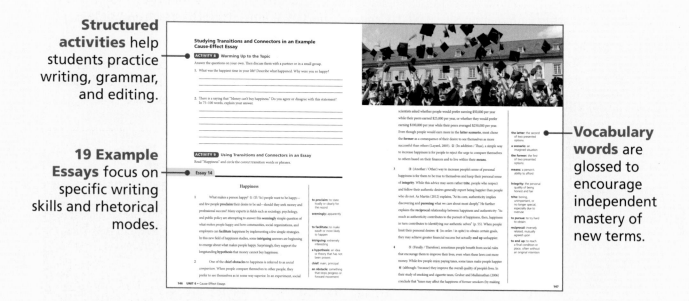

Vocabulary words are glossed to encourage independent mastery of new terms.

Inside a Unit

Grammar for Writing

Consistent Verb Tense Usage

Good writers are careful to use the same verb tense throughout an essay. While it is true that an essay may have, for example, some information about the past and some information about the present, most of the information will be about one time, most likely either past or present. Do not change verb tenses without a specific reason for doing so.

Explanation	Examples
When describing an event in the past tense, maintain the past tense throughout your explanation.	In our experiment, we **placed** three live fresh-water plants (each approximately 20 centimeters in length) into a quart jar that **was filled** with fresh water at 70 degrees Fahrenheit. We **left** the top two centimeters of the jar with air. We then carefully **added** a medium goldfish.
When talking about facts that are always true, use present tense in your explanation.	The sun **is** the center of the solar system. The earth and other planets **revolve** around the sun. Most of the planets **have** at least one moon that **circles** the planet, and these moons **vary** tremendously in size, just as the planets **do**.
In writings such as a report, it is possible to have different verb tenses reflecting different times.	According to this report, the police now **believe** that two men **stole** the truck and the money in it.

Grammar for Writing

New **Grammar for Writing** charts provide clear explanations and examples, giving learners easy access to the structures they will use in their writing.

Building Better Vocabulary

Practicing Three Kinds of Vocabulary from Context activities highlight words from the Academic Word List and help students to apply and expand their vocabulary and knowledge of important collocations.

Building Better Vocabulary

ACTIVITY 10 Practicing Three Kinds of Vocabulary from Context

Read each important vocabulary word or phrase. Locate it in the essay if you need help remembering the word or phrase. Then circle the best synonym, antonym, or collocation from column A, B, or C.

Type of Vocabulary	Important Vocabulary	A	B	C
Synonyms	1. pursue	chase	mount	overlook
	2. obstacle	difficulty	extinction	forecast
	3. authentic	challenging	likely	real
	4. scenario	demeanor	example	verification
Antonyms	5. intriguing	accurate	uninteresting	worthwhile
	6. the former	the incentive	the latter	the organizer
	7. hinder	facilitate	navigate	range
	8. chief	essential, vital	far, remote	minor, lesser
Collocations	9. the means ___ something	do	doing	to do
	10. care about something ___	deeply	happily	tritely
	11. my overall ___ of	core	example	impression
	12. obtain a ___	desire	goal	tax

Original Student Writing: Cause-Effect Essay

In this section, you will follow the seven steps in the writing process to write a cause-effect essay. If you need help, refer to Unit 2, pages 34–46.

ACTIVITY 15 Step 1: Choose a Topic

Your first step is to choose a topic for your essay. For a cause-effect essay, you want to choose a topic for which you can develop three causes of one effect or three effects from one cause. Your teacher may assign a topic, you may think of one yourself, or you may choose one from the suggestions in the chart. As you consider possible topics, ask yourself, "What do I know about this topic? What do my readers know? What else do I need to know? Do I need to research this topic?"

Humanities	Literature: The effects of writing a novel on a computer
	History: The causes of an important historical event such as World War I
	Philosophy: The effects of Socrates on modern thought
Sciences	Biology: The causes of cancer
	Geology: The effects of burning oil and gas
	Meteorology: The causes of climate change
Business	Economics: The causes of inflation
Personal	The effects of your attitude toward challenges in life

Original Student Writing gives students the chance to combine the grammar, vocabulary, and writing skills together in one writing piece.

Peer Editing activities increase awareness of commonly made errors and help students become better writers and editors.

Timed Writing prepares students for success on standardized and high-stakes writing exams.

Timed Writing

How quickly can you write in English? There are many times when you must write quickly, such as on a test. It is important to feel comfortable during those times. Timed-writing practice can make you feel better about writing quickly in English.

1. Read the essay guidelines below. Then take out a piece of paper.

2. Read the writing prompt below the guidelines.

3. Write a basic outline including either **one cause** and more than one effect or a few causes and **one effect**. You should spend no more than five minutes on your outline.

4. Write a five-paragraph essay.

5. You have 40 minutes to write your essay.

Cause-Effect Essay Guidelines

- Use the focus-on-causes or the focus-on-effects organization for this essay. Do not write about multiple causes and multiple effects.
- Remember to give your essay a title.
- Double-space your essay.
- Write as legibly as possible (if you are not using a computer).
- Include a short introduction (with a thesis statement), three body paragraphs, and a conclusion.
- Try to give yourself a few minutes before the end of the activity to review your work. Check for mistakes in spelling and consistent verb tense, and look for sentence fragments.

We all face personal troubles in our lives. Think about a recent challenging situation in your life at home, at work, at school, or with friends. What were the causes of this situation? What were its effects? Although you will discuss both causes and effects, remember to emphasize either the causes of the situation or the effects of the situation.

The **Brief Writer's Handbook with Activities** includes many resources for the developing writer, including a new **Useful Vocabulary for Better Writing** section.

Brief Writer's Handbook with Activities

Technology

Great Writing 5: From Great Essays to Research

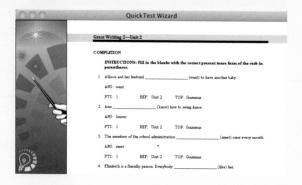

For Instructors:

Assessment CD-ROM with ExamView® allows instructors to create and customize tests and quizzes easily.

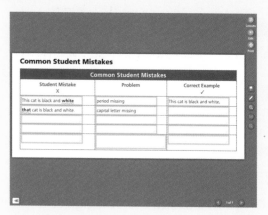

Presentation Tool CD-ROM contains time-saving, interactive activities from the student book, a set of whiteboard tools, and additional content to help the teacher guide learners through the editing process.

Teacher's Notes, Answer Keys, and Peer Editing Sheets are available online for instructors.

For Students:

The Online Workbook: Powered by MyELT, this independent student resource features instructor-led and self-study options and includes additional vocabulary, grammar, writing, and editing practice with immediate feedback.

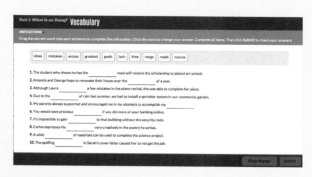

Great Writing eBooks are available for all levels and are compatible with tablets, laptops, and smartphones.

Acknowledgements

We would like to thank the hundreds of ESL and English composition colleagues who have generously shared their ideas, insights, and feedback on second language writing, university English course requirements, and textbook design.

We would also like to thank our editors at National Geographic Learning, Laura LeDréan, Thomas Jefferies, and Vanessa Richards for their guidance. We are extremely grateful for the support given to us by our development editor Kathleen Smith. We also remain forever grateful to our previous editors at Houghton Mifflin—Susan Maguire and Kathy Sands-Boehmer—for their indispensable guidance throughout the birth and growth of this writing project.

As well, we are indebted to the following reviewers who offered ideas and suggestions that shaped our revisions:

Laura Taylor, Iowa State University, Iowa
Mary Barratt, Iowa State University, Iowa
Abdelhay Belfakir, University of Central Florida, Florida
Taoufik Ferjani, Zayed University, United Arab Emirates
Cheryl Alcorn, Pasadena City College, California
Paul McGarry, Santa Barbara City College, California
Fernanda Ortiz, University of Arizona, Arizona
Michelle Jeffries, University of Arkansas – Fayetteville, Arkansas
Suzanne Medina, California State University – Dominguez Hills, California
Kristi Miller, American English Institute, California
Kevin Van Houten, Glendale Community College, California
Izabella Kojic-Sabo, University of Windsor, Canada
Wayne Fong, Aston School, China
Yiwei Shu, New Oriental School, China
Raul Billini, John F. Kennedy Institute of Languages, Dominican Republic
Rosa Vasquez, John F. Kennedy Institute of Languages, Dominican Republic
Mike Sfiropoulos, Palm Beach State College, Florida
Louise Gobron, Georgia State University, Georgia
Gabriella Cambiasso, City College of Chicago – Harold Washington, Illinois
Lin Cui, Harper College, Illinois
Laura Aoki, Kurume University, Japan
Rieko Ashida, Konan University, Japan
Greg Holloway, Kyushu Institute of Technology, Japan
Collin James, Kansai Gaigo University, Japan
Lindsay Mack, Ritsumeikan Asia Pacific University, Japan
Robert Staehlin, Morioka University, Japan
Jenny Selvidge, Donnelly College, Kansas
Phan Vongphrachanh, Donnelly College, Kansas
Virginia Van Hest Bastaki, Kuwait University, Kuwait
Jennifer Jakubic, Century College, Minnesota
Trina Goslin, University of Nevada – Reno, Nevada
Margaret Layton, University of Nevada – Reno, Nevada
Amy Metcalf, University of Nevada – Reno, Nevada
Gail Fernandez, Bergen Community College, New Jersey
Lynn Meng, Union County College – Elizabeth, New Jersey

Zoe Isaacson, Queens College, New York
Sherwin Kizner, Queens College, New York
Linnea Spitzer, Portland State University, Oregon
Jennifer Stenseth, Portland State University, Oregon
Rebecca Valdovinos, Oregon State University, Oregon
Renata Ruff, Prince Mohammed University, Saudi Arabia
Ya Li Chao, National Taichung University of Science and Technology, Taiwan
Kuei-ping Hsu, National Tsing Hua University, Taiwan
Morris Huang, National Taiwan University of Science and Technology, Taiwan
Cheng-Che Lin, Tainan University of Technology, Taiwan
Rita Yeh, Chia Nan University of Pharmacy and Science, Taiwan
Nguyen Chanh Tri, Vietnam Australia International School, Vietnam
Mai Minh Tien, Vietnam Australia International School, Vietnam
Tuan Nguyen, Vietnam Australia International School, Vietnam
Nguyen Thi Thanh The, Vietnam Australia International School, Vietnam
Nguyen Vu Minh Phuong, Vietnam Australia International School, Vietnam
Colleen Comidy, Seattle Central Community College, Washington
Cindy Etter, University of Washington, Washington
Kris Hardy, Seattle Central Community College, Washington
Liese Rajesh, Seattle Central Community College, Washington

Finally, many thanks go to our ESL and native-speaking students who have taught us what advanced composition ought to be. Without them, this work would have been impossible.

Keith S. Folse
Tison Pugh

Photo Credits

When a man has done what he considers to be his duty to his people and his country, he can rest in peace. I believe I have made that effort and that is, therefore, why I will sleep for the eternity.

A street artist completes a mural of Nelson Mandela in Cape Town, South Africa.

What accomplishments do you hope to achieve in your life?

How Is an Essay Organized?

ESSAY	a short written composition on one subject that expresses the views of the writer

In an **essay,** a writer shares his or her thoughts about a topic with an audience—a teacher, fellow students, or the world beyond the classroom. An essay expresses the writer's point of view. In this book, you will study how to communicate your ideas effectively through essays and longer papers.

Although essays vary greatly in their subject matter and style of writing, the most common academic essays share a similar structure. They are usually made up of at least five paragraphs organized in three basic parts: an **introduction**, a **body**, and a **conclusion**.

INTRODUCTION	Paragraph 1
BODY	Paragraph 2
	Paragraph 3
	Paragraph 4
	(Additional paragraphs, depending on the assignment or the complexity of the topic)
CONCLUSION	Paragraph 5

There are many different ways to write an essay. The method that a writer chooses is often determined by the **topic**, the **purpose**, and the **audience**. Good writers consider these three elements when writing any type of essay.

The writer needs to consider what kind of essay will convey his or her ideas in the clearest and most accurate way. This book contains examples of four common kinds of essays: **process** (Unit 4), **comparison** (Unit 5), **cause-effect** (Unit 6), and **argument** (Unit 7).

Students in a writing class usually practice one kind of essay at a time. For example, you may write a comparison essay that discusses two plans. However, outside a writing class, it is rare for an essay to be completely one kind.

In fact, many essays are actually a combination of different kinds of essays. For example, an essay titled "Two Plans for the Future of Our City" may have a paragraph that compares two plans of action (comparison-contrast), a paragraph that discusses the effects of each plan (cause-effect), and then a paragraph that attempts to persuade the reader that one plan is better than the other (argument). If you learn how to write these different kinds of essays, you will also be able to write a mixed essay effectively. In addition, you will be better able to write a much longer composition, such as a research paper.

	Essay with One Type of Writing	Essay with Different Types of Writing
Title	*Two Plans for the Future of Our City*	*Two Plans for the Future of Our City*
Type of Essay	comparison	mixed
Purpose	to show the differences between Plan A and Plan B	to compare plans, to show the effect of each plan, and to persuade readers that one plan is better.
Organization	1. Introduction		1. Introduction	
	Body	2. Compare the objectives of Plan A and Plan B.	**Body**	2. Compare Plan A and Plan B.
		3. Compare the costs of Plan A and Plan B.		3. Discuss the effects of Plan A and Plan B.
		4. Compare the feasibility of Plan A and Plan B.		4. Persuade readers why Plan B will benefit us more.
	5. Conclusion		5. **Conclusion:** Plan B is better than Plan A for these reasons …	

Common Essay Forms

The most common essay form taught in textbooks is the five-paragraph essay. This form has a very simple, clear organization, yet it allows writers tremendous freedom to explain their ideas on a topic. The traditional classroom assignment is also a five-paragraph essay. In this form, the introduction is paragraph one; the body includes paragraphs two, three, and four; and the conclusion is paragraph five.

Though many people first learn to write a five-paragraph essay, an essay can have as many paragraphs as the writer thinks are necessary. The only requirement is that an essay should have a beginning, a middle, and an ending. If you understand how to write an essay with a clear introduction, a detailed body, and a logical conclusion, you can easily include more paragraphs that address increasingly complex and sophisticated ideas. The goal is to understand the organization of an essay and write a good one, no matter the number of paragraphs.

For more complex subjects, writers often choose to write a **research paper**. A research paper uses ideas and material from other sources, in addition to your own ideas. A research paper is usually measured in number of pages or number of words, not just paragraphs. You will study research papers in Unit 8.

ACTIVITY 1 **Studying an Example Essay**

This essay is about voting. Discuss the Preview Questions with a partner. Then read the example essay and answer the questions that follow.

Preview Questions

1. Have you ever voted? If so, what was the process like?

2. How safe do you think elections are? Is there any chance that someone could change the outcome of an election?

3. How do you think voting may change in the next fifty years?

Against E-Voting

1   The computer, which is the most important advance in modern communication technology, is in fact a **threat** to our democratic elections. With computer technology advancing daily, many activities that used to require many long hours can now be **accomplished** in a few minutes and sometimes even seconds. For the most part, these technological **innovations** promise to save time and money and to make people's lives easier and more comfortable, but not every aspect of life should be taken care of by computers. In particular, societies should not vote with computers or other electronic media because elections are too important to trust to cyberspace.

2   In years past, people voted on paper **ballots** and marked them with ink or some similar means. Voters could look over their ballots to ensure that they did not make a mistake. Also, when there was a **dispute** over the results of an election, paper ballots allowed election officials to count votes by hand. This process was **tedious**, but the results could be easily **verified** to see if there were any **deviations** between vote tallies. Several countries still use this traditional system of voting, and it provides a **crucial** foundation for ensuring fairness.

a threat: a danger

to accomplish: to complete; to do

an innovation: something new

a ballot: a piece of paper used for voting

a dispute: a disagreement

tedious: boring or tiresome because of length or dullness

to verify: to check for accuracy

a deviation: an action, behavior, or result different from what is expected

crucial: essential; necessary

3   Without this traditional system of voting, however, voters do not really know whether e-voting systems count their votes accurately. It is quite possible that a computer programmer could develop a program so that a person could select one candidate on a computer screen, yet the vote would be counted for another candidate. Although some people might think this scenario sounds unlikely, serious problems with computer security have occurred throughout the world. The simple fact is that hackers can gain access to many computer systems for illegal purposes. By illegally entering an online polling site, they could easily change the **outcome** of an election. Citizens should also question whether electronic voting **enhances** the voting process. As Celeste, Thornburgh, and Lin (2006) point out, "the desirability of electronic voting systems should be judged on the basis of whether their use will **significantly** improve the process of election administration" (p. 131). As the old saying tells us, "If something isn't broken, don't fix it."

an outcome: a result

to enhance: to improve

significantly: greatly

4   If government officials decide to use electronic voting machines, they should ensure that all voters receive receipts for their votes that could then be collected for **subsequent** verification. These paper receipts would clearly state that the voters really voted for the candidates that they selected. Furthermore, if any candidate suspects that an election is unfair, these receipts could be counted by hand and checked against the results that the computers provided. At the very least, as Alvarez and Hall (2008) argue, voting should be a simple, secure, and consistent process, regardless of the voting procedure that is being used.

subsequent: next; following

5   Computer technologies have improved the quality of our lives **vastly**, but these technologies are not a cure for all of society's problems. Sometimes a little more human work ensures a better, more precise result. Since voting is critically important to the effective and honest working of society, citizens should rely on a much older technology—paper and ink—rather than on computers for all elections.

vastly: greatly

References

Alvarez, R. M., & Hall, T. (2008). *Electronic elections: The perils and promises of digital democracy*. Princeton, NJ: Princeton University Press.

Celeste, R., Thornburgh, D., & Lin, H. (Eds.). (2006). *Asking the right questions about electronic voting*. Washington, DC: National Academy Press.

Post-Reading

1. Write the number(s) of the introduction paragraph(s). _____

2. Write the number(s) of the body paragraph(s). _____

3. Write the number(s) of the conclusion paragraph(s). _____

4. A good opening paragraph often grabs the reader's attention. Was there anything in the first paragraph that grabbed your attention? Explain your answer.

_____

_____

5. A good ending paragraph often repeats information from the opening paragraph in an attempt to tie the introduction and conclusion together. Can you identify two or three pieces of information in the introduction that are repeated in the conclusion?

_____

_____

_____

6. If you were going to rewrite this essay in your own voice, which parts would you change and how?

_____

_____

_____

Building Better Vocabulary

ACTIVITY 2 **Practicing Three Kinds of Vocabulary from Context**

Read each important vocabulary word or phrase. Locate it in the essay if you need help remembering the word or phrase. Then circle the best synonym, antonym, or collocation from column A, B, or C.

Type of Vocabulary	Important Vocabulary	A	B	C
Synonyms	1. accomplish	complete	ensure	improve
	2. enhance	analyze	improve	memorize
	3. rely	depend	fix	subtract
	4. outcome	citizen	receipt	result
Antonyms	5. crucial	comfortable	efficient	unimportant
	6. subsequent	accurate	prior	reliable
	7. similar	different	possible	verified
	8. unlikely	basic	interesting	probable
Collocations	9. ___ people's lives easier	advance	make	take
	10. a traditional ___	citizen	fact	system
	11. ___ a mistake	do	make	take
	12. gain ___ to	access	basis	verification

How Do You Write an Introduction?

The first paragraph of an essay is the introduction. A good introduction accomplishes four objectives:

INTRODUCTION	1. starts with a hook that grabs readers' attention
	2. mentions the topic, or subject, of the essay
	3. gives background information to connect the reader to the topic
	4. includes a thesis statement that summarizes the main point of the essay and explains the writer's idea or position about the topic

Essays begin with a paragraph called the **introduction** that introduces the reader to the topic. The thesis statement gives the writer's plan for the essay and is often the last sentence in the introductory paragraph.

ACTIVITY 3 Comparing Introductions of Essays

For each pair of essays, read the introductions. Then select the introduction you prefer. Give at least one reason for your choice.

1. Essay 1 "Against E-Voting," pages 6–7 and Essay 3 "Varieties of Animal Camouflage for Survival," pages 18–19

   Your preferred introduction: Essay ____

   Reason(s): _____

   _____

   _____

   _____

2. Essay 4 "Effects of Computers on Higher Education," pages 20–22 and Essay 6 "The Dangers of Texting While Driving," pages 44–45

   Your preferred introduction: Essay ____

   Reason(s): _____

   _____

   _____

   _____

3. Essay 11 "Fight for Survival," pages 117–119 and Essay 12 "Two Extremely Dangerous Reptiles," pages 124–126

   Your preferred introduction: Essay ____

   Reason(s): _____

   _____

   _____

   _____

4. Essay 14 "Happiness," pages 146–148 and Essay 17 "Empty Oceans," pages 176–178

Your preferred introduction: Essay ____

Reason(s): _____

_____

_____

_____

The Hook

The **hook** is the opening sentence of any essay. It is the writer's attempt to make you want to read the essay. There are several different ways to write an effective hook.

Type of hook	Example hook
shocking statement	Each year thousands of teenagers die in driving accidents.
definition	The dictionary defines gossip as "casual conversation," but gossip is in reality a much more negative interaction.
quote from a famous person	The poet Emily Dickinson once said, "Saying nothing … sometimes says the most."
question	Have you ever thought about where your salad came from?
scene	On January 8, 2011, the worst snowstorm in the history of my state paralyzed our area.
humorous statement	Many business advertisements offer a free gift, but isn't every gift free?
dilemma	After college, I had to decide between a low-paying job that seemed like fun and a more mundane job that paid really well.
comparison (simile or metaphor)	My life has been like a roller coaster. OR My life has been a roller coaster.

Locate the hooks in these essays and copy them here. Then use the chart on page 10 to identify the type of hook. Write your comments about the hook. For example, is the hook interesting, difficult, effective, or dull?

1. Essay 14 "Happiness," pages 146–148

   Hook: _____

   _____

   _____

   Type of hook: _____

   Your comments on the hook: _____

2. Essay 17 "Empty Oceans," pages 176–178

   Hook: _____

   _____

   _____

   Type of hook: _____

   Your comments on the hook: _____

3. Essay 18 "No More Spam," pages 183–185

   Hook: _____

   _____

   _____

   Type of hook: _____

   Your comments on the hook: _____

ACTIVITY 5 **Comparing Hooks**

Compare the strengths and weaknesses of the three hooks in Activity 4.

1. In your opinion, which hook is the most effective?   1   2   3

2. Explain your choice. _____

_____

3. In your opinion, which of these hooks is the weakest?   1   2   3

4. How would you improve it? Rewrite the hook here.

_____

_____

_____

5. Search the Internet for an essay hook that you think is good. Write it here.

   Essay title: _____

   Source: _____

   Hook: _____

   _____

   Reason you like this hook: _____

   _____

ACTIVITY 6 **Writing a Hook**

Read this essay about one person's experience with a foreign language. Write a hook that gets readers' attention and makes them want to read the essay.

Essay 2

Bread in a Foreign Land

1   _____

_____

I am a teacher of English as a second language (ESL). In June 2008, I accepted an overseas job in a **rural** area of Japan called Niigata and found myself faced with this language problem. One event **in particular** really **stands out** as an example of my inability to express my ideas to the people around me **due to** my **lack** of vocabulary.

2   I had been in Japan only a few days, and I was already feeling homesick. For some reason, I had this incredible urge to make some fresh bread, so I decided to go to the store with the simple intention of buying

rural: countryside; the opposite of *urban*

in particular: especially

to stand out: to be different from the group (adjective: *outstanding*)

due to: because of

lack: something that you don't have and is needed

a basic **commodity**—some flour. I had taken some Japanese language classes before I arrived in Japan, so I knew a little Japanese. Although I knew my Japanese skills were limited, my lack of knowledge did not stop me from going to the store to buy flour. I thought that I would locate the section where the grains were displayed and find the bag that had a picture of either bread or flour on it.

3   The small town where I lived had one tiny store. I walked around the store a few times, but I did not see a bag of anything that appeared to be flour. In my home country, flour usually comes in a paper bag with pictures of biscuits or bread on it, so this was what I was looking for. I finally found a few clear plastic bags that had bread **crumbs** inside, so I thought that flour might be located nearby. No matter how many bags I examined, however, I could not find any flour.

a crumb: small piece of bread that breaks off

4   I desperately wanted to ask one of the three **elderly** women clerks where the flour was, but I could not do this straightforward **task**. I knew how to ask where something was, but I did not know the word for "flour." I tried to think of how to say "flour" using different words such as "white powder" or "the **ingredient** that you use to make bread," but I did not know "powder" and I did not know "ingredient." Just then, I saw one of my students leaving the store. I ran outside to his car and explained that I needed to know a word in Japanese. "How do you say 'flour'?" I asked. He told me effortlessly that the word was *hana*.

elderly: older people

a task: a small job

an ingredient: something you use to make something else

5   I ran back into the store, which was about to close for the evening. I found one of the elderly clerks and asked in my best Japanese, "*Sumimasen. Hana wa doko desu ka?*" or "Excuse me. Where is the *hana*?" The petite old woman said something in Japanese and moved as quickly as she could to the far right side of the store. "Finally," I thought to myself with a sense of success, "I'm going to get my flour and be able to go home to make bread." However, my hopes ended

rather quickly when I followed the clerk to the fresh vegetable section. I saw green onions, tomatoes, and even **pumpkins**, but I could not understand why flour would be there. The woman then pointed to the beautiful yellow **chrysanthemums**—a type of flower—next to the green onions.

6   At first I was **puzzled**, but suddenly it all made sense, and I understood my error. I had been in the country long enough to know that people in Japan sometimes eat chrysanthemums in salads. I was standing in front of the f-l-o-w-e-r display, not the f-l-o-u-r display. When I asked my student for the Japanese word for "flour," I did not **specify** whether I meant "flour" or "flower" because it had never **occurred to** me that grocery stores, especially small ones, might sell flowers to eat.

7   I did not buy any chrysanthemums that night. I was not able to find the flour either. My lack of knowledge about Japanese food and my very limited knowledge of Japanese caused me to go home empty-handed. However, I learned the often **underestimated** value of simple vocabulary in speaking a second language. For me, this event in a small store in rural Japan really opened my eyes to the importance of vocabulary in a second language.

a pumpkin: a large round orange vegetable

a chrysanthemum: a flower that is a national symbol of Japan

puzzled: confused

to specify: to state very clearly

to occur to (someone): the person realizes (something)

to underestimate: to guess a lower number or value for

Building Better Vocabulary

ACTIVITY 7   **Practicing Three Kinds of Vocabulary from Context**

Read each important vocabulary word or phrase. Locate it in the essay if you need help remembering the word or phrase. Then circle the best synonym, antonym, or collocation from column A, B, or C.

Type of Vocabulary	Important Vocabulary	A	B	C
Synonyms	**1.** tiny	difficult	powder	small
	2. specify	identify	rush	witness
	3. an urge	a desire	an event	a section
	4. locate	find	label	yield
Antonyms	**5.** rural	different	green	urban
	6. puzzled	certain	especially	limited
	7. petite	empty	large	valuable
	8. elderly	cheap	unfriendly	young
Collocations	**9.** a ___ of	crumb	lack	skill
	10. express my ___	ideas	languages	shortages
	11. rather ___	empty-handed	ingredient	quickly
	12. ___ sense	get	make	run

What Is the Role of the Thesis Statement?

An essential part of any essay is the **thesis statement.** The thesis statement explains the writer's position about the topic. It tells the general topic, gives details of specific aspects of the topic that will be discussed, and provides a blueprint for the organization of the entire essay. Although the location of a thesis statement can vary, the most common location is the last sentence in the introductory paragraph.

TOPIC	the subject of the essay
THESIS STATEMENT	the writer's position about the topic

All writers must determine what their main idea is and why it is important to them. This idea is contained in a special sentence called the thesis statement. The difference between a topic and a thesis statement is illustrated in the following example:

Topic: cell phones in school

Thesis statement: Student use of cell phones in schools should be prohibited.

Note that the topic does not usually show the writer's idea or position. However, the writer's opinion is clearly contained in the thesis statement. In this case, the main idea that controls the thesis statement is the word *prohibited*. As a result, we expect the essay to contain reasons that support the prohibition of cell phone use in schools.

Thesis Statements and Controlling Ideas

Good thesis statements include the writer's position about a topic as well as reasons or information to support that position. These extra pieces of information that provide support for the writer's idea are called **controlling ideas**.

For example, in the essay "Against E-Voting," pages 6–7, the writer's position is that "societies should not vote with computers or other electronic media." The reason to support this position is "because elections are too important to trust to cyberspace." The controlling ideas are *elections* and *too important to trust to cyberspace.*

ACTIVITY 8 **Studying Examples of Thesis Statements**

Locate the thesis statement in each essay and copy it here. Then explain how you, as the reader, expect the information in the essay to be organized. Your answer should be based on the controlling ideas in the thesis statement.

1. Essay 1 "Against E-Voting," pages 6–7

Thesis Statement	*In particular, societies should not vote with computers or other electronic media because elections are too important to trust to cyberspace.*
Expected Organization	*I expect the writer to explain the reasons that we should not allow our elections to happen in cyberspace. I expect the writer to give some examples of possible problems with electronic elections.*

2. Essay 5 "Studying Study Skills, " pages 25–26

Thesis Statement	
Expected Organization	

3. Essay 8 "How a Caterpillar Becomes a Butterfly," pages 86–88

Thesis Statement	
Expected Organization	

4. Essay 12 "Two Extremely Dangerous Reptiles," pages 124–126

Thesis Statement	
Expected Organization	

ACTIVITY 9 **Comparing Thesis Statements**

Answer these questions that compare the thesis statements in Activity 8.

1. In your opinion, which of the thesis statements is the best?   1   2   3   4

2. Explain your choice. _____

_____

3. In your opinion, which of the thesis statements is the weakest?   1   2   3   4

4. How would you improve it? Rewrite the thesis statement here.

_____

_____

_____

ACTIVITY 10 Finding Thesis Statements and Other Information about Essays

Search the Internet or books for essays related to the general topics below. Write the essay title, the author (if given), the thesis statement, and the source where you located the essay.

1. Topic: Business

   Essay title: _____

   Author: _____

   Thesis statement: _____

   _____

   Source: _____

2. Topic: Sciences

   Essay title: _____

   Author: _____

   Thesis statement: _____

   _____

   Source: _____

3. Your choice of topic: _____

   Essay title: _____

   Author: _____

   Thesis statement: _____

   _____

   Source: _____

What Is in the Body of an Essay?

BODY	1. usually consists of three or more paragraphs
	2. explains and supports the thesis statement

The **body** of the essay follows the introduction. In the body paragraphs, writers explain and support their position and controlling ideas in the thesis statement. In a good essay, the body paragraphs develop the writer's thesis statement so that the reader fully comprehends the writer's point of view. The thesis statement also provides the writing plan for the body paragraphs.

ACTIVITY 11 Organizing the Body Paragraphs of an Essay

This essay contains six paragraphs. Read the introductory paragraph and the concluding paragraph on this page. Then number the paragraphs on page 19 as *2*, *3*, *4*, and *5* to indicate the correct sequence of the four body paragraphs. Finally, copy the topic sentence from each body paragraph on the lines provided in the essay. The topic sentences for the body paragraphs will give you a clear picture of the organization of this essay, but the essay will not be complete below.

Essay 3

Varieties of Animal Camouflage for Survival

1   Animals must protect themselves from **predators** if they are to survive and reproduce, and many accomplish this goal through **camouflage**. If they hide themselves well, their predators will not see them and thus will not eat them. The four primary strategies of camouflage include **concealing** coloration, **disruptive** coloration, disguise, and **mimicry**. These varieties of camouflage show many **evolutionary** factors, but they develop primarily as responses to animals' environments. By **blending** in with their surroundings, animals greatly reduce the chance that a predator will locate and kill them.

2   _____

_____

3   _____

_____

4   _____

_____

5   _____

_____

6   No one of these strategies of camouflage is more effective than the other, and they all show the range of possibilities that nature offers animals to survive. Many animals combine camouflage with their "fight or flight" responses, which gives them additional time to decide whether they should stay and fight or whether they should **flee**. Furthermore, animals that use camouflage for protection share a potential problem as well, as Street (1977) observes, "The disadvantage of camouflage is that if any animal has to move from its normal surroundings, it may become very **conspicuous** against a different background" (p. 7). The most effective camouflages keep animals safe from their predators. Whether by concealing coloration, disruptive coloration, disguise, or mimicry, animals need the protections of camouflage if they are to escape their natural **foes**.

References

Hamilton, W. (1973). *Life's color code*. New York: McGraw-Hill.

Street, P. (1977). *Colour in animals*. Middlesex, England: Kestrel.

a predator: an animal that hunts other animals to eat

camouflage: the use of colors or other designs to become less visible to an enemy

to conceal: to hide

disruptive: disturbing or interrupting the normal situation

mimicry: a method of copying the actions of another person or animal

evolutionary: relating to *evolution*; the process of development or growth

to blend: to mix

to flee: to escape for your life

conspicuous: obvious, usually not in a good way

a foe: an enemy

___ With mimicry, an animal's coloring makes it resemble another, more dangerous creature so that they are virtually identical. The red, black, and yellow rings of scarlet kingsnakes resemble those of coral snakes. Scarlet kingsnakes are not poisonous, but coral snakes are one of the deadliest species of reptiles. Consequently, the coloring of scarlet kingsnakes scares away their predators, who mistake them for their venomous **kin** and do not target them for a meal.

kin: relatives; related by blood

___ Animals such as zebras and giraffes show disruptive coloration. It may seem strange to think that zebras camouflage themselves through their **stripes** since these features appear quite **distinctive** to humans. The main predators of zebras, however, are lions, and they are color blind. Thus, a zebra's stripes help it to blend in with the landscapes of grassy plains. Due to their height, giraffes are among the most easily recognized animals on the planet, yet their disruptive coloring allows them to blend in with trees, particularly when they are young and **vulnerable**. Disruptive coloration creates an optical illusion for predators, tricking them about what stands right before their eyes, and so these animals are rarely detected.

a stripe: a line of color

distinctive: different

vulnerable: weak; easily attacked

___ With disguise, some animals resemble specific elements of their surroundings rather than their environment as a whole. The insect known as a walking stick looks very much like a stick, so it is difficult to find it when looking at a tree or bush. Another insect species is referred to as leaf insects or walking leaves because their bodies so closely look like the plants where they live. Animals camouflage themselves in the seas and oceans as well. The tan coloring and markings of flatfish make them almost impossible to recognize due to the sand around them, despite **fluctuations** in tides that disturb the ocean's floor.

a fluctuation: a shift back and forth

___ Concealing coloration helps animals to blend into their surroundings and create a visual illusion. For example, the white coats or feathers of many animals living in arctic zones, such as polar bears and snowy owls, allow them to blend into a uniform background. If a predator looks across a white snow-covered field, it is quite difficult to pick out its white **prey**. Of course, not all species in cold climates are white, but Hamilton (1973) points out the role of this color in camouflage: "White coloration in the arctic is largely restricted to species with the greatest need for camouflage in predator-prey relationships" (p. 62).

prey: an animal that another animal hunts to eat

Building Better Vocabulary

Practicing Three Kinds of Vocabulary from Context

Read each important vocabulary word or phrase. Locate it in the essay if you need help remembering the word or phrase. Then circle the best synonym, antonym, or collocation from column A, B, or C.

Type of Vocabulary	Important Vocabulary	A	B	C
Synonyms	**1.** a factor	a coloring	a reason	a trick
	2. primary	colorful	main	various
	3. resemble	look at	look for	look like
	4. a role	a lesson	a purpose	a set of stripes
Antonyms	**5.** conceal	allow	compare	display
	6. flee	determine	pick out	remain
	7. a foe	a disadvantage	a friend	a sound
	8. kin	a stranger	a stripe	a variety
Collocations	**9.** accomplish a ___	goal	predator	zone
	10. has the ___ need	best	greatest	worst
	11. blend ___ with the trees	at	in	on
	12. an ___ illusion	ocean	optical	owl

Connectors and Transition Words

All good writing contains words or phrases that connect information from one sentence to another. Within the body of an essay, some words or phrases help the reader transition from one paragraph to the next. These **connectors** and **transitions**—"glue" words—help the reader better understand the content of an essay.

Identifying Connectors and Transition Words

Read the essay. Circle the connectors and transition words that make the most sense for the content of this essay.

Essay 4

Effects of Computers on Higher Education

1   People have always created conveniences to make life easier. One **such** modern invention is the computer, which has improved many aspects of our lives, in particular in the **sphere** of education and learning.

such: like this

a sphere: an area of influence or activity

1 (Therefore / Because of) computer technology, higher education today has three major conveniences: **lecture** variety, easy research, and time-saving writing.

a lecture: an academic speech or presentation

2   One important effect of computer technology on higher education is the availability of lectures. **2** (For this reason / As a result of) the development of computer networks, we can access lectures from many universities in real time. We are now able to sit down in front of a digital screen and listen to a lecture being given at another university. In addition, by **utilizing** interactive media, we can question the lecturer and exchange opinions with other students through e-mail. Such computerized lectures give us access to knowledge that we did not have before. **3** (For this reason / Because), professors in specialized fields can transfer their knowledge to their students, regardless of where the professors are teaching.

to utilize: to use

3   The development of computers also makes it possible for us to have access to more information through the Internet and databases.

4 (Since / Consequently), when we research a topic, we do not have to go to the library to locate information because the computer offers an impressive number of resources. It is easy to use the Internet and databases because all we have to do is type in a few key words and wait a few moments. In addition, we can do this research at home, which is certainly convenient for busy students.

4   Another effect of computer technology on higher education is time-saving writing techniques. E-mail assignments are becoming more common at universities. **5** (As a result / Due to), the assignments are much quicker and easier to finish than before. When it is time to hand in our assigned papers or homework, we simply send them to our professors electronically. This method is beneficial for students and convenient for teachers, who will not **risk** losing their students' work in a mountain of papers. Another time-saving device is the word processor.

to risk: to put in danger of losing

6 (Thus / Because of) improved word-processing programs, we have the added benefit of spell-checking and grammar-checking programs. If we type a grammatically incorrect sentence, one of these programs automatically **highlights** the incorrect parts of the sentence and corrects them. In addition, without using a dictionary, we can write papers that have no spelling mistakes. **7** (Since / As a result of) these two functions, e-mail and word processing, both teachers and students can save a great deal of time.

to highlight: to draw attention to; to make more visible

5   To summarize, computer technology has three main positive effects on higher education: lecture variety, easy research, and time-saving writing. **8** (Because of / Because) **the advent of** computers in education, we can improve our knowledge and save **precious** time. Academic life will never be the same and will result in a more **dynamic** learning experience for many.

the advent of: the beginning of

precious: valuable

dynamic: energetic

Building Better Vocabulary

ACTIVITY 14 **Practicing Three Kinds of Vocabulary from Context**

Read each important vocabulary word or phrase. Locate it in the essay if you need help remembering the word or phrase. Then circle the best synonym, antonym, or collocation from column A, B, or C.

Type of Vocabulary	Important Vocabulary	A	B	C
Synonyms	1. utilize	improve	therefore	use
	2. since	because	meaning	under
	3. highlight	produce	resemble	stress
	4. precious	expensive	front	valuable
Antonyms	5. key	convenient	difficult	unimportant
	6. positive	advanced	lecture	negative
	7. specialized	intelligent	ordinary	reluctant
	8. major	greedy	jealous	minor
Collocations	9. save precious ___	education	methods	time
	10. a digital ___	benefit	screen	wonder
	11. spelling ___	conveniences	effects	mistakes
	12. the advent of ___	computers	fields	parts

What Does the Conclusion of an Essay Do?

CONCLUSION	1. summarizes the writer's main point
	2. uses key vocabulary from the introduction
	3. usually offers a suggestion, opinion, or prediction

Most good essays end with a **conclusion** that summarizes the writer's main point. The conclusion should not include any new information. Adding new information does not make your essay sound stronger or more convincing. Instead, it may actually confuse your reader.

Good conclusions often end with a sentence that expresses a suggestion, an opinion, or a prediction. The writer suggests what should be done now, offers a final opinion about the topic, or predicts what will happen next. Without a conclusion, essays often seem incomplete and unfinished.

ACTIVITY 15 **Comparing Conclusions of Essays**

For each pair of essays, read the conclusions. Then select the conclusion you prefer. Give at least one reason for your choice.

1. Essay 2 "Bread in a Foreign Land," pages 12–14 and Essay 6 "The Dangers of Texting While Driving," pages 44–45

   Your preferred conclusion: Essay ___

   Reason(s): _____

   _____

   _____

   _____

2. Essay 13 "How Weather Has Changed World History," pages 139–141 and Essay 14 "Happiness," pages 146–148

   Your preferred conclusion: Essay ___

   Reason(s): _____

   _____

   _____

   _____

3. Essay 16 "The Best Classroom," pages 167–169 and Essay 18 "No More Spam," pages 183–185

   Your preferred conclusion: Essay ___

   Reason(s): _____

   _____

   _____

   _____

ACTIVITY 16 Writing a Conclusion Paragraph

Read the essay and write an appropriate conclusion paragraph. For ideas, study the introduction paragraph and the thesis statement as well as the topic sentences of the body paragraphs.

Essay 5

Studying Study Skills

1   Many students **dread** them, but tests are an **integral** part of the educational experience. To be prepared for the various exams they must endure over the years of their education, students must develop study skills that help them learn a range of new academic materials efficiently yet with maximum comprehension. A wide variety of study skills and techniques can aid students as they achieve their objectives in all of their classes.

2   One of the most important and simplest ways to prepare for exams is to attend all classes and to take notes on lectures and discussions. For effective studying, however, students' notes must be meaningful and **coherent**, as Palmer (2004) points out: "All notes that are not accompanied by solid understanding are useless" (p. 129). Palmer cautions students not simply to write down everything that they hear but instead to write down key words and phrases that will remind them of the issues that were discussed. It is impossible—and would **ultimately** not be helpful—to write down every word the teacher says. By focusing on the most important topics of the lecture or discussion in their note-taking, students improve their understanding of the lesson. After class, students should review the notes they have taken to clarify their meaning and to reinforce their understanding of the relevant topics covered and also to determine what information is supplementary, but not essential, to the lessons.

3   Sometimes studying for an exam requires memorizing large amounts of information. Study techniques such as **mnemonic** devices and flashcards can help students accomplish this task. Mnemonic devices are named after Mnemosyne, the Greek goddess of memory, and they are simple cues to help a student's memory. In one common mnemonic device, the exact colors of what we see as white light are associated with the corresponding made-up name "ROY G. BIV," an **acronym** that stands for red, orange, yellow, green, blue, indigo, violet. While mnemonic devices can be helpful, sometimes it can be more challenging to learn the mnemonic than simply to memorize the information it represents. Which is easier: to learn to spell the word "arithmetic" or to remember the lengthy phrase, "A rat in Tom's house might eat Tom's ice cream," in which the first letters of the words spell out "arithmetic"? Flashcards also help students to develop their memory and to learn new information by repeatedly testing themselves on new information. Typically, students will write a term on one of side of the card and its definition on the reverse. The use of flashcards is an appropriate memorization technique when a student is learning a lot of new information, such as vocabulary words of a new language or scientific terms necessary for a biology class. Students can also rearrange the cards to ensure that they are learning each term separately and not simply memorizing the order of the cards.

to dread: to feel anxious or extremely worried about something that will happen

integral: key; of primary importance

coherent: logical; well-organized; easy to understand

ultimately: finally; in the end

mnemonic: related to memory

an acronym: a group of letters that stands for another term, such as UFO for Unidentified Flying Object

25

4   While memorization is an important part of studying, students should also seek to enhance their understanding of the main concepts in their courses. To this end, Reynolds (2002) **advocates** the SQ3R (Survey, Question, Read, Recite, Review) method to help students understand the importance of the subject matter throughout their reading and study (pp. 152–155). Before each assignment, students should look over the material to get a general sense of the information they are expected to learn and its overall **context**. Next, students formulate questions about this material, trying to anticipate what they will be expected to learn from it. Students then read the assignment, looking for the answers to the questions they created in the previous step. For the fourth step, students recite or restate what they learned. To enhance this part of the SQ3R process, students might draw a diagram of the reading material, make an outline of it, or write a summary. Finally, students must frequently review the materials. Reynolds cautions students that "most forgetting takes place within twenty-four hours," and so they must "review the reading selection to **retain**" the information (p. 155).

5   Time management skills are another necessary component for effective studying. Many students simply "**cram** for the exam," but this strategy limits long-term learning because people then forget information they have put in their short-term memory. Turner (2002) advises students to **pace** themselves throughout the course of the semester: "It is difficult to take in a lot at any one time, especially when things are new to you. Spreading your learning over a period of time can help you to remember things" (p. 37). Thus, the single most effective strategy for studying is to see it as a long process stretching over the course of a semester rather than as a rushed session the night before each test.

6   _____

_____

_____

_____

_____

_____

_____

to advocate: to promote; to speak well of

the context: the situation in which something appears or happens

to retain: to keep

to cram: to push into a small time or space

to pace: to go at a slow, steady speed

References

Palmer, R. (2004). *Studying for success*. London: Routledge.

Reynolds, J. (2002). *Succeeding in college: Study skills and strategies* (2nd ed). Upper Saddle River, NJ: Prentice Hall.

Turner, J. (2002). *How to study: A short introduction*. London: Sage.

Building Better Vocabulary

ACTIVITY 17 Practicing Three Kinds of Vocabulary from Context

Read each important vocabulary word or phrase. Locate it in the essay if you need help remembering the word or phrase. Then circle the best synonym, antonym, or collocation from column A, B, or C.

Type of Vocabulary	Important Vocabulary	A	B	C
Synonyms	**1.** a component	an acronym	a device	a part
	2. clarify	challenge	explain	manage
	3. typically	possibly	throughout	usually
	4. a term	a place	a skill	a word
Antonyms	**5.** dread	enhance	enjoy	require
	6. accompanied	alone	especially	memorized
	7. seek	achieve	attempt	locate
	8. stretch	caution	shrink	spread
Collocations	**9.** over the ___ of a year	course	formula	time
	10. over a ___ of time	period	recital	spread
	11. a ___ of materials	concept	range	step
	12. reinforce your ___	answers	scores	understanding

Original Student Writing: Practicing the Steps

In this section, you will follow seven steps in the writing process to write a five-paragraph essay with a title, introduction (including an interesting hook and a thesis statement), body paragraphs that develop the topic, and a strong conclusion. If you need help with the steps in the writing process, refer to Unit 2, pages 34–46.

ACTIVITY 18 Step 1: Choose a Topic

Your first step is to choose a topic for your essay. Your teacher may assign a topic, you may think of one yourself, or you may choose one from the suggestions in the chart on the next page. As you consider possible topics, ask yourself, "What do I know about this topic? What do my readers know? What else do I need to know? Do I need to research this topic?"

Humanities	*Literature:* Analyze a favorite poem and discuss its meaning. *History:* Write an essay about an invention. *Philosophy:* Some parents educate their children at home instead of sending them to a traditional school. What are the advantages of homeschooling?
Sciences	*Biology:* Write about three kinds of animals found only in one place (such as Australia). *Meteorology:* Write about one kind of bad weather such as lightning, a tornado, or a hurricane.
Business	*Consumer Affairs:* Compare two restaurants that have similar menus.
Personal	How would your life be different if there were no electricity? Explain the three biggest impacts on your life.

1. What topic did you choose? _____

2. Why did you choose this topic? _____

   _____

3. How well do you know this topic? What is your experience with it?

   _____

   _____

ACTIVITY 19 **Step 2: Brainstorm**

Use this space to jot down as many ideas about the topic as you can.

Brainstorming Box

ACTIVITY 20 **Step 3: Outline**

Prepare a simple outline of your essay.

Title: _____

  I. Introduction

    A. Hook: _____

_____

    B. Connecting information: _____

_____

    C. Thesis statement: _____

_____

_____

  II. Topic of Body Paragraph 1: _____

Two to four ideas to include:

    A. _____

    B. _____

    C. _____

    D. _____

 III. Topic of Body Paragraph 2: _____

Two to four ideas to include:

    A. _____

    B. _____

    C. _____

    D. _____

 IV. Topic of Body Paragraph 3: _____

Two to four ideas to include:

    A. _____

    B. _____

    C. _____

    D. _____

  V. Conclusion: _____

_____

_____

Peer Editing of Outlines

Exchange books with a partner. Read your partner's outline. Then use the following questions to help you to comment on your partner's outline. Use your partner's feedback to revise your outline.

1. Is there any aspect of the outline that is unclear to you? Give details here.

_____

_____

_____

2. Can you think of an area in the outline that needs more development? Make specific suggestions.

_____

_____

_____

3. If you have any other ideas or suggestions, write them here.

_____

_____

_____

ACTIVITY 21 **Step 4: Write the First Draft**

Use the information from Steps 1–3 to write the first draft of your essay. Use at least four of the vocabulary words or phrases from the Building Better Vocabulary activities in this unit. Underline these words and phrases in your essay. Try to also use at least two of the words from the Academic Word List in the *Brief Writer's Handbook with Activities* on pages 230–231.

ACTIVITY 22 **Step 5: Get Feedback from a Peer**

Exchange papers from Step 4 with a partner. Read your partner's first draft. Then use Peer Editing Sheet 1 (available online at NGL.Cengage.com/GW5) to help you comment on your partner's writing. Be sure to offer positive suggestions and comments that will help your partner improve his or her essay.

ACTIVITY 23 **Step 6: Revise the First Draft**

Read the comments on Peer Editing Sheet 1 about your essay. Then reread your essay. Can you identify places where you should make revisions? List the improvements you plan to make.

1. _____

_____

2. _____

_____

3. _____

_____

Use all the information from the previous steps to write the final version of your paper. Often, writers will need to write a third or even a fourth draft to express their ideas as clearly as possible. Write as many drafts as necessary to produce a good essay.

ACTIVITY 24 **Step 7: Proofread the Final Draft**

Be sure to proofread your paper several times before you submit it so you find all the mistakes and correct them.

Additional Topics for Writing

Here are five more ideas for topics for essay writing.

PHOTO TOPIC: Look at the photo on pages 2–3. What accomplishments do you hope to achieve in your life? Consider the areas of education, work, and family.

TOPIC 2: What are some causes of divorce?

TOPIC 3: Explain several ways for people to improve their spelling.

TOPIC 4: Compare and contrast two jobs you have had.

TOPIC 5: Do you agree or disagree that participating in team sports helps to build a person's character? Explain your reasons.

Timed Writing

How quickly can you write in English? There are many times when you must write quickly, such as on a test. It is important to feel comfortable during those times. Timed-writing practice can make you feel better about writing quickly in English.

1. Take out a piece of paper.

2. Read the writing prompt below.

3. Write a basic outline, including the introduction and thesis, the body paragraphs, and the conclusion. You should spend no more than five minutes on your outline.

4. Your essay needs at least five paragraphs.

5. You have 40 minutes to write your essay.

If you could meet one famous person, living or dead, who would it be? Explain why you would choose to meet this person and what you would hope to gain from the experience.

Understanding the Writing Process: The Seven Steps

Climber Conrad Anker descends through the
Khumbu Icefall on Mount Everest, Nepal.

Have you ever had a real adventure?

The Writing Process

A good essay is always the result of good planning, from brainstorming to finding the right topic, to outlining basic ideas for the first draft, to revising the essay from self and peer editing, to carefully proofreading the final version of the paper. The length of the paper does not change the basic writing process very much. All essays start with planning!

Following is a list of seven steps that good writers may use as they move from the initial idea for their essay to the final draft that is ready for the reader. It is important to understand each of these steps well. Keep in mind that writing an essay is not a linear process. You will likely go back and forth between steps.

The Seven Steps in the Writing Process

| **Step 1**
Choose a topic | **Step 2**
Brainstorm | **Step 3**
Outline | **Step 4**
Write the first draft | **Step 5**
Get feedback from a peer | **Step 6**
Revise the first draft | **Step 7**
Proofread the final draft |

Step 1: Choose a Topic

Every essay addresses a specific topic. The choice of the topic is important because you do not want a topic that is so general, such as "pets," that it cannot be covered in any one essay. Likewise, you do not want a topic that is so specific, such as "The weather in New York on August 25," that it may be difficult to write more than one or two paragraphs about it.

After you have selected the topic, your next task will be to develop ideas about that topic. In this explanation of the seven steps in the writing process, the general topic is "technology and people."

> **Writer's Note**
>
> **At the Beginning: Don't Write—THINK!**
>
> Many writers make the mistake of trying to write an essay without thinking or planning. The first part of writing is not writing; it is thinking. If you start writing too soon, your essay will be unorganized and unfocused.
>
> Think about your topic. What do you already know about it? What do your readers know about it? What do you need to find out about this topic? Only after you have thought about and answered these questions are you ready to begin writing.

ACTIVITY 1 Narrowing Topics

Read the general topic, which would not be good for an essay. Then narrow it down to three topics that are more specific and could work for a five-to-eight paragraph essay.

General Topics	More Specific Topic
1. Pets	**a.** Why Cats are the Best Pet **b.** **c.**
2. Technology and people	**a.** The Dangers of Texting While Driving **b.** **c.**
3. Weather	**a.** **b.** **c.**
4. Food	**a.** **b.** **c.**
5. Jobs	**a.** **b.** **c.**
6. Sports	**a.** **b.** **c.**
7. Health	**a.** **b.** **c.**
8. Hobbies	**a.** **b.** **c.**

Step 2: Brainstorm

The next step in writing an essay is to generate ideas about your topic by brainstorming. Here is an example writing assignment:

Assignment: Write a narrative essay illustrating some aspect of how technology impacts people's lives.

The general topic is "technology and people." Because the assignment is a narrative essay, the writer must address the topic through a personal story. Study below how the writer brainstormed ideas about four areas that relate to the general topic: applying for a job, cell phones and driving, e-mail problems, and health. As you can see, the writer chose "cell phones and driving." The personal story will be about a car accident that the student had while texting. He chose the one topic that he thinks he can present with the best support, and he crossed out the other three.

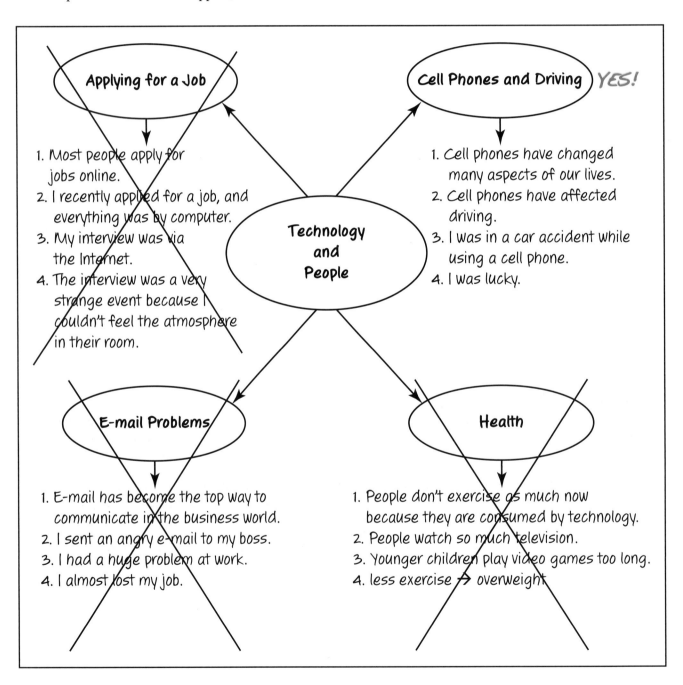

Here you will practice brainstorming a different topic. In the box, write some ideas about the following topic: "The pros and cons of limiting children's TV access to two hours per day." When you are finished, compare your brainstorming notes with a partner's.

Step 3: Outline

After you brainstorm your ideas, the next step is to make an outline. An outline helps to organize how you will present your information. It also helps you to see which areas of the essay are strong and which are weak.

Formal outlines use Roman numerals, capital letters, and many different levels of information. Some outlines consist of only words or phrases. Others have full sentences. You should use the type of outline that will best help you write a great essay.

On the next page, there is an example of an outline that uses words, phrases, and sentences.

Title: The Negative Impact of Computers on Society

I. Introduction

    A. Hook

    B. Background information

    C. Thesis statement: *Computers have had a negative impact on society in three significant areas: personal relationships, health, and the economy.*

II. Topic of Body Paragraph 1: Effects on personal relationships

    A. Topic sentence

    B. Effect 1

    C. Effect 2

III. Topic of Body Paragraph 2: Effects on health

    A. Topic sentence

    B. Effect 1

    C. Effect 2

IV. Topic of Body Paragraph 3: Effects on economy

    A. Topic sentence

    B. Effect 1

    C. Effect 2

V. Conclusion

    A. Restated thesis

    B. Brief discussion

    C. Prediction that in time, these three areas will steadily worsen if the situation continues.

Write a general outline for the brainstorming information from Activity 2.

_____

_____

_____

_____

_____

_____

_____

_____

_____

_____

_____

_____

Writer's Note

Using a Hook to Gain Readers' Attention

Good writers grab their readers' attention with the first sentence of an essay, which is called the **hook**. Just as people use a hook to catch fish, a writer will use a good hook to generate readers' interest in the essay.

Look at the two versions of a hook below for an essay about a vacation experience.

Boring hook (be verb): My worst vacation **was** in Nagano.

Better hook (action verbs): It might seem unlikely to **catch** the flu, **lose** my wallet, and **get** a speeding ticket in the same week, but these incidents **ruined** my ski vacation in Nagano.

The first hook, which uses the verb *be* (*was*), is simple and boring. In contrast, the second hook gets readers' attention by providing more details associated with the active verbs *catch*, *lose*, *get*, and *ruin*. Using specific verbs forces the writer to provide interesting details that create a better hook.

ACTIVITY 4 **Understanding the Organization of an Essay**

Read this partial outline of the essay "The Dangers of Texting While Driving" on pages 44–45. Use the information in the box to complete the outline.

- A police officer gave me a ticket.

- People think using a cell phone does not affect their ability to do other things at the same time.

- I was expecting a text message.

- Obey the protocols of safe driving and turn your cell phone off.

- My car accident was completely avoidable because I was texting while driving.

- I took my eyes off the road.

- Texting causes the same delayed reaction as driving while drinking.

Title: The Dangers of Texting While Driving

I. Introduction

    A. Establish that texting while driving is dangerous.

    B. Briefly state that I had an accident while driving because I was texting.

    C. Thesis statement: _____

II. Topic of Body Paragraph 1: Beginning of the story

    A. _____

    B. I answered the message.

    C. _____

III. Topic of Body Paragraph 2: Because I was texting while driving, I had an accident.

    A. I had an accident; I hit a parking meter.

    B. _____

    C. I had to pay for the parking meter, so I learned how much it costs.

IV. Topic of Body Paragraph 3: People feel a strong need to answer their cell phones.

    A. Cell phones are addictive.

    B. Humans are rational, but answering a text while driving is not rational.

V. Topic of Body Paragraph 4: _____

    A. Humans think we can multitask well.

    B. The Occupational Safety and Health Administration warns drivers that reaction time is greatly slowed down.

    C. Example: _____

VI. Conclusion

    A. The story is not good, but the ending is not as bad as it could have been.

    B. Various websites give some incredible statistics on deaths.

    C. _____

Step 4: Write the First Draft

After you have completed your outline and received peer feedback on it, it is time to write the first draft of your essay. Writing an essay is never a linear process. As you write, you will make numerous changes. In fact, after you write the hook or other sentences, you may rewrite them and later add additional words and sentences.

The most important thing in writing a first draft is to write it. Too many students spend hours thinking about what they will say. A much better strategy is to get your ideas on paper and then edit your words to match what you really intend to say.

Another useful strategy is to write your paper and then set it aside for a few hours or even a few days. When you read your paper again, you will probably find several places where you want to change words or add ideas. In this case, the time between when you wrote the paper and when you read the paper again helps you see the paper from a different perspective.

Step 5: Get Feedback from a Peer

A good way to generate ideas about improving your writing is to ask a friend or classmate to look at your ideas and organization, beginning with your outline. If something is not clear to that person, then perhaps you should rework or rewrite that part. Sometimes information is confusing because there is a language problem. Other times, the problem comes from unclear ideas or a lack of good supporting ideas. Peer editing is commonly used for first drafts, but it can also be useful for hooks and outlines and in every step in the writing process.

When you are editing someone else's work, remember to be helpful. If something is not clear, do not write, for example, "No." Such a simple remark is not helpful. You should write something like "This sentence is not clear" or "Can you think of three reasons to support this idea?"

The peer editing sheets for your essays in Units 1–7 (available online at NGL.Cengage.com/GW5) will help you to focus on specific areas to examine in each essay. Here are a few general points that a good peer editor examines in an essay:

- Does every sentence have a subject and a verb and express a complete thought?

- Are there any sentences or sections that do not make sense?

- Even if I do not agree with the writer's viewpoint, do I understand the writer's line of thinking?

Peer editing a draft is a critical step toward the final goal of a polished essay. As the writer of the essay, you will be greatly helped by the fresh perspective a new reader can give. No matter how good a writer you are, it is often difficult for you to see the weaknesses in your own writing. Remember that even professional writers have editors, so do not be embarrassed to ask for help.

ACTIVITY 5 Practice Using a Peer Editing Sheet

Most readers can give better feedback if they use a peer editing sheet that has questions and space for specific feedback. Study this sample peer editing sheet. Read each question and decide if it would be easy or difficult for you to answer if you were reading another writer's paper. On the line next to each number, identify whether the question would be easy (*E*) or difficult (*D*) to answer.

Sample Peer Editing Sheet

Writer: _____ Date: _____

Peer Editor: _____

Essay Title: _____

_____ 1. What is the general topic of the essay?

_____

_____ 2. How many paragraphs are there? _____

_____ 3. Do you think the introduction does a good job of introducing the topic?   ☐ **Yes**   ☐ **No**

Do you have any suggestions for improving it? If so, write them here.

_____

_____

_____ 4. Can you identify the thesis statement? If so, write it here.

_____

_____

_____ **5.** If you see any spelling errors, write them here.

_____

_____

_____ **6.** If you see any grammar errors, write them here.

_____

_____

_____ **7.** Do you agree with the writer's ideas about this topic? Why or why not? Explain your answer and give examples of things you agree or disagree with. _____

_____

_____ **8.** Do you have any ideas about changing how the conclusion is written? If so, share them here. _____

_____

Step 6: Revise the First Draft

Once you have received feedback from a peer editor, you can use that feedback to improve your essay in the second draft. You have at least four choices in responding to the feedback:

1. **Do nothing.** If you think the writing in your essay is clear enough, then do nothing. However, if one reader had a problem with an element in your essay, perhaps other readers will encounter the same problem.

2. **Add information.** If the reader found any unclear language or needed any parts clarified, then you might want to add more information. For example, you might need to add an adjective or identifying information, so instead of writing "The solution is actually quite easy," you could write, "The <u>best</u> solution <u>to this problem that plagues modern society</u> is actually quite easy."

3. **Cut information.** If the reader thinks that your writing is wordy or that a certain sentence is not related to the topic, then you should edit out the wordiness or omit the sentence. The saying "less is often best" is true for good writing.

4. **Correct errors.** If the reader found any grammatical errors, correct them. Thus, if your draft has language errors, then you should make those corrections.

   Example: "Computers <u>has</u> had a negative impact <u>for</u> society <u>with</u> three significant <u>area</u>: personal relationships, health, <u>__</u> the economy."

   If a peer reader underlined these errors in your writing, you would then rewrite the sentence with these changes: "Computers <u>have</u> had a negative impact <u>on</u> society <u>in</u> three significant <u>areas</u>: personal relationships, health, <u>and</u> the economy."

This essay has six paragraphs, and each paragraph has one sentence that is not necessary or does not contain important information for the essay. Underline the six sentences that should be eliminated because the information is not directly connected to the topic of the paragraph.

Essay 6

The Dangers of Texting While Driving

1   Everyone knows that texting while driving is dangerous, but many people continue to do so. Fortunately, my own experiences with texting and driving did not result in a horrible accident, and the **damage** to my car was relatively minor. While I did not suffer bodily injury, the damage to my ego was truly **humbling**. My car accident was completely avoidable because I was texting while driving. The vehicle I was driving at the time was approximately five years old.

2   I have always thought of myself as a good driver. I pay attention to the road, anticipate the actions of other drivers, and am very aware of how road conditions can **shift** instantly. One day when I was driving to my job on roads I have traveled countless times, my cell phone beeped to indicate

damage: harm to property that reduces its value

humbling: a feeling of not being important

to shift: to change

that I had a new text message. Every day I receive **up to** 50 text messages. I knew a friend would text me that morning to let me know about his plans for the evening, and I also knew that I should write back quickly to tell him that I could not join him. Unfortunately, that is when I took my eyes off the road, thereby setting the stage for the accident.

3   Thankfully, I was not on a major highway, but rather on a quiet street early in the morning. The only result of my accident was that I drove onto a sidewalk and **knocked down** a parking meter. The police came and gave me a ticket, and I also learned how much parking meters cost. The police who arrived at the accident scene were very polite.

4   The trouble with cell phones and texting is that they are **virtually addictive**. When phones make that sweet sound of new texts waiting, people want to read those messages **at once**. We may like to believe that we usually make **rational** decisions, but reading a text while driving is not a rational choice at all. Just last week, one of my teachers got mad at me for checking a text message in class.

5   Some cell phones are better for drivers. Drivers think they can successfully **multitask**, but on this issue they are simply incorrect. No matter how good drivers might be, they can only fully concentrate on one activity at a time, and to do so they must eliminate all distractions, including cell phones. The Occupational Safety and Health Administration (2012), a division of the United States Department of Labor, warns drivers: "Reaction time is **delayed** for a driver talking on a cell phone as much as it is for a driver who is legally drunk." Many people who would never think of drinking and driving see no **harm** at all in texting and driving, but they must learn that the two activities are interchangeable in the dangers they create on the road.

6   Why do people continue to mix texting and driving? Other than the cost of a ticket and a parking meter, my story has a happy ending. Many other people, both drivers and innocent **pedestrians**, are not so lucky, as documented by the **tragic** stories on various websites. Learn from my experiences and those detailed online, obey the **protocols** of safe driving, and turn your cell phone off so that you will arrive safely at your next **destination**.

Reference

Occupational Safety and Health Administration. (2012). Distracted driving: No texting [Brochure]. Retrieved from https://www.osha.gov/

---

up to (a number): no more than (a number)

to knock down: to hit or move so that something falls

virtually: in fact; for all purposes

addictive: causing a strong feeling that a habit must be satisfied

at once: immediately

rational: reasonable or sensible; based on facts and not opinions or emotions

to multitask: to do several things at the same time

to delay: to cause to be late

harm: danger or damage

a pedestrian: a person who is walking

tragic: very serious, shocking, or sad

a protocol: a rule or procedure

a destination: the final place to which a person is traveling

Building Better Vocabulary

ACTIVITY 7 **Practicing Three Kinds of Vocabulary from Context**

Read each important vocabulary word or phrase. Locate it in the essay if you need help remembering the word or phrase. Then circle the best synonym, antonym, or collocation from column A, B, or C.

Type of Vocabulary	Important Vocabulary	A	B	C
Synonyms	**1.** instantly	honestly	immediately	legally
	2. minor	adult	small	terrible
	3. a destination	a location	a person	a time
	4. anticipate	expect	justify	persuade
Antonyms	**5.** delay	concentrate	postpone	rush
	6. up to 100	approximately 100	less than 100	more than 100
	7. tragic	empty	happy	knowledgeable
	8. polite	innocent	rude	virtual
Collocations	**9.** a rational ___	beverage	ceiling	decision
	10. anticipate a ____ problem	fortunate	future	past
	11. you must ___ concentrate	fully	incorrectly	neatly
	12. a countless ___	number	people	traffic

Step 7: Proofread the Final Draft

Do not forget to proofread! When you proofread, you correct grammar and spelling errors. Careless mistakes make your writing look sloppy and get in the way of clear communication. Proofreading is not just about grammar and spelling, however. Even at this late stage, you can add or change words to make your essay sound better. It is essential to proofread your final essay carefully before you turn it in to your teacher.

Again, if it is possible to wait a few days between your editing stage (Step 6) and the final proofreading, you will be able to see your paper more objectively.

Original Student Writing: Practicing the Steps

In this section, you will follow the seven steps of the writing process to write a five-paragraph essay with a title, introduction (including an interesting hook and a thesis statement), body paragraphs that develop the topic, and a strong conclusion. If you need help with the steps in the writing process, refer to pages 34–46.

ACTIVITY 8 **Step 1: Choose a Topic**

Your first step is to choose a topic for your essay. Your teacher may assign a topic, you may think of one yourself, or you may choose one from the suggestions in the chart. As you consider possible topics, ask yourself, "What do I know about this topic? What do my readers know? What else do I need to know? Do I need to research this topic?"

Humanities	*Linguistics:* How difficult is it to learn English compared to learning another language? *Literature:* Some people consider Shakespeare to be the greatest writer of the English language. Write an essay that offers three reasons to support this claim. *History:* Write an essay in which you explain the causes of a very difficult economic period in a country or region.
Sciences	*Biology:* The number of cases of skin cancer (melanoma) has increased in the past few decades. Write an essay in which you explain this fact. *Climate:* What is global warming? What can be done to slow this process down?
Business	Many new businesses fail in their first three years of operation. What are the characteristics of a successful new business?
Personal	In your opinion, what are the three most important qualities of a good friend? Explain why each of these qualities is integral to your definition of a good friend.

1. What topic did you choose? _____

2. Why did you choose this topic? _____

_____

3. How well do you know this topic? What is your experience with it?

_____

_____

ACTIVITY 9 Step 2: Brainstorm

Use this space to jot down as many ideas about the topic as you can.

Brainstorming Box

ACTIVITY 10 Step 3: Outline

Prepare a simple outline of your essay.

Title: _____

  I. Introduction

    A. Hook: _____

    _____

    B. Connecting information: _____

    _____

    C. Thesis statement: _____

    _____

    _____

II. Topic of Body Paragraph 1: _____

Two to four ideas to include:

A. _____

B. _____

C. _____

D. _____

III. Topic of Body Paragraph 2: _____

Two to four ideas to include:

A. _____

B. _____

C. _____

D. _____

IV. Topic of Body Paragraph 3: _____

Two to four ideas to include:

A. _____

B. _____

C. _____

D. _____

V. Conclusion: _____

_____

_____

Peer Editing of Outlines

Exchange books with a partner. Read your partner's outline. Then use the following questions to help you to comment on your partner's outline. Use your partner's feedback to revise your outline.

1. Is there any aspect of the outline that is unclear to you? Give details here.

_____

_____

_____

2. Can you think of an area in the outline that needs more development? Make specific suggestions.

_____

_____

_____

3. If you have any other ideas or suggestions, write them here.

_____

_____

_____

ACTIVITY 11 **Step 4: Write the First Draft**

Use the information from Steps 1–3 to write the first draft of your essay. Try to use at least four of the words from the Academic Word List in the _Brief Writer's Handbook with Activities_ on pages 230–231.

ACTIVITY 12 **Step 5: Get Feedback from a Peer**

Exchange papers from Step 4 with a partner. Read your partner's first draft. Then use Peer Editing Sheet 2 (available online at NGL.Cengage.com/GW5) to help you to comment on your partner's writing. Be sure to offer positive suggestions and comments that will help your partner improve his or her essay.

ACTIVITY 13 **Step 6: Revise the First Draft**

Read the comments on Peer Editing Sheet 2 about your essay. Then reread your essay. Can you identify places where you should make revisions? List the improvements you plan to make.

1. _____

_____

_____

2. _____

_____

_____

3. _____

_____

_____

Use all the information from the previous steps to write the final version of your paper. Often, writers will need to write a third or even a fourth draft to express their ideas as clearly as possible. Write as many drafts as necessary to produce a good essay.

Be sure to proofread your paper several times before you submit it so you find all the mistakes and correct them.

Additional Topics for Writing

Here are five more ideas for topics for essay writing.

PHOTO
TOPIC: Look at the photo on pages 32–33. Think about an adventure that you have had. Were you alone? What happened? Describe your experience.

TOPIC 2: What are the effects of daily exercise?

TOPIC 3: Explain how to make a pizza.

TOPIC 4: Explain why you do or don't like to travel.

TOPIC 5: Do you support government-sponsored lotteries? Why or why not?

Timed Writing

How quickly can you write in English? There are many times when you must write quickly, such as on a test. It is important to feel comfortable during those times. Timed-writing practice can make you feel better about writing quickly in English.

1. Take out a piece of paper.

2. Read the writing prompt below.

3. Write a basic outline, including the introduction and thesis, the body paragraphs, and the conclusion. You should spend no more than five minutes on your outline.

4. Your essay needs at least five paragraphs.

5. You have 40 minutes to write your essay.

Some people believe that all students should study a foreign language before they can graduate. Others do not support this requirement. Write an essay in which you agree with one of these two positions.

Paraphrasing, Summarizing, Synthesizing, and Citing Sources

Many countries, including Brazil, Indonesia, and Kenya, export coffee.

OBJECTIVES To learn how to paraphrase, summarize, and synthesize original material
To learn how to cite information from sources
To know when to paraphrase and when to use direct quotations

What products do you use that come from another country?

Using Information from Sources

The majority of the words in an essay should be the writer's own. Sometimes, however, writers want to use ideas that they have read in another work to serve as good supporting details or examples. In particular, using a quotation from a famous person adds credibility to what the writer is trying to say. For example, writers who are writing about an election may want to use a quotation from a politician. In this case, the writer must indicate that the idea or the words came from someone else by giving direct credit to that source.

The action of indicating that a writer's words are not original but are from another source is called **citing** (from the verb *to cite*). In academic writing, it is necessary to use sources to make the paper stronger, but it is equally important to cite the source of this information correctly.

When writers want to include material from another source in a paper, they have two choices: using a **direct quotation** or **paraphrasing**. A direct quotation uses the exact words from the original source, and there is no change in the way the idea is expressed. A paraphrase restates the ideas from the original in the writer's own words, which means the same idea from the original is expressed in different words.

Using a Source	Examples
Direct Quotation	What is important in learning a foreign language? According to Wilkins (1972), **"While without grammar very little can be conveyed, without vocabulary nothing can be conveyed"** (p. 111).
Paraphrase	What is important in learning a foreign language? According to Wilkins (1972), **communication depends much more on vocabulary than on grammar** (p. 111).

If a writer uses a direct quotation from a source, the borrowed words must be placed in **quotation marks**. In contrast, paraphrasing does not require quotation marks because the writer is not using the exact words from the original source. Whether a writer is using an exact quotation or a paraphrased version, the information is not original and must be cited.

Methods of Citing Sources in Your Paper

There are a few different methods for composing citations in your paper. Two of the most common styles are **APA** (American Psychology Association) and **MLA** (Modern Language Association). In general, APA is used in the sciences, while MLA is used in the humanities.

In this book, we use APA because of the topics in the essays. When you write a research paper for a class, you should confirm with the teacher which method to use for your paper.

Examples of APA Style Citations in Context

A Direct Quotation

Study this excerpt from the book *Vocabulary Myths* (Folse, 2004). The example contains a direct quotation. When you use a direct quotation in APA style, you must state the **name of the author**, the **date of the publication**, and the **page number of the direct quotation**.

> One of the first observations that second language learners make in their new language is that they need vocabulary knowledge to function well in that language. How frustrating it is when you are unable to say something because you don't know the word for a simple noun even! In spite of the obvious importance of vocabulary, most courses and curricula tend to be based on grammar or a combination of grammar and communication strategies rather than vocabulary. As a result, even after taking many courses, learners still lack sufficient vocabulary knowledge. Vocabulary knowledge is critical to any communication. Wilkins (1972) summarizes the situation best with "While without grammar very little can be conveyed, without vocabulary nothing can be conveyed" (p. 111).

A Longer Quotation

Notice that the following paragraph from *Vocabulary Myths* (Folse, 2004) contains a longer direct quotation. The longer quotation is indicated in a different way from the rest of the writing. While shorter quotations are set off with quotation marks, longer quotations must be indented, without quotation marks. Shorter quotations are much more common in papers than longer quotations. In general, a paper should not use more than one or two longer quotations, and, except for very rare cases, a longer quotation should not exceed ten lines.

> As more and more empirical research in second language study is made available and results provide important insight into our questions about vocabulary learning and teaching, the education pendulum is swinging back toward some more "traditional" methods, including those which rely on explicit instruction from the teacher. This in turn begs the question of what kinds of classroom activities, especially vocabulary activities, are effective for L2 learners. Carter and McCarthy (1988) conclude that
>> although it suffered neglect for a long time, vocabulary pedagogy has benefited in the last fifteen years or so from theoretical advances in the linguistic lexicon, from psycholinguistic investigations into the mental lexicon, from the communicative trend in teaching, which has brought the learner into focus, and from developments in computers. What is perhaps missing in all this is more knowledge about what happens in classrooms when vocabulary crops up. (p. 51)

A Paraphrase

Notice that the following paragraph from *Vocabulary Myths* (Folse, 2004) contains a paraphrase, or restatement, of a concept from a work written by Eskey in 1988. Instead of using any phrases or sentences from Eskey's work, Folse uses his own words (underlined sentence) to restate Eskey's work and connect that idea to the current paragraph and audience. When you paraphrase material, you must state the name of the author, the date of the publication, and the page number(s).

> While lack of vocabulary knowledge is a problem across all skill areas, it is especially apparent in ESL reading. Eskey (1988) found that not being able to recognize the meaning of English words automatically causes students who are good readers in their native language to do excessive guesswork in the second language and that this guessing slows down the process of reading (pp. 27–28).

Key Words to Introduce a Direct Quotation or a Paraphrase

One of the most common ways to introduce a direct quotation or a paraphrase is to use the preposition **according to + the name of the journal** or **the name of the author**.

Example with Direct Quotation

According to a report in the ***New England Journal of Medicine***, "Senior citizens who have experienced acute chest pains at least twice in the past six months often find themselves back in the hospital within a month if they have not sought professional treatment"(p. 37).

Example with Paraphrase

According to a report in ***New England Journal of Medicine***, elderly patients who have suffered chest pains two times in six months should get medical treatment or they may require serious medical treatment again within thirty days (p. 37).

In addition to **according to**, you should use **common reporting verbs** to add variety to your writing:

As Poundstone **suggests**, "Where possible, give a good answer that the interviewer has never heard before" (p. 129).

In their study of online learning, Hiltz and Shea (2013) **conclude** that many online courses "elicit more active participation from students than does the typical face-to-face course" (p. 145).

Common Reporting Verbs		
admit	insist	report
agree	maintain	show
concede	note	suggest
conclude	observe	reveal
disagree	point out	think
explain	predict	warn
find	propose	write

Plagiarism: Be Very Careful!

If writers do not give credit for borrowed ideas or words, they make a serious error. In fact, it is academic theft, and such stealing of ideas or words cannot be tolerated at all. It is not acceptable to use even a few words from another source without citing the source; the amount of information that you borrow is irrelevant. If you steal one sentence or one paragraph, it is still stealing. Stealing someone else's ideas or words and using them in a piece of writing as if they were the writer's original ideas is called **plagiarism**.

In most schools, there are extremely serious academic consequences for plagiarizing any work. For example, some schools require that the student receive no credit for the paper. Other schools will expel the student permanently. In some instances, schools will take both actions.

Does this mean then that writers cannot use other people's words or ideas? No, not at all. In fact, good writing can be strengthened by using facts from sources or quotations to support key points or ideas, so writers should borrow appropriate information. The key to avoiding plagiarism is to cite the source of the information. Your paper should consist of your words, and any words or ideas that are not your original work must be cited.

Many students have a difficult time knowing when to use a citation, especially if they believe the information is general knowledge. When should you cite? If the ideas are not yours, you should cite those ideas. In addition, when the ideas are not common knowledge, you should cite them.

Paraphrasing, Summarizing, Synthesizing

In writing longer essays, you will often have to write information based on something you have read. Therefore, it is important to learn how to **paraphrase** (use different language to say the same thing), **summarize** (express the same idea in fewer words), and **synthesize** (combine information from two or more sources).

The diagram below shows how you may paraphrase a source, summarize a source, and then use these skills to synthesize information from two or more sources into your original writing.

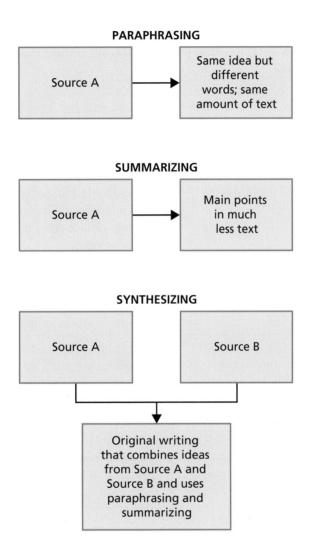

PARAPHRASING

Source A → Same idea but different words; same amount of text

SUMMARIZING

Source A → Main points in much less text

SYNTHESIZING

Source A   Source B

↓

Original writing that combines ideas from Source A and Source B and uses paraphrasing and summarizing

Paraphrasing

Using ideas and information from other sources strengthens your writing. One option when using other people's ideas is to include their exact words as a direct quotation and put quotation marks around them. Including direct quotations is a dramatic way to show that you are using other sources in your work. However, direct quotations should not be overused in a paper. In general, you should not include more than two direct quotations per page.

A much more common way to use other people's ideas is to restate them in your own words, which is called a **paraphrase**.

Paraphrasing can be difficult for some writers because it requires a large vocabulary that will allow you to express the ideas in different words.

Basic Steps for Paraphrasing
1. Read the source material and understand it well.
2. Decide which material you want to use.
3. Think of a different way to say that information.
4. Use different and original vocabulary.
5. Use different and original sentence structure.

Examples of Paraphrasing

Paraphrasing is an extremely important skill for all academic writers. Study these examples of good and poor paraphrasing.

Original (13 words) Selling a product successfully in another country often requires changes in the product.	Main idea to keep: Companies must change their products to succeed in another country
✓ The most successful exporting companies have succeeded because they made important changes in their products. (15 words)	1. It keeps the idea that change is necessary. 2. Grammar is different (subject: *exporting companies*; verb: *have succeeded*; dependent clause: *because they made important changes in their products*). 3. Vocabulary is different (*successful exporting companies, have succeeded because, important*). 4. Length is similar to original.
X To sell a product successfully in another country, you need to change the product. (14 words)	1. The ideas are the same, but the wording is too similar (*successfully, in another country*). In fact, it is almost exactly the same. (Reread the original above.) This is plagiarism! 2. Though the length is similar to the original, only minor changes were made (*Selling = To sell; often requires = you need to*) 3. The use of *you* is usually not acceptable in academic writing.

Practice with Paraphrasing

In this section, you will practice paraphrasing from an original source. Read the paragraph about the U.S. city of Orlando, Florida. If you have any questions about the paragraph, discuss them with your classmates.

Orlando: From Tiny Town to Major Metropolitan Area*

The city of Orlando, located in sunny central Florida, has experienced enormous growth and is internationally known as a popular tourist destination. Founded in 1844, Orlando was a small town for more than a century. With the arrival of the South Florida Railroad in 1880, Orlando was on its way to rapid growth. However, no one could have predicted the extent of what was to come. This growth was intensified with the development of the Cape Canaveral space complex in 1950. Two decades later, Orlando experienced rapid growth again on an incredible scale when Walt Disney World opened its gates to tourists in 1971. Located 22 miles southwest of Orlando, the Disney complex alone covers some 28,000 acres. In addition to having Florida's largest hotel (with 1,509 rooms), Walt Disney World has a variety of thrilling attractions, including the Magic Kingdom, Epcot, Disney's Hollywood Studios, and Animal Kingdom. Though Orlando has other industries, the tourist industry is by far the leading area of employment for the region. Because of this increase in tourism, Orlando has undergone an amazing amount of growth, which will likely continue given the popularity of this city as a world tourist destination.

Adapted from: http://www.britannica.com/bcom/eb/
    article/7/0,5716,58827+1+57392,00.html

Paraphrasing: Multiple Choice

Read the original sentences about Orlando and then read the three possible paraphrases. Mark which is the best (*B*), which is too similar (*TS*), and which has a different meaning or wrong information (*X*).

1. With the arrival of the South Florida Railroad in 1880, Orlando was on its way to rapid growth.

    _____ **a.** With the arrival of the South Florida Railroad in 1880, the city of Orlando was on its way to fast growth.

    _____ **b.** The city of Orlando began to grow tremendously when the South Florida Railroad reached the city in 1880.

    _____ **c.** Most people were genuinely shocked at how quickly Orlando grew after the South Florida Railroad arrived in 1880.

2. These theme parks pull more than 55 million people a year to what was until recently an empty area of land.

    _____ **a.** Because the theme parks in the Orlando area are so popular, there is no more space for additional parks.

    _____ **b.** The theme parks in Orlando attract over 55 million people every year, and this area was empty until recently.

    _____ **c.** Over 55 million tourists visit this recently developed Florida city because of its numerous theme parks.

ACTIVITY 2 **Paraphrasing Practice**

Read the original sentences. Circle what you consider to be the most important ideas. Then in number 1, put a check mark (✔) next to the best paraphrase for the original sentence. In number 2, write your own paraphrase of the sentence.

1. Two decades later, Orlando experienced rapid growth again on an incredible scale when Walt Disney World opened its gates to tourists in 1971.

    _____ **a.** Twenty years later, rapid growth on an incredible scale was seen in Orlando when Walt Disney World opened its gates to tourists.

    _____ **b.** In 1971, Walt Disney World opened for business in Orlando.

    _____ **c.** The opening of Walt Disney World in 1971 caused a massive increase in the number of tourists to Orlando.

2. Orlando, which was a quiet farming town a little more than 40 years ago, has more people passing through it than any other place in the state of Florida.

    Your paraphrase: _____

    _____

    _____

Summarizing

In addition to quoting and paraphrasing, another way to include information from another source is by **summarizing** it. When you summarize, you do not include all of the information from the source. Instead, you use only the parts you think are the most important. Remember that summaries do not contain any of your original ideas.

Summarizing involves not only writing but also reading and critical thinking.

Basic Steps for Summarizing
1. Read the source material and understand it well.
2. Decide which parts of the source material are the most important.
3. Put the important parts in the same order they appear in the original.
4. Paraphrase, using different grammar and vocabulary (see page 58).

A summary is always shorter than the original writing. A ten-page article might become a few paragraphs in a summary. A two-hundred page book might become an essay.

Examples of Summarizing

Summarizing is a very useful skill for a good writer. It is especially important when you are taking information from long sources. Study these examples of good and poor summarizing.

Original (184 words)	Main ideas to keep:
Selling a product successfully in another country often requires changes in the product. Domino's Pizza offers mayonnaise and potato pizza in Tokyo and pickled ginger pizza in India. Heinz varies its ketchup recipe to satisfy the needs of specific markets. In Belgium and Holland, for example, the ketchup is not as sweet as it is in the United States. When Häagen-Dazs served up one of its most popular American flavors, Chocolate Chip Cookie Dough, to British customers, they left it sitting in supermarket freezers. What the premium ice-cream maker learned is that chocolate chip cookies are not popular in Great Britain, and children do not have a history of snatching raw dough from the bowl. So the company had to develop flavors that would sell in Great Britain. Because dairy products are not part of Chinese diets, Frito-Lay took the cheese out of Cheetos in China. Instead, the company sells Seafood Cheetos. Without a doubt, these products were so successful in these foreign lands only because the company realized that it was wise to do market research and make fundamental changes in the products.	1. Companies must change their products to succeed. 2. Examples of companies that did this: Domino's, Heinz, Häagen-Dazs, Frito-Lay.
Reference	
Pride, W. M., Hughes, R. J., & Kapoor, J. R. (2014). *Business* (12th ed.). Mason, Ohio: South-Western Cengage Learning.	

✓ Companies must adapt their products if they want to do well in foreign markets. Many well-known companies, including Domino's, Heinz, Häagen-Dazs, and Frito-Lay, have altered their products and proved this point. (31 words) **Reference** Pride, W. M., Hughes, R. J., & Kapoor, J. R. (2014). *Business* (12th ed.). Mason, Ohio: South-Western Cengage Learning.	1. It covers the main ideas. 2. It is a true summary, not an exact repeat of the specific examples. 3. It includes some new grammar, for example: Original text: *often requires changes* Summary: modal is used: *companies must adapt* 4. It includes some new vocabulary, for example: Original text: Specific country names Summary: *foreign markets*
X Changes in a product are important if a company wants to sell it successfully in another country. For example, Domino's Pizza offers mayonnaise and potato pizza in Tokyo and pickled ginger pizza in India. In addition, Heinz has changed its ketchup recipe to satisfy the needs of specific markets. In Belgium and Holland the ketchup is less sweet. When Häagen-Dazs served up one of its most popular American flavors, Chocolate Chip Cookie Dough, to British customers, the British customers left it sitting in supermarket freezers. The luxury ice-cream maker learned that chocolate chip cookies are not popular in Great Britain, and children do not take uncooked dough from the bowl. So the company developed flavors to sell in Great Britain. Since dairy products are not usually eaten in China, Frito-Lay removed the cheese from Cheetos in China. In its place, the company has Seafood Cheetos. Certainly, these items were so successful in these countries only because the company was smart enough to do market research and implement fundamental changes in the products. (172 words) **Reference** Pride, W. M., Hughes, R. J., & Kapoor, J. R. (2014). *Business* (12th ed.). Mason, Ohio: South-Western Cengage Learning.	1. It is almost as long as the original and, therefore, not really a summary. 2. It includes almost the same vocabulary, for example: Original text: *the premium ice-cream maker* Summary: *the luxury ice-cream maker* This is plagiarism! 3. It includes almost the same grammar, for example: Original text: *So the company had to develop flavors that would sell in Great Britain.* Summary: *So the company developed flavors to sell in Great Britain.* This is plagiarism!

Practice with Summarizing

In this section, you will practice summarizing from an original source. Read another paragraph about the U.S. city of Orlando, Florida. If you have any questions about the paragraph, discuss them with your classmates.

The Effects of Tourism on One Florida City*

Orlando, which was a quiet farming town a little more than 40 years ago, has more people passing through it than any other place in the state of Florida. The reason, of course, is Walt Disney World, Universal Studios, Sea World, and a host of other theme attractions. These theme parks pull more than 55 million people a year to what was until recently an empty area of land. Few of these people visit the actual city of Orlando. Instead, they prefer to stay in one of the countless motels 15 miles to the south along Highway 19 or five miles southwest on International Drive. Despite enormous expansion over the last two decades, the city itself remains free of the commercialism that surrounds it. However, the city has not been able to escape the traffic congestion and other problems associated with the visit of so many millions of tourists as well as the thousands of people who work in the tourist industry. Without a doubt, tourism has changed life for the residents of Orlando and the surrounding area.

*Adapted from: http://search.britannica.com/frm_redir
.jsp?query=Orlando&redir=http://city.net/countries/
united_states/florida/orlando/*

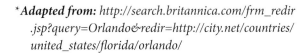

ACTIVITY 3 **Summarizing: Identifying the Most Important Ideas**

Read the paragraph "The Effects of Tourism on One Florida City." Make a list of four important facts and ideas. Then paraphrase the facts and ideas.

Facts	Your Paraphrase
1.	
2.	
3.	
4.	

ACTIVITY 4 **Summarizing: Putting It in Your Own Words**

Use your ideas from Activity 3 to write two to five sentences that summarize the original message of "The Effects of Tourism on One Florida City."

_____

_____

_____

_____

_____

_____

_____

Synthesizing

A **synthesis** is a combination of information from two or more sources. When you synthesize, you take information from different sources and blend them smoothly into your paragraph.

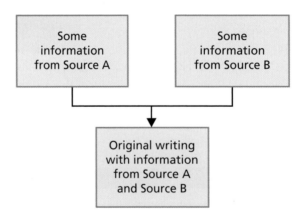

Basic Steps for Synthesizing

1. Read the material from all of the sources.
2. Choose the important ideas from each source. You must analyze the information. Ask yourself, "What is the author's purpose for writing this information?" Then decide which pieces of information are most important in accomplishing what the author intended. It is always important in synthesizing to use only the important, relevant information.
3. Group together the ideas that are connected and that support each other.
4. Combine the ideas in each group into sentences, using your paraphrasing skills (see page 58).
5. Organize the sentences logically and combine them into one continuous piece of writing. Do not forget to include your original ideas, too.
6. Check your work for accuracy and smoothness.

Examples of Synthesizing

Synthesis is an important skill for academic writers, who often use more than one source when writing papers. Study these examples of good and poor synthesizing.

Source A (81 words)	Main ideas to keep:
Switzerland is a great example of linguistic diversity because there are three different national languages. People in the central and northern areas speak German. People in the western area speak French. People in the southeastern area of the country speak Italian. Most Swiss can speak more than one language. One interesting fact is that the name of the country on its coins and stamps is not in any of these languages. Instead, "Helvetia," the Latin name for this country, is used.	1. Geographical areas of Switzerland speak different languages. 2. Central and northern regions = German 3. Western part = French 4. Southeastern region = Italian 5. The Latin name for Switzerland is used as well.
Source B (68 words)	Main idea to keep:
You might think that most of the people in Switzerland speak the same language because it is a rather small country. However, you would be wrong. Yes, the country is tiny, but there are four national languages. German is spoken by more people than any other language. The second most commonly spoken language is French, and Italian is third. A very small percentage of the people speak Romansch.	Most Swiss speak German, then French, then Italian, and finally a few people in Switzerland speak Romansch.

✓ Although Switzerland is a small country, several languages are spoken there. In fact, this tiny country has four national languages. The most commonly spoken language is German, which is used in the central and northern regions. The second most widely spoken language is French, which is used in the western area of the country. The third most commonly used language is Italian, which is spoken in the southeastern area of Switzerland. A fourth language, Romansch, is spoken by only a very small percentage of the population. Ironically, the name for Switzerland on Swiss currency is not in any of these languages. Instead, "Helvetia," the Latin term for this country, is used. (111 words)	1. It has ideas from both sources (for example, Source A: *German is spoken in central and northern regions*; Source B: *the most common language is German*) 2. The ideas are woven together. (*The most commonly spoken language is German, which is used in the central and northern regions.*) 3. The sequence of the material is logical. (first, second, third, fourth most common languages)
X Switzerland is tiny, but there are four national languages. The languages in order of usage are: German, French, Italian, and Romansch. Portuguese and Greek are not spoken in this country. People in the western area speak French. People in the southeastern area of the country speak Italian. People in the central and northern areas speak German. One interesting fact is that the name of the country on its coins and stamps is not in any of these languages. Instead, "Helvetia," the Latin name for this country, is used. (88 words)	1. The ideas are not woven together very well. It is easy to see where one source ends and another begins. Source B information ends after *The languages in order of usage are German, French, Italian, and Romansch.* Source A information takes up the rest of the paragraph. 2. The third sentence is an unrelated idea about Portuguese and Greek that is not from either source. 3. The sequence of the languages by geographical areas is illogical because it does not match the list of languages given at the beginning of the paragraph.

Original Student Writing: Using Two Sources to Create Your Paper

In this section, you will follow seven steps in the writing process to write a short essay with a title, introduction (with an interesting hook and a thesis statement), body paragraphs that develop the topic, and a strong conclusion. If you need help with the steps in the writing process, refer to Unit 2, pages 34–46.

ACTIVITY 5 **Step 1: Choose a Topic**

In this unit, the topic has been chosen for you. Imagine that you are a student in a sociology class. Write a short essay that synthesizes the information from the two paragraphs about Orlando ("Orlando: From Tiny Town to Major Metropolitan Area," page 59, and "The Effects of Tourism on One Florida City," page 63). According to your teacher's instructions, you may need additional sources.

You should ask yourself, "What do I know about this topic? What do my readers know? What else do I need to know? Do I need to research this topic more?"

1. What are the first questions that come to mind when you see this writing assignment?

_____

_____

_____

_____

2. How well do you know this topic? What is your experience with it?

_____

_____

_____

_____

ACTIVITY 6 **Step 2: Brainstorm**

Use this space to jot down as many ideas about the topic as you can.

Brainstorming Box

```



```

ACTIVITY 7 | Step 3: Outline

Prepare a simple outline of your essay. This outline is set up for five paragraphs, but you may write fewer paragraphs or more, depending on your answers in Activity 5 on pages 66–67.

Title: _____

   I. Introduction

      A. Hook: _____

         _____

      B. Connecting information: _____

         _____

      C. Thesis statement: _____

         _____

         _____

   II. Topic of Body Paragraph 1: _____

     Two to four ideas to include:

      A. _____

      B. _____

      C. _____

      D. _____

  III. Topic of Body Paragraph 2: _____

     Two to four ideas to include:

      A. _____

      B. _____

      C. _____

      D. _____

  IV. Topic of Body Paragraph 3: _____

     Two to four ideas to include:

      A. _____

      B. _____

      C. _____

      D. _____

V. Conclusion: _____

_____

_____

Peer Editing of Outlines

Exchange books with a partner. Read your partner's outline. Then use the following questions to help you to comment on your partner's outline. Use your partner's feedback to revise your outline.

1. Is there any aspect of the outline that is unclear to you? Give details here.

_____

_____

_____

2. Can you think of an area in the outline that needs more development? Make specific suggestions.

_____

_____

_____

3. If you have any other ideas or suggestions, write them here.

_____

_____

_____

ACTIVITY 8 **Step 4: Write the First Draft**

Use the information from Steps 1–3 to write the first draft of your essay. Try to use at least four of the words from the Academic Word List in the *Brief Writer's Handbook with Activities* on pages 230–231.

ACTIVITY 9 **Step 5: Get Feedback from a Peer**

Exchange papers from Step 4 with a partner. Read your partner's first draft. Then use Peer Editing Sheet 3 (available online at NGL.Cengage.com/GW5) to help you comment on your partner's writing. Be sure to offer positive suggestions and comments that will help your partner improve his or her essay.

Read the comments on Peer Editing Sheet 3 about your essay. Then reread your essay. Can you identify places where you should make revisions? List the improvements you plan to make.

1. _____

_____

_____

2. _____

_____

_____

_____

3. _____

_____

_____

Use all the information from the previous steps to write the final version of your paper. Often, writers will need to write a third or even a fourth draft to express their ideas as clearly as possible. Write as many drafts as necessary to produce a good essay.

ACTIVITY 11 **Step 7: Proofread the Final Draft**

Be sure to proofread your paper several times before you submit it so you find all the mistakes and correct them.

Additional Topics for Writing

Here are five more ideas for topics for essay writing. Your teacher may require you to consult one or more sources.

PHOTO
TOPIC: Look at the photo on pages 52–53. Discuss the international origin of at least three popular foods.

TOPIC 2: What are some of the causes of cheating on exams?

TOPIC 3: Explain how a person can quit a bad habit.

TOPIC 4: What are the major differences between a debit card and a credit card? Does one offer more advantages than the other? Explain.

TOPIC 5: Should passengers on airplanes be allowed to use their cell phones?

Timed Writing

How quickly can you write in English? There are many times when you must write quickly, such as on a test. It is important to feel comfortable during those times. Timed-writing practice can make you feel better about writing quickly in English.

1. Take out a piece of paper.

2. Read the writing prompt below.

3. Write a basic outline, including the introduction and thesis, the body paragraphs, and the conclusion. You should spend no more than five minutes on your outline.

4. Your essay needs at least five paragraphs.

5. You have 40 minutes to write your essay.

A kindergarten teacher has one of the most difficult jobs. Write an essay in which you present three arguments to support this statement.

A woman makes bamboo umbrellas near Chiang Mai, Thailand.

OBJECTIVES To learn how to write a process essay
To use effective transitions and connectors in process writing
To use subject-verb agreement correctly
To add the correct suffixes based on a word's part of speech

What do you know how to build or create?

What Is a Process Essay?

A **process essay** explains in detail how a certain objective is accomplished. You might think of a process essay as a set of instructions explaining the most effective means to achieve a desired goal.

Although all process essays describe how to accomplish a particular goal, the more interesting essays also include relevant information about the wider context of the process. Why is this process important? How is it useful to the reader who is learning about it? What are the benefits and/or limitations of the process? When you answer such questions before you write the essay, your writing will be better tailored to your specific audience.

When you write a process essay, you need to pay special attention to your **audience.** You should always consider what your readers already know or do not know. How much information do they need so that they can understand the process? For example, if you write an essay describing the causes of heart disease, it is important to know whether your readers are high school students or doctors.

How Is a Process Essay Organized?

The most common way of organizing a process essay is **chronologically**. In a **chronological process essay,** the writer describes the steps in the order in which they happen. In some process essays, a person is in charge of doing certain steps in chronological order. This method is helpful for teaching a person a new skill, such as how to repair a computer or how to change the oil in a car. In addition, this method is also used when reporting the sequence of events in a natural event such as how a hurricane is formed or how a butterfly is created.

A simple process, such as how to make a tomato sandwich, may have as few as three steps. A more complicated process, such as how a car is manufactured, has many more steps. At first, you may think that a good way to organize a process essay is to write one paragraph for each step. This system may work for steps that need extended explanation and supporting information. In contrast, when many steps are needed that are not complicated, your paragraphs would consist of only one sentence, such as *Now cut the tomatoes into thin slices*. However, a paragraph should not be only one sentence long, so this is not good writing. A better way to write this kind of essay would be to organize the smaller steps into groups of steps that have something in common.

For example, if your essay explains the steps in evaluating the quality of a restaurant, you might write about how you evaluate the restaurant before you eat there and then after you eat there. In other words, you could group all of the steps into two bigger categories. Such an essay could look like this:

INTRODUCTION	Paragraph 1	Hook Connecting information Thesis
BODY	Paragraph 2	Before you visit a restaurant • Step 1: Check the quality of the restaurant's website. • Step 2: Analyze the restaurant's location. • Step 3: Compare the restaurant's prices with prices of competing restaurants.
	Paragraph 3	After you visit a restaurant • Step 4: Write about the restaurant's atmosphere. • Step 5: Describe the food. • Step 6: Analyze the restaurant's strengths and weaknesses.
CONCLUSION	Paragraph 4	Restated thesis Suggestion/opinion/prediction

For this same essay, you could write a paragraph about each of the six steps if you have enough information about each step to avoid any one-sentence paragraphs. In this case, the essay would have eight paragraphs and might look like this:

INTRODUCTION	Paragraph 1	Hook Connecting information Thesis
BODY	Paragraph 2	Step 1: Check the quality of the restaurant's website.
	Paragraph 3	Step 2: Analyze the restaurant's location.
	Paragraph 4	Step 3: Compare the restaurant's prices with prices of competing restaurants.
	Paragraph 5	Step 4: Write about the restaurant's atmosphere.
	Paragraph 6	Step 5: Describe the food.
	Paragraph 7	Step 6: Analyze the restaurant's strengths and weaknesses.
CONCLUSION	Paragraph 8	Restated thesis Suggestion/opinion/prediction

Great Topics for Process Essays

What is a great topic for a process essay? Obviously, this type of essay should tell how something happens. Simply put, a process essay explains the steps involved in a process.

Process essay topics can range from a task as simple as how to access a website about the geography of a country to a task as complex as how electricity is produced.

Here are some general topics that lend themselves well to a process essay. Notice how the topics in the left column would use steps to accomplish a goal, while the topics in the right column would include more complex processes, such as what happens during a natural event.

For a Goal	For a Complex Process
how to train a pet to do a trick	explaining a solar eclipse
explaining the steps in a lab report about an experiment you conducted	describing how an airplane can fly
creating a great PowerPoint® presentation	describing how tornadoes form
using Twitter	explaining how cats keep themselves clean

ACTIVITY 1   Identifying Topics for Process Essays

Read these eight topics. Put a check mark (✔) next to the four that could be good topics for process essays.

_____ 1. The steps in applying for a bank loan to purchase a vehicle

_____ 2. Dubai versus Istanbul as a vacation destination

_____ 3. How to get a passport most efficiently

_____ 4. Steps to convince citizens to support a candidate

_____ 5. An analysis of driving routes in a certain community

_____ 6. Reasons that a person should stop smoking

_____ 7. An argument against deforestation

_____ 8. How a new laptop is manufactured

Can you think of two additional topics that would be excellent for a process essay?

9. _____

10. _____

Supporting Details

Many of the everday tasks we do, such as paying bills and cooking meals, involve processes with seemingly simple steps. However, if you made a list of all of the actual steps in that process, you would quickly see that no process is as simple as it seems.

When you brainstorm your plan for writing an essay, a useful technique is to think of details for each step. As you explain each step, make sure that a reader who does not know much about the topic can easily follow the steps, based on your instructions.

ACTIVITY 2 Brainstorming Steps in a Process

Choose one task and use the space in the box to brainstorm the steps necessary to perform the task. Then read your steps to a partner to check whether you included all of the necessary steps.

1. making your favorite lunch

2. directing someone to a building on the other side of the city

3. washing your clothes

4. taking care of your pet

ACTIVITY 3 Studying an Example Process Essay

This essay explains how to do well in a job interview. Discuss the Preview Questions with a partner. Then read the essay and answer the questions that follow.

Preview Questions

1. How many job interviews have you had?

2. What was your most difficult job interview? What made it difficult?

3. What are two or three ways to do well in a job interview?

Essay 7

How to Succeed in a Job Interview

1   While most people want jobs, few look forward to interviewing for them. Job interviews are stressful situations for even the most qualified **candidates** because applicants have only one opportunity to demonstrate that they will succeed and will do better than the other applicants in the position they are **seeking**. To approach a job interview successfully, applicants should prepare well so that their interviewers will clearly **perceive** their **assets** as a candidate, as one capable of contributing effectively to the company.

2   First, applicants should research the company and learn as much about it as possible. They should not focus **exclusively** on the specific department that will hire them but on the company as a whole and how

a candidate: a person competing for a specific job or other position

to seek: to look for; to search for

to perceive: to feel; to believe; to think

an asset: a useful and valuable thing or quality

exclusively: available for only one person or one group

they can contribute to its mission. Stein (2003) cautions job seekers that interviewers frequently ask a variation of the following question: "What do you know about our company, and why would you like to work here?" (p. 59). To answer this kind of question **effectively**, and to answer it more effectively than their **fellow** job seekers, applicants must have done sufficient research to understand the needs of the company.

3   In addition, applicants should **bear in mind** that the interviewer is repeating the same questions to different candidates over an interval of several days, or even several weeks. Therefore, applicants should consider ways to make their answers unique so that they will **stand out**. As Poundstone (2003) suggests, an applicant's goal should be to make a unique impression on the interviewer by giving a good answer that the interviewer has never heard before. Applicants can expect certain questions about their training and skill sets, but rather than simply answering them and then moving on to the next question, they should use this opportunity to give specific examples and **anecdotes** about their experiences that make them **ideal** candidates for the job. Of course, applicants should not talk too much about how wonderful they are, but answers that are too brief are a wasted opportunity to illustrate specific strengths. Curtis (2000) advises interviewers to "spend 75 to 80 percent of their time listening and 20 to 25 percent talking or **soliciting**" (p. 39), which implies that during the majority of the interview, applicants should discuss how they match the job's requirements. Applicants must recognize that the interviewer wants to learn about them, so they should give full, detailed, and unique answers to the questions.

effectively: in a way that produces the desired goal or objective

fellow: one who is in a similar group

to bear in mind: to keep in mind; to consider; to remember

to stand out: to be different from the other members of a group

an anecdote: a personal story

ideal: perfect

to solicit: to ask; to request

4　　As an interview **proceeds**, applicants should be careful about their nonverbal communication. Bunting (2005) cautions job applicants to consider the importance of nonverbal communications because, as she notes, "Gestures, expressions and actions can speak a great deal louder than any words" (p. 29). Bunting advises job applicants to pay attention to their body language, facial expressions, and **posture**, and to **be aware of** the ways in which their nonverbal communications **contribute to** or **undermine** their verbal answers. If an applicant gives an **eloquent** answer while **glancing** at his or her watch or cell phone, the interviewer will likely feel that this person is insufficiently interested in the position. Applicants should display their motivation to succeed.

5　　Finally, applicants should recognize that frequently their interviewers will be older than they are, which means that there might be a generation **gap**. While this is not always the case, most interviewers have worked with the company long enough to rise through its **hierarchy** to now be in charge of hiring. Therefore, applicants should be careful not to use slang that the interviewer might not understand. At the same time, they should not assume that their interviewers will understand references to television shows, movies, or other aspects of popular culture. Communicating in a job interview requires applicants to consider the **challenging** situation of speaking effectively about themselves to a person or group of people they have only just met. **Ultimately**, the goal for applicants is to phrase their answers so they are sure to be understood.

6　　In the end, a successful job interview can improve a person's **prospects** by promoting opportunities for employment and future advancement. Although an applicant can never **anticipate precisely** how an interview will **unfold**, careful planning, detailed answers, attention to nonverbal communication, and appropriate word choice will make the process of applying for a job less stressful and more **likely** to be successful. Throughout every interview, whether during the **preliminary** round or in the final meeting, candidates must present a sharp, professional image, one that reveals their strengths while implicitly shielding their weaknesses, if they are to win the jobs they seek.

References

Bunting, S. (2005). *The interviewer's handbook: Successful interviewing techniques for the workplace.* London: Kogan Page.

Curtis, J. (2000). *Strategic interviewing: Skills and tactics for savvy executives.* Westport, CT: Quorum Books.

Poundstone, W. (2003). *How would you move Mount Fuji? How the world's smartest companies select the most creative thinkers.* New York: Little, Brown.

Stein, M. (2003). *Fearless interviewing: How to win the job by communicating with confidence.* New York: McGraw-Hill.

---

to proceed: to continue

posture: the way you carry your body; the position of your body

to be aware of: to be conscious of; to know about

to contribute to: to be an important role in causing something to happen

to undermine: to weaken the position of

eloquent: using clear and powerful language

to glance: to look at very briefly

a gap: a space or separation

hierarchy: the order or sequence ranked by importance or power

challenging: somewhat difficult; requiring effort to accomplish

ultimately: eventually; in the end

a prospect: a future possibility

to anticipate: to see in advance; to expect

precisely: exactly

to unfold: to develop; to reveal itself

likely: probable

preliminary: something that comes first to prepare for something else

Post-Reading

1. What is the topic of the essay? _____

2. What is the writer's thesis? _____

   _____

3. What are four suggestions the writer offers for a successful interview?

   a. _____

   _____

   b. _____

   _____

   c. _____

   _____

   d. _____

   _____

4. In your opinion, which of these four suggestions is the most important for a successful interview and why?

   _____

   _____

   _____

   _____

5. Can you think of any information that the writer could have included to make the message of the essay stronger?

   _____

   _____

   _____

Building Better Sentences: For further practice, go to Practice 1 on pages 238–239 in the Appendix.

Building Better Vocabulary

ACTIVITY 4 **Practicing Three Kinds of Vocabulary from Context**

Read each important vocabulary word or phrase. Locate it in the essay if you need help remembering the word. Then circle the best synonym, antonym, or collocation from column A, B, or C.

Type of Vocabulary	Important Vocabulary	A	B	C
Synonyms	1. seek	call off	look for	make up
	2. anticipate	chase	expect	gather
	3. undermine	comprehend	multiply	weaken
	4. challenging	difficult	healthy	local
Antonyms	5. proceed	explain	purchase	stop
	6. ideal	dishonest	imperfect	unhappy
	7. brief	long	mysterious	selfish
	8. insufficient	enough	important	original
Collocations	9. ___ research	do	make	put
	10. in ___ of	anger	charge	trouble
	11. ___ forward to	look	make	put
	12. bear in ___	brain	head	mind

Writer's Note

Outlines

The purpose of an outline is to help you organize your ideas and include sufficient and logical details that support your ideas. Formal outlines usually contain only nouns or only full sentences. However, some writers prefer to include nouns, phrases, sentences, or a mixture of these.

Note that the outline for "How to Succeed in a Job Interview" (pages 82–83) includes a mixture. If your instructor has not given you instructions for your outline, choose the system that is most comfortable for you.

ACTIVITY 5 **Analyzing the Organization**

Use the information from the box to complete the outline of "How to Succeed in a Job Interview." Reread the essay on pages 77–79 if you need help.

> - should seek to communicate as clearly as possible with their interviewers
> - cite scholar W. Poundstone
> - research the company and learn as much about it as possible
> - applicants to be careful about their nonverbal communication
> - careful planning, detailed answers, attention to nonverbal communication, and appropriate word choice
> - to succeed in a job interview, applicants should prepare well so that their interviewers will clearly perceive their assets as a candidate

Title: How to Succeed in a Job Interview

I. Introduction

    A. Establish that most people find job interviews stressful

    B. Thesis statement: _____ .

II. Body Paragraph 1

    A. Advise job applicants to _____ .

    B. Cite scholar M. Stein, who advises job seekers about the types of questions they are likely to face in interviews.

    C. Reiterate the need for job seekers to research the company they are applying to.

III. Body Paragraph 2

    A. Establish the fact that job interviewers are asking similar questions of many candidates, so effective applicants need to make their answers unique.

    B. _____, who advises candidates to give answers that the interviewers have never heard before.

    C. Candidates should be prepared to discuss their strengths for the position during the majority of the interview.

IV. Body Paragraph 3

    A. Establish the necessity for _____ .

    B. Cite scholar S. Bunting about the importance of nonverbal communication.

    C. Discuss the negative effects that arise when applicants are not careful about their nonverbal communication.

V. Body Paragraph 4

    A. Advise job applicants about the necessity of preparing for the generation gap—the likelihood that their interviewers will be older than they are.

    B. Discuss how references to popular culture might hamper candidates' ability to communicate with their interviewer.

    C. Emphasize that job applicants _____ .

VI. Conclusion

    A. Conclude by stressing that successful job interviews can build successful futures.

    B. Summarize the necessity of _____

_____ for successful

job interviews.

Strong Thesis Statements for Process Essays

A strong thesis statement for a process essay tells the reader that you are going to explain how to do something or tell how something happens. The simplest thesis statements often directly say the number of steps involved in the process you are writing about. Other thesis statements merely imply the existence of steps and do not mention the number. Sometimes a thesis statement for a process essay is more interesting or more intriguing if you include some information that expresses a condition or a judgment. The thesis statement may use hedging words such as **may, might, can, seem, appear,** or **some** or a condition with **if, provided that, unless,** or a similar word.

Type of thesis	Example thesis statement
thesis with the number of steps	Children go through **four** stages in learning to speak.
	Buying almost anything online involves **three** distinct steps.
thesis without the number of steps	Adapting to a new culture can be incredibly difficult **unless** you know what to expect.
	Playing chess **may appear** to be complicated, but it is actually an easy game **if** you understand the basic rules.

Write a thesis statement for each topic. When you finish, compare your answers with a partner's.

1. how chocolate is made

_____

_____

2. writing a thank-you note

_____

_____

3. cooking (any type of food you want) _____

_____

_____

Transitions and Connectors in Process Essays

Transitions and connectors are important in process essays because they help the reader visualize the order of the steps more clearly. Careful use of transitions helps the reader know when one step is complete and the next one is beginning.

Transitions and Connectors Often Used at the Beginning of the Process		
as you start	(the) first	initially
at first	(the) first step	to begin with
first	in the beginning	when you begin

Transitions and Connectors Often Used in the Middle of the Process			
after	before this	meanwhile	soon
after a few hours	continuing with	next	subsequently
after that	during	(the) next	then
afterward	eventually	(the) next step is	third
as	immediately before (or following)	previously	until
as you continue	in addition	second	when
at the same time	in the meantime	simultaneously	when this step is finished
before	later	since	while

Transitions and Connectors Often Used Near the End of the Process			
as you finish	finally	last	later
at last	in the end	(the) last step	toward the end
eventually	in the future	lastly	ultimately

ACTIVITY 7 Identifying Transitions and Connectors in an Essay

Reread "How to Succeed in a Job Interview" on pages 77–79. Find five transitions or connectors. Copy the sentences here, underline the transition or connector, and write the paragraph number in the parentheses.

Transition/Connector in the Introduction

1. _____ ( )

Transitions/Connectors in the Body Paragraphs

1. _____ ( )

2. _____ ( )

3. _____ ( )

Transition/Connector in the Conclusion

1. _____ ( )

Studying Transitions and Connectors in an Example Process Essay

ACTIVITY 8 Warming Up to the Topic

Answer the questions on your own. Then discuss them with a partner or in a small group.

1. What do you know about butterflies? What do you know about the life cycle of a butterfly?

_____

_____

2. Did you know that butterflies migrate great distances just like birds do? How far do you think a fragile butterfly can travel? Write your guess here. Then, to check your answer, do an Internet search about the migration of the monarch butterfly in Mexico.

_____

_____

ACTIVITY 9 Using Transitions and Connectors in an Essay

Read "How a Caterpillar Becomes a Butterfly" and circle the correct transition words or phrases.

Essay 8

How a Caterpillar Becomes a Butterfly

1   **1** (When / Soon) famed author Vladimir Nabokov (2000) was a child, he was amazed by the beauty of butterflies: "From the age of seven, everything I felt in connection with a rectangle of framed sunlight was dominated by a single passion. If my first glance of the morning was for the sun, my first thought was for the butterflies" (p. 81). Graceful, colorful, and **delicate**, very few animals **inspire** such delight and wonder as butterflies. The process of how the much less beautiful caterpillar **transforms** into a beautiful butterfly, which is truly one of the **miracles** of nature, requires four **discrete stages** for complete **metamorphosis**.

2   In **2** (first / the first) stage of a butterfly's life cycle, a **mature** female butterfly lays eggs. **3** (After / In addition) these eggs mature, the caterpillar, or *larva*, **emerges**. Larvae (plural of larva) are immature insects that have not yet developed fully; they are often wingless and wormlike. Dickens (1972) explains the purpose of the larval stage: "The **sole** purpose, one may think, of the larva or caterpillar is to eat. This certainly appears to be true, for the larva will eat so fast that it has to discard its non-elastic skin four or five times during its life" (p. 14). Typically, the larval stage lasts from two weeks to two months.

delicate: fragile

to inspire: to cause others to do something based on strong words or emotions

to transform: to change greatly in appearance

a miracle: an event that is so incredible that no one can explain how it is possible

discrete: separate; unrelated

a stage: a step in a process

a metamorphosis: a great change in appearance or condition

mature: fully grown or developed

to emerge: to come out of; to exit

sole: only; unique

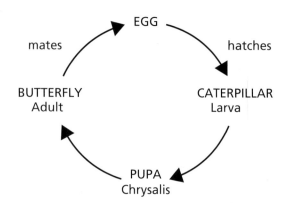

3   **4** (Next / The next) sequence in a butterfly's life cycle is referred to as the *pupa*, or *chrysalis*. The term *pupa* **denotes** this life stage for all insects, **whereas** *chrysalis* denotes this stage specifically for the life cycle of butterflies. **5** (Until / During) this stage, the insect **apparently** lies **dormant**; however, **6** (at the same time / afterward), within its protective **cocoon**, much activity is taking place. Its cell structure is breaking down, and the organism is undergoing its transformation into a butterfly. The chrysalis stage typically takes from one week to one month.

4   **7** (Finally / As you finish), the insect **transitions** from a chrysalis into a butterfly **8** (since / when) it emerges from its cocoon. This adult stage of a butterfly's life cycle is also referred to as the *imago* phase. A butterfly's wings are not yet fully developed when it leaves its cocoon, so, **9** (previously / immediately following), it must spend the first half hour after leaving its cocoon expanding them. During this stage of the life cycle, reproduction can begin again, **10** (as / before) adult butterflies **mate** and lay eggs to produce the next generation; hence, the life cycle of a new generation begins as well.

to denote: to indicate; to show

whereas: although; but

apparently: based on what people can see or think they know (although it may not be true)

dormant: inactive; sleeping

a cocoon: a protective covering that insects produce during certain stages of their life cycle

to transition: to make a change from one position or stage to the next

to mate: to copulate for the purpose of producing offspring

5   Butterflies' lives are brief, typically lasting only one to two months, but their life cycle as a whole is one of the wonders of nature. Few people truly appreciate the delightful appeal of caterpillars, but butterflies prove that nature's inspiring beauty often has surprising roots. The life cycle of the butterfly, from egg to larva to chrysalis to adult, provides a **vivid** example of the complexity of nature and the **remarkable** power of metamorphosis.

vivid: strong

remarkable: amazing; extraordinary

References

Dickens, M. (1972). *The world of butterflies.* New York: Macmillan.

Nabokov, V. (2000). *Nabokov's butterflies.* B. Boyd & R. M. Pyle (Eds.) (D. Nabokov, Trans.). Boston: Beacon.

Building Better Vocabulary

ACTIVITY 10 **Practicing Three Kinds of Vocabulary from Context**

Read each important vocabulary word or phrase. Locate it in the essay if you need help remembering the word. Then circle the best synonym, antonym, or collocation from column A, B, or C.

Type of Vocabulary	Important Vocabulary	A	B	C
Synonyms	1. transform	change	mention	require
	2. discrete	dangerous	jealous	separate
	3. expand	grow	knock	prove
	4. delicate	beautiful	fragile	illegal
Antonyms	5. remarkable	average	changing	friendly
	6. emerge	hide	inquire	unlock
	7. complex	colorful	immature	simple
	8. dormant	active	likely	reluctant
Collocations	9. develop ___	finely	fully	importantly
	10. the sole ___	morning	purpose	rectangle
	11. discard ___	information	money	trash
	12. as a ___	stage	transition	whole

Grammar for Writing

Subject-Verb Agreement

In any sentence, the subject and verb must agree in number.

Explanation	Examples
A singular verb must be used with a singular subject. A plural verb must be used with a plural subject.	singular subject singular verb An important **export** **is** cocoa. plural subject plural verb Important **exports** **are** cocoa and palm oil.
Words that come between the subject and the verb can sometimes cause writers to choose the wrong number for the verb. Remember that the object of a preposition is never the subject of a sentence.	singular subject object of preposition singular verb The main **export** of **Honduras, Guatemala, and Colombia is** coffee. plural subject object of preposition plural verb The main **exports** of **Guatemala** **are** coffee, sugar, and bananas.

ACTIVITY 11 Working with Subject-Verb Agreement

Write the correct form of the verb in parentheses.

1. After horrendous events, people often (react) _____ quite differently.

2. Rice and beans, my favorite dish, (remind) _____ me of my native Puerto Rico.

3. Most of the countries in OPEC (export) _____ millions of dollars worth of petroleum each day.

4. Surprisingly, our company has found that a survey covering more than 100 colleges often (reveal) _____ as much information as a survey of five key colleges in the central part of the state.

5. The characters in Pearl Buck's *The Good Earth* (live) _____ very simple lives.

Grammar for Writing

Suffixes

One way to become a better writer is to learn suffixes, or word endings, which will help you to understand how words are constructed. Recognizing word endings and learning what they mean will increase your vocabulary at the same time that it improves your writing.

Adjective Endings		
Suffix	**Meaning**	**Examples**
-able	able to	enjoyable, acceptable
-al	having the quality of	criminal, musical
-ant	having the quality of	reluctant, defiant
-ar / -ary	relating to	spectacular, ordinary
-ate	characterized by	considerate, passionate
-ative / -itive	having the quality of	talkative, primitive
-ed / -en	past participle	selected, chosen
-en	made of	golden, wooden
-ent	having the quality of	consistent, dependent
-ful	full of	beautiful, stressful
-ible	able to	inflexible, possible
-ing	present participle	confusing, existing
-ish	having the quality of	childish, foolish
-ive	having the quality of	expensive, protective
-less	without	wingless, harmless
-ly	having the quality of	finally, exclusively
-ory	relating to	mandatory, obligatory
-ous	full of	advantageous, spacious
-y	tending to	clearly, frequently

Noun Endings		
Suffix	Meaning	Examples
-ance / -ence	condition, state	importance, excellence
-ant / -ent	person who	applicant, student
-ar	person who	liar, scholar
-ation	action, state	exploitation, exploration
-er / -or	person who	employer, donor
-ery	relating to	bribery, slavery
-ing	gerund (action)	interviewing, shopping
-ion / -sion / -tion	action, state	opinion, explosion, transition
-ism	belief, practice	socialism, skepticism
-ment	result of action	agreement, requirement
-ness	quality, state	darkness, politeness
-ship	condition, quality	partnership, scholarship
-ty / -ity	quality, condition	eligibility, complexity

Verb Endings		
Suffix	Meaning	Examples
-ate	cause, make	anticipate, illustrate
-en	make	ripen, widen
-ify	make	beautify, simplify
-ize	make	recognize, maximize

ACTIVITY 12 **Editing Suffixes**

Read the paragraph. Write the correct form of the word in parentheses.

Paragraph 3

Sources of Energy

From the energy that is **1** (expend) _____ by a **2** (destroy) _____ hurricane or a **3** (dead) _____ earthquake to the energy that is **4** (require) _____ to make an automobile run, energy affects our lives in ways that are **5** (impossible) _____ to ignore. Often, when we talk about **6** (energy) _____, we are referring to the energy that people have channeled to provide **7** (heat) _____, light, and **8** (power) _____ for homes and industries. As the sources we have relied on for this energy are depleted or are found to pose **9** (threatens) _____ to our environment, efforts to develop **10** (practice) _____ new sources are increasing.

For more work with suffixes, see the *Brief Writer's Handbook with Activities*, pages 224–225.

Ten of the fifteen words in parentheses contain an error involving one of the grammar topics featured in this unit. If the word or phrase is correct, write *C*. If it is incorrect, fill in the blank with a correction.

Essay 9

Getting the Best Deal

1   **Bargaining** is a difficult process. The buyer wants to purchase a product at its minimal price; conversely, the seller **1** (want) _____ to maximize the **potential** for **profit** and revenue. The desires of the buyer and the seller **2** (opposes) _____ each other, and thus it is in the best interest of buyers to strategize exactly how they will convince sellers to **3** (lower) _____ their prices. Although prices are sometimes **inflexible**, buyers should always attempt to bargain with the seller.

bargaining: the act of a buyer and a seller arriving at a sales price

potential: possibility

profit: money remaining after a business transaction after all expenses have been deducted

inflexible: unable to bend or change

2   First, buyers should assume that the **price tag** represents the starting point of **negotiations**, not the final word on the **matter**. Assuming that the price tag indicates the **4** (finally) _____ price of an item is the single worst mistake that a buyer can make in the bargaining process. Buyers should begin by asking the salesperson whether any sales or discounts will soon be advertised. If customers do not request a special deal, the salesperson probably will not **volunteer** to give one to them. Salespeople often work on **commission**, so it is **5** (frequent) _____ to their advantage to hide this information from their customers. Buyers should also consider the bargaining **range** of the purchase. Pruitt and Carnevale (1993) define the bargaining range as the " **6** (distance) _____ between two parties' price limits," which includes numerous points of possible **7** (agree) _____ ranging from the advantageous to the disadvantageous (p. 51). Both buyer and seller should determine at what price their willingness to finish the deal overlaps.

3   Second, buyers must be prepared to walk away from an item when they are bargaining, even if they really want it. Dolan (2006) **stresses** that negotiators need to find out whether the seller has lowered prices in the past and, if so, by how much. For example, if the buyer learns that the seller has offered discounts to other customers in the past, he or she can request a **8** (similarity) _____ price. This step in the bargaining process **9** (requires) _____ **perseverance**, but it can **pay off 10** (financially) _____. Also, it is important that buyers never let sellers know that they need their products because the seller then has less of an **incentive** to lower the price.

4   Finally, buyers must be **11** (**patience**) _____. Looking for bargains takes time and energy, as buyers must **compile** a good deal of information about the merchandise. Sometimes buyers might need to purchase a product at a more expensive price simply because they do not have the time necessary to shop **further**. The buyer's time is important, too, and sometimes it is worth spending extra money if he or she needs the item immediately. However, sometimes simply by waiting two weeks or even two months, the buyer will save a

a price tag: a small piece of paper with a price written on it

a negotiation: a discussion between two parties to reach an agreement

the matter: the topic being discussed

to volunteer: to give freely without being forced to do so

a commission: an amount of money earned by a salesperson on a sale

a range: a variation between a low point and a high point

to stress: to emphasize

perseverance: continuing to attempt something despite difficulties

to pay off: to result in success

an incentive: a reward that causes someone to try harder

patience: remaining quiet or calm and without complaints despite imperfect conditions

to compile: to collect or gather

further: additional

12 (considerate) _____ amount of money. Under these **circumstances**, it can be **worthwhile** to wait.

5   Many people enjoy 13 (shopping) _____ for bargains, and many bargainers 14 (finds) _____ that it becomes an **addictive** game in which they compete with the salesperson to save their own money. Practitioners of the art of bargaining often improve in their 15 (subsequently) _____ negotiations and earn more money to bargain with the next time they go shopping.

a circumstance:
  a condition

worthwhile:
  beneficial; valuable

addictive: causing someone to be unable to stop doing something

References

Dolan, J. (2006). *Smart negotiating: It's a done deal.* Irvine, CA: Entrepreneur Media.

Pruitt, D., & Carnevale, P. (1993). *Negotiation in social conflict.* Pacific Grove, CA: Brooks/Cole.

Building Better Vocabulary

ACTIVITY 14 **Practicing Three Kinds of Vocabulary from Context**

Read each important vocabulary word or phrase. Locate it in the essay if you need help remembering the word or phrase. Then circle the best synonym, antonym, or collocation from column A, B, or C.

Type of Vocabulary	Important Vocabulary	A	B	C
Synonyms	**1.** request	ask for	listen to	wait for
	2. an item	a beverage	an idea	a thing
	3. stress	emphasize	mention	rely
	4. potential	permission	possibility	prohibition
Antonyms	**5.** profit	game	loss	wisdom
	6. numerous	flexible	illogical	sole
	7. purchase	release	sell	terrify
	8. subsequent	prior	technical	wasteful
Collocations	**9.** ___ from 1 to 9	flexing	purchasing	ranging
	10. my hard work paid ___	off	on	over
	11. ___ these circumstances	for	into	under
	12. ___ shopping	go	make	take

Original Student Writing: Process Essay

In this section, you will follow the seven steps in the writing process to write a process essay. If you need help, refer to Unit 2, pages 34–46.

ACTIVITY 15 **Step 1: Choose a Topic**

Your first step is to choose a topic for your essay. For a process essay, you want to explain how to do something in a few or several steps. Your teacher may assign a topic, you may think of one yourself, or you may choose one from the suggestions in the chart. As you consider possible topics, ask yourself, "What do I know about this topic? What do my readers know? What else do I need to know? Do I need to research this topic?"

Humanities	Write a process essay in which you describe how to research a subject on the Internet (or in a library).
Sciences	Scientists often write process papers describing how they achieved a particular set of results from an experiment. Write a process essay describing an experiment so that someone could duplicate your results.
Business	Managers often create standard procedures to be followed across the company. Write a process essay describing the necessary procedure for a key function of a business in which you have been involved, such as advertising, marketing, or selling a product.
Personal	Think of your favorite hobby. How would you explain it to a friend who is interested in learning about it? Write a process essay in which you explain how to be good at your hobby.

1. What topic did you choose? _____

2. Why did you choose this topic? _____

_____

3. How well do you know this topic? What is your experience with it?

_____

_____

ACTIVITY 16 **Step 2: Brainstorm**

Use the space to jot down as many ideas about the topic as you can.

Brainstorming Box

```
┌─────────────────────────────────────────────┐
│                                             │
│                                             │
│                                             │
│                                             │
│                                             │
│                                             │
│                                             │
│                                             │
│                                             │
│                                             │
│                                             │
└─────────────────────────────────────────────┘
```

ACTIVITY 17 **Step 3: Outline**

Prepare a simple outline of your essay. You need at least three steps, but there is no maximum number. Use as many body paragraphs as you think are necessary.

Title: _____

  I. Introduction

    A. Hook: _____

    _____

    B. Connecting information: _____

    _____

    C. Thesis statement: _____

    _____

II. Body Paragraph 1 (Step 1): _____

   Details: _____

   _____

   _____

III. Body Paragraph 2 (Step 2): _____

   Details: _____

   _____

   _____

IV. Body Paragraph 3 (Step 3): _____

   Details: _____

   _____

   _____

V. Body Paragraph 4 (Step 4): _____

   Details: _____

   _____

   _____

VI. Body Paragraph 5 (Step 5): _____

   Details: _____

   _____

   _____

VII. Body Paragraph 6 (Step 6): _____

   Details: _____

   _____

   _____

VIII. Conclusion: _____

   _____

   _____

   _____

Peer Editing of Outlines

Exchange books with a partner. Read your partner's outline. Then use the following questions to help you comment on your partner's outline. Use your partner's feedback to revise your outline.

1. Is there any aspect of the outline that is unclear to you? Give details here.

_____

_____

_____

_____

2. Can you think of an area in the outline that needs more development? Make specific suggestions.

_____

_____

_____

_____

3. If you have any other ideas or suggestions, write them here.

_____

_____

_____

_____

ACTIVITY 18 **Step 4: Write the First Draft**

Use the information from Steps 1–3 to write the first draft of your process essay. Use at least four of the vocabulary words or phrases from the Building Better Vocabulary activities in this unit. Underline these words and phrases in your essay. Try to also use at least two of the words from the Academic Word List in the *Brief Writer's Handbook with Activities* on pages 230–231.

Step 5: Get Feedback from a Peer

Exchange papers from Step 4 with a partner. Read your partner's first draft. Then use Peer Editing Sheet 4 (available online at NGL.Cengage.com/GW5) to help you to comment on your partner's writing. Be sure to offer positive suggestions and comments that will help your partner improve his or her essay.

ACTIVITY 20 **Step 6: Revise the First Draft**

Read the comments on Peer Editing Sheet 4 about your essay. Then reread your essay. Can you identify places where you should make revisions? List the improvements you plan to make.

1. _____

_____

_____

2. _____

_____

_____

3. _____

_____

_____

Use all the information from the previous steps to write the final version of your paper. Often, writers will need to write a third or even a fourth draft to express their ideas as clearly as possible. Write as many drafts as necessary to produce a good essay.

Be sure to proofread your paper several times before you submit it so you find all the mistakes and correct them.

> **Writer's Note**
>
> **Read Aloud**
>
> One suggestion for better proofreading is to read your essay aloud. Reading aloud forces you to read more slowly so you have a better chance of spotting your errors.

Additional Topics for Writing

Here are ten more ideas for topics for additional process essay writing.

PHOTO TOPIC: Look at the photograph on pages 72–73. Think of something you know how to build or create. What materials are necessary? What is the process you need to follow?

TOPIC 2: Explain the process of finding volunteer work.

TOPIC 3: Explain how to settle a dispute between two friends.

TOPIC 4: Describe how to apply for a job.

TOPIC 5: Explain how to plan and prepare for a vacation.

TOPIC 6: Explain the steps to follow to invest in the stock market.

TOPIC 7: Describe how to create your own website.

TOPIC 8: Explain how to drive a car with a manual transmission.

TOPIC 9: Explain how to get a top score in a course.

TOPIC 10: Explain how blood moves through the heart.

Timed Writing

How quickly can you write in English? There are many times when you must write quickly, such as on a test. It is important to feel comfortable during those times. Timed-writing practice can make you feel better about writing quickly in English.

1. Read the essay guidelines below. Then take out a piece of paper.

2. Read the writing prompt below the guidelines.

3. Write a basic outline, including the thesis and your three main points or steps. You should spend no more than five minutes on your outline.

4. Your essay needs at least three body paragraphs for three steps. You can write more if you would like.

5. You have 40 minutes to write your essay.

Process Essay Guidelines

- Determine the multiple steps that make up the process that will be discussed in the essay.
- Make sure that you give each step adequate attention.
- Use transitions and connectors appropriately to help your readers move from one step to the next.
- Remember to give your essay a title.
- Double-space your essay.
- Write as legibly as possible (if you are not using a computer).
- Include a short introduction (with a thesis statement), at least three body paragraphs, and a conclusion.
- Try to give yourself a few minutes before the end of the activity to review your work. Check for mistakes in spelling, subject-verb agreement, and suffixes.

How do you prepare for final exams? Explain the process of studying for and succeeding in exams to a student four years younger than you.

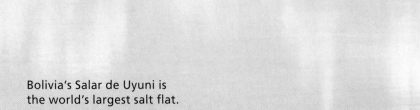

Bolivia's Salar de Uyuni is
the world's largest salt flat.

OBJECTIVES To learn how to write a comparison essay
To use effective transitions in comparative writing
To use comparative forms correctly
To understand parallel structure

*What do you think is
an interesting travel
destination?*

What Is a Comparison Essay?

A **comparison essay** analyzes how two related subjects are similar or different. For example, you might select Julius Caesar and Alexander the Great for an essay on historical military figures. As another example, if your general topic addresses forms of urban transportation, you could choose to write a comparison essay on the car and the bicycle.

The subjects that you compare should have some characteristics in common. These common characteristics must be logical to your readers. For example, you could write a comparison essay about the differences between a politician in Britain in 1950 and a military leader in China in the 1700s, but why would you want to compare the lives of these two people? What do they have in common? On the other hand, a comparison essay that addresses the lives of two politicians or of two military leaders would have a more unified focus and a stronger thesis because the two subjects would share characteristics in common.

A comparison essay can do one of three things:

- It can say that the two subjects are more different than similar.

- It can say that the two subjects are more similar than different.

- It can show how the two subjects share both similarities and differences.

In other words, your essay may focus on comparing, on contrasting, or on both.

How Is a Comparison Essay Organized?

There are two basic ways to organize a comparison essay: **point-by-point method** and **block method**. Both styles include an introduction and a conclusion, but the body paragraphs are organized differently. Of these two organizations, the point-by-point method is more common in academic writing and the one that you should study with greater attention.

The Point-by-Point Method

In the **point-by-point method**, one point of comparison provides the topic for each body paragraph. In each paragraph, the writer discusses both subjects in relation to that one point.

For example, you might compare two modes of transportation, such as a car and a bicycle, for convenience and ease of use, for safety, and for cost. A point-by-point essay using these three points might have five paragraphs and look like this:

INTRODUCTION	Paragraph 1	Hook Connecting information Thesis
BODY	Paragraph 2	Point 1: convenience and ease of use • car • bicycle
	Paragraph 3	Point 2: safety • car • bicycle
	Paragraph 4	Point 3: cost • car • bicycle
CONCLUSION	Paragraph 5	Restated thesis Suggestion/opinion/prediction

In addition to the five-paragraph, point-by-point essay organization, another common variation is to add an additional paragraph in which the writer uses the information from the previous paragraphs to evaluate which subject (the car or the bicycle) is better or more suitable. In other words, the writer makes a longer recommendation or a suggestion to the reader. In this case, the organization for this essay could have six paragraphs and would look like this:

INTRODUCTION	Paragraph 1	Hook Connecting information Thesis
BODY	Paragraph 2	Point 1: convenience and ease of use • car • bicycle
	Paragraph 3	Point 2: safety • car • bicycle
	Paragraph 4	Point 3: cost • car • bicycle
	Paragraph 5	Writer's evaluation of the car and the bicycle using information from paragraphs 2, 3, and 4
CONCLUSION	Paragraph 6	Restated thesis Suggestion/opinion/prediction

The Block Method

In the **block method**, you present all of the relevant information about one subject first and then present all of the relevant information about the other subject. In this method, you must be very careful to list the same kind of information in the same order for each subject, a technique called **parallel structure**. For example, if you again compare two modes of transportation—a car and a bicycle—for their convenience and ease of use, for safety, and for cost, you must provide this information for both modes of transportation and you must list this information in the same order. Maintaining parallel structure in your sentences and in your paragraphs greatly improves the organization of your writing.

A simple block method essay would include four paragraphs and look like this:

INTRODUCTION	Paragraph 1	Hook Connecting information Thesis
BODY	Paragraph 2	The car • Point 1: convenience and ease of use • Point 2: safety • Point 3: cost
	Paragraph 3	The bicycle • Point 1: convenience and ease of use • Point 2: safety • Point 3: cost
CONCLUSION	Paragraph 4	Restated thesis Suggestion/opinion/prediction

For this same essay, you may want to include a paragraph in which you evaluate what you have compared about a car and a bicycle and make a longer recommendation or a suggestion to the reader. In this case, the essay using the block method would have five paragraphs and might look like this:

INTRODUCTION	Paragraph 1	Hook Connecting information Thesis
BODY	Paragraph 2	The car • Point 1: convenience and ease of use • Point 2: safety • Point 3: cost
	Paragraph 3	The bicycle • Point 1: convenience and ease of use • Point 2: safety • Point 3: cost
	Paragraph 4	Compares the car and the bicycle and makes a recommendation or suggestion
CONCLUSION	Paragraph 5	Restated thesis Suggestion/opinion/prediction

Great Topics for Comparison Essays

What is a great topic for a comparison essay? Obviously, it should address two subjects that are related in some way. You must have a logical reason for making the comparison or contrast.

When selecting the topics to compare or to contrast, a good writer should consider relevant questions such as:

- What features do the subjects share in common?

- What features do they not share in common?

- Can you develop a thesis by comparing and contrasting their traits?

- Can you find enough information about both topics? If not, your essay will not appear balanced.

Here are some general topics that lend themselves well to a comparison essay. Some topics are very broad and would need to be narrowed further.

General Topics for Comparison	
two countries	women today and women a century ago
two professional athletes	two websites for learning English
an early and a later Shakespearean drama	a current leader in your country and a former leader
courses of study at two different colleges	World War I and World War II
a book and the movie based on the book	vegetarian and non-vegetarian diets

ACTIVITY 1 Identifying Topics for Comparison Essays

Read these eight topics. Put a check mark (✔) next to the four that could be good topics for comparison essays.

_____ 1. The steps in collecting data for a research study

_____ 2. Rio de Janeiro versus Tokyo as a site for the Summer Olympic Games

_____ 3. Reproductive processes of mammals and reptiles

_____ 4. Societies with small families and societies with large families

_____ 5. An analysis of voting trends and results in recent elections in Ecuador

_____ 6. The career choice of becoming a teacher or a lawyer

_____ 7. Daily life in Saudi Arabia

_____ 8. A description of llamas in the Andes Mountains in Peru

Can you think of two additional topics that would be excellent for a comparison essay?

9. _____

10. _____

Supporting Details

After you have selected a topic and the two subjects within that topic, your job is to identify the similarities and differences between the two subjects. This process will also help you to identify supporting details for your essay, which is a very important step in constructing a solid essay.

When you brainstorm your plan for this essay, a useful technique is to fill in a Venn diagram illustrating the similarities and differences. A Venn diagram usually consists of two overlapping ovals that each represent one of the two subjects. The shared area in the middle highlights their similarities. The areas not shared highlight their differences.

Here is a Venn diagram for an essay comparing the two countries of Malaysia and Thailand:

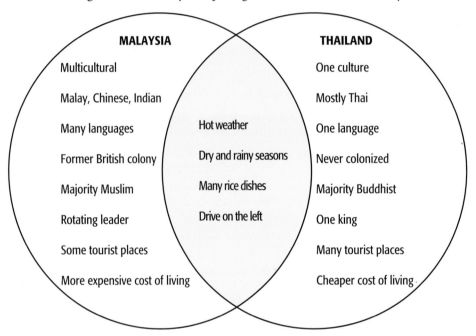

ACTIVITY 2 Brainstorming Details for a Successful Comparison

Select a topic from the list of ten topics in Activity 1 on page 107. Using your own knowledge or information from the Internet, fill in the Venn diagram with the two subjects and lists of their similarities and differences. When you have finished, discuss your ideas with a partner.

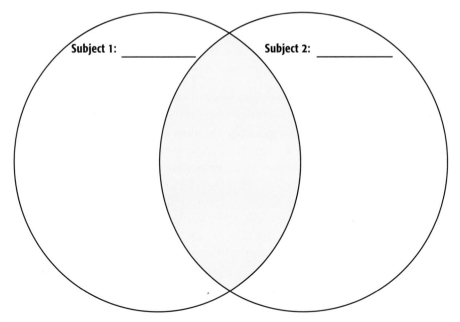

This essay compares online classes with face-to-face classes. Discuss the Preview Questions with a partner. Then read the essay and answer the questions that follow.

Preview Questions

1. What was the last online class you took? Was it a good experience?

2. Can you think of one course that would be better online than face-to-face? Can you think of one course that would be better face-to-face than online?

3. Do you think online classes will completely replace face-to-face classes in the future? Why or why not?

Essay 10

Online and Face-to-Face Learning in the Digital Age

1   As computers become increasingly important in education, many schools, colleges, and universities have begun offering online courses and **allocating** resources for the development of online degrees. In this new type of education, some students need never set foot on campus to earn a degree. Online learning is causing a revolution in education, but its benefits need to be measured against its **liabilities** when compared to traditional face-to-face instruction. Students should not assume that either online or face-to-face classes are **inherently superior**; instead, students should focus on what they need to learn from a particular course and which learning **paradigm** will best **facilitate** their education.

2   Although face-to-face courses are more familiar to many students, online courses offer several advantages. One of the most important of these advantages is that online courses offer greater convenience. In online courses, students may do their coursework according to their own schedules. Because so many of today's students have work and family responsibilities **beyond** their coursework, it is **vital** that they have the necessary flexibility to **fulfill** their other obligations while also **tending to** their studies. As a result, some students complete their coursework on weekends or in the middle of the night after they have finished their work and family duties. They no longer have to choose between school and work or between school and family and can pursue their commitments to both as their schedules allow. Clearly, online courses are more convenient than face-to-face classes.

3   Contrary to many lecture classes, online courses can increase student participation. In large classrooms with fifty or more students, it is often impossible for many students to say anything because the room is so big that not everyone can hear other students well. In addition, some shy students who would hesitate to speak up in a big class may feel more comfortable contributing to class discussions in which they can type their thoughts without having to speak them. In their investigation of online learning strategies, Hiltz and Shea (2005) concluded that many online courses "elicit more active participation from students than does the typical face-to-face course (at least those conducted on the lecture model)" (p. 145). Online courses allow students to participate in forums and discussions where they do not feel the pressure of public speaking.

---

to allocate: to divide and give something out to someone or something

a liability: a disadvantage

inherently: naturally

superior: better

a paradigm: an example that serves as a model

to facilitate: to make easier

beyond: more than

vital: essential; necessary

to fulfill: to complete

to tend to: to take care of

4   Another prime difference between these two types of education involves the lack of face-to-face communication, which can be a **drawback** to online classes. Despite some students' **reluctance** to speak in class, communicating with others in person is a vital skill for the real job market. Students who **isolate** themselves during learning situations may lack the necessary communication skills to succeed in the future. Also, many courses are more difficult to offer online than in face-to-face settings. For example, courses in foreign languages benefit from classroom environments where students practice speaking to one another. Many science classes require laboratories where students **conduct** experiments, and drama classes allow students to perform plays. **Duplicating** these experiences online is challenging for even the best instructors.

5   While face-to-face classes typically do not rely on technology in the classroom to a great extent, online courses require students to have certain computer skills as well as sufficient technological access to take the courses. Computer usage is **widespread**, but even today, not all students have their own computers, and many may lack sufficient computer literacy to **navigate** a course's website easily. Under these circumstances, some students may require so much time to find an accessible computer or to learn how to use the course's online tools that they end up with insufficient time and opportunity to complete the coursework.

6   Finally, one very important difference between traditional and online classes is that students in online courses do not enjoy as many opportunities to build personal relationships with teachers and classmates throughout the duration of their education. In fact, because teachers do not know their students personally, many educators worry about

a drawback: a disadvantage

reluctance: hesitation to do something

to isolate: to separate from all others

to conduct: to perform; to complete; to do

to duplicate: to copy

widespread: common; in many places

to navigate: to move through

the potential for cheating in online courses. It is quite easy for students to register for an online course and then to hire someone else to take the course for them. Furthermore, many professors hesitate to write recommendation letters for their online students, even those who earn the highest grades in their classes, because they feel uncomfortable **advocating** for people whom they have never met in person. Teachers of online courses cannot comment on a student's punctuality, presentations before groups, or interpersonal skills due to the online environment, which does not promote live, human interactions.

7   Both face-to-face and online courses share the same goal of educating students. While students may prefer either online or face-to-face courses as a matter of personal taste, it is essential that online courses **address** some of their liabilities and that face-to-face courses take advantage of some of the opportunities available from online learning. Some schools and universities offer mixed-mode courses that combine face-to-face courses with online **components**. However, mixed-mode courses do not necessarily offer a simple solution to a complex problem, as they have their own set of benefits and liabilities. Students need to **assess** their learning styles, and teachers need to assess their instructional styles, so that both students and teachers can create learning environments where everyone is likely to **prosper**. In the future, these instructional modes could **merge** in interesting ways, as Lever-Duffy, McDonald, and Mizell (2005) suggest: "Eventually, perhaps, there will be no distinctions among traditional education, alternative education, and distance education" (p. 372). In such a future, only the best features from these worlds will survive.

to advocate for: to support; to speak in favor of

to address: to discuss; to deal with

a component: a key part

to assess: to evaluate

to prosper: to be successful

to merge: to blend together to form one

References

Hiltz, S., & Shea, P. (2005). The student in the online classroom. In S. Hiltz & R. Goldman (Eds.), *Learning together online: Research on asynchronous learning networks* (pp. 145–168). Mahwah, NJ: Erlbaum.

Lever-Duffy, J., McDonald, J., & Mizell, A. (2005). *Teaching and learning with technology* (2nd ed.). Boston: Pearson.

Post-Reading

1. What is the topic of the essay? _____

2. What is the writer's thesis? _____

   _____

3. What features of traditional classes does the writer discuss?

   _____

   _____

4. What features of online classes does the writer discuss?

   _____

   _____

5. What is your opinion about these two types of classes? Which one do you prefer and why?

   _____

   _____

   _____

6. Putting your opinion aside and considering only the ideas and supporting details in the essay, which type of class sounds better to you? _____

   What information from the essay influenced your answer the most?

   _____

   _____

7. Write one detail that strongly supports the thesis statement.

   _____

   _____

8. How is the essay organized?

   ☐ block method   ☐ point-by-point method

9. Can you think of any information that the author should have included to make the message of the essay stronger?

   _____

   _____

Building Better Sentences: For further practice, go to Practice 2 on page 239 in the Appendix.

Building Better Vocabulary

ACTIVITY 4 **Practicing Three Kinds of Vocabulary from Context**

Read each important vocabulary word or phrase. Locate it in the essay if you need help remembering the word or phrase. Then circle the best synonym, antonym, or collocation from column A, B, or C.

Type of Vocabulary	Important Vocabulary	A	B	C
Synonyms	**1.** facilitate	make easier	make lighter	make sadder
	2. a drawback	a disadvantage	a failure	a hesitation
	3. fulfill	complete	elicit	guess
	4. inherently	angrily	completely	naturally
Antonyms	**5.** widespread	quiet	rare	sufficient
	6. vital	optional	shy	well-known
	7. address	behave	ignore	succeed
	8. prosper	fail	leave	tend
Collocations	**9.** a ___ solution	furthermore	personal	simple
	10. a matter of personal ___	potential	register	taste
	11. ___ foot on a place	make	set	take
	12. quite ___	duplicating	easy	facilitated

ACTIVITY 5 **Analyzing the Organization**

Use the information from the box to complete the outline of "Online and Face-to-Face Learning in the Digital Age" on page 114. Reread the essay on pages 109–111 if you need help.

- when these instructional modes merge in interesting ways

- the need for adequate computer access and skills to take online courses

- the different rates of student participation in online and face-to-face courses

- the potential benefits of face-to-face courses in enhancing communication skills

- how online and face-to-face classes differ in their ability to foster personal relationships

- Students should not assume that either online or face-to-face classes are inherently superior; instead, students should focus on what they need to learn from a particular course and which learning paradigm will best facilitate their education.

- examples of how scheduling time for online courses is more convenient than for face-to-face courses

---

Title: Online and Face-to-Face Learning in the Digital Age

I. Introduction

    A. Describe the increasing importance of computers in education.

    B. Briefly contrast online education with traditional face-to-face classes.

    C. Thesis statement: _____

    _____ .

II. Body Paragraph 1

    A. Discuss the convenience of online courses compared to face-to-face courses.

    B. Provide _____ .

III. Body Paragraph 2

    A. Discuss _____ .

    B. Provide scholarly evidence that supports the argument that online courses increase student participation.

IV. Body Paragraph 3

    A. Provide an example of _____

    _____ .

    B. Provide an example of specific classroom settings that benefit from face-to-face interaction, such as foreign-language courses.

V. Body Paragraph 4

    A. Discuss _____

    _____ .

    B. Provide the suggestion that some students use too much time learning how to use the computer technology rather than concentrating on the course's subject matter.

VI. Body Paragraph 5

    A. Discuss _____

    _____ .

    B. Provide an example of how teachers cannot write effective recommendation letters for students they do not know personally.

VII. Conclusion

    A. Suggest that mixed-mode courses, which combine online learning with face-to-face instruction, can potentially strengthen student learning.

    B. Predict that this issue will be resolved in the future _____

    _____ .

Strong Thesis Statements for Comparison Essays

A strong thesis statement for a comparison essay indicates whether the essay focuses on similarities, differences, or both. In addition, the thesis statement sometimes uses hedging words such as **may**, **might**, **can, seem**, **appear**, or **some**. A common structure employs a contrasting connector such as **although, while,** or **despite**.

Focus	Example thesis statement
more differences	**Although** Joe's Diner and Burger Town both serve hundreds of hamburgers each day, the similarities end there. **Although** Malaysia and Thailand **may seem** similar because these neighboring nations share a common border, they have striking differences.
more similarities	**Despite** obvious differences in the two languages, English and French share a number of important similarities. **While** Nite Owl and Rorschach, the heroes of Alan Moore's *Watchmen*, **appear** to be exact opposites, they share three important qualities that enable their heroic acts.
both differences and similarities	**Although** both Barbara Ehrenreich's *Nickel and Dimed* and Jeffrey Sachs's *The End of Poverty* discuss the topic of poverty, they approach this topic in very different ways.

ACTIVITY 6 **Writing Strong Thesis Statements for Comparison Essays**

Write a thesis statement for each topic. When you finish, compare your answers with a partner's.

1. a book and the movie based on the book

2. vegetarian and non-vegetarian diets

3. a current leader (or historical person) with a previous leader (or historical person)

Transitions and Connectors in Comparison Essays

Transitions and connectors are important in comparison essays because they help clarify the relationship between the two subjects. Transitions and connectors are especially useful in the point-by-point method in which both subjects are discussed in relation to each point. Precise use of transitions helps the reader to follow the writer's comparisons.

Transitions and Connectors That Focus on Similarities			
also	compared to	in the same way	a similarity
as	equally	like	similar to
as well (as)	have in common	likewise	similarly
both	in addition	(the) same as	too

Transitions and Connectors That Focus on Differences			
an advantage	a / another difference	instead	though
although	different from	on the contrary	unless
but	a disadvantage	on the other hand	unlike
contrary to contrasted	even though	(the) opposite	whereas
contrasted (to / with)	however	rather	while
X differs from Y	in contrast (to)	(the) reverse	yet

ACTIVITY 7 **Identifying Transitions and Connectors in an Essay**

Reread "Online and Face-to-Face Learning in the Digital Age" on pages 109–111. Find six transitions or connectors. Copy the sentences here, underline the transition or connector, and write the paragraph number in the parentheses.

Transition/Connector That Shows Similarities

1. _____

   _____ ( )

Transitions/Connectors That Show Differences

1. _____

   _____ ( )

2. _____

   _____ ( )

3. _____

   _____ ( )

4. _____

   _____ ( )

5. _____

   _____ ( )

Studying Transitions and Connectors in an Example Comparison Essay

ACTIVITY 8 **Warming Up to the Topic**

Answer the questions on your own. Then discuss them with a partner or in a small group.

1. How many zoos have you visited? Which ones and where? _____

_____

2. Do you think animals are better off in a zoo or an animal reserve? Explain your answer.

_____

_____

ACTIVITY 9 **Using Transitions and Connectors in an Essay**

Read "Fight for Survival" and circle the correct transition words or phrases.

Essay 11

Fight for Survival

1   Many animals are facing **extinction**, which threatens the diversity of animal life on earth. Gorillas, eagles, rhinoceroses, water buffalo, elephants, and tigers are just a few of the **species** across the globe whose existence is **threatened**. To ensure that these creatures are protected and survive in the future, many environmentalists **advocate** that they should be in zoos or animal **reserves**. Zoos keep animals in exhibits where visitors can learn about them, **1** (therefore / whereas) reserves allow animals to **roam** freely in **vast** expanses of land that better **simulate** their natural living conditions. Both zoos and reserves create **habitats** where animals can reproduce and thus protect their species from extinction, **2** (but / unless) both have liabilities as well.

2   **3** (Although / Because) zoos tend to the physical needs of the animals in their care, the animals become **tamer** than they were in **the wild**. For instance, rather than killing their prey themselves, animals are fed by zookeepers. Perhaps the biggest liability of zoos is that they take animals out of their natural habitats and expose them to new climates and conditions, which can present unforeseen dangers and diminish the animals' ability to fend for themselves. Ewen and his colleagues

extinction: no more of a species in existence

a species: one type of animal

to threaten: to endanger

to advocate: to support

a reserve: an area of land for protecting animals

to roam: to move from place to place without a specific destination

vast: very great area; huge

to simulate: to copy or reproduce in order to look or behave like something

a habitat: the natural place where a creature lives

tame: domesticated; gentle

the wild: a large area where people do not live and where plants grow and animals live freely

(2012) cite several dangers of long-term captivity for animals, including inbreeding, adaptation to captivity, and exposure to non-native **parasites**. No matter how hard zoos attempt to simulate natural living conditions of animals, some do not succeed. **4** (By chance / For example), Kemmerer (2010) documents that "sixty percent of zoo-kept elephants suffer from painful and dangerous foot **ailments** caused by standing on unnatural surfaces" (p. 38). **5** (However / While) trying to protect animals, some zoos harm them instead due to the conditions of the animals' confinement.

3   Animal reserves, **6** (on one hand / on the other hand), better **mimic** the conditions of the wild. Animals must hunt and kill their own prey, and the conservationists do not interact with the animals frequently. **7** (Thus / Whereas), the animals in reserves do not become accustomed to or dependent on humans. **8** (Although / In fact), most animal reserves are located within the same geographic region as the **indigenous** animals. **9** (As a result / As a matter of fact), the animals do not need to **adjust** to a new climate, nor do they **encounter alien** parasites or predators they cannot defend themselves against.

4   **10** (However / While) reserves may appear to provide a more **hospitable** environment for animals than zoos for these reasons, zoos

a parasite: an animal or plant that lives off another

an ailment: a health problem

to mimic: to copy; to reproduce

indigenous: native to an area

to adjust: to change

to encounter: to meet

alien: foreign

hospitable: having an environment where plants, animals, or people can live or grow easily

better protect animals from their principal, most dangerous predator: humans. Because reserves are so much larger than zoos, it is quite difficult to police their borders; **11** (also / consequently), **poachers** can break into animal reserves and kill the very animals that the reserves are intended to protect. Such a situation occurs frequently when poachers kill rhinoceroses and elephants to steal and sell their horns and tusks on the **black market**. **12** (Consequently / In addition), some animal reserves act as large-scale zoos for tourists, even though these environments are supposedly set aside to protect and preserve animals.

5   Both zoos and reserves attempt to ensure that animals will survive for future generations, but, whether intentionally or not, both habitats potentially harm the animals they seek to protect. To ensure that future generations of animals will escape extinction, the best answer might be neither zoos nor animal reserves but simply for humans to leave animals alone in their natural habitat. At the very least, humans must find an **ethical** and humane way to preserve all species with which we share the planet.

a poacher: a person who kills and takes animals illegally

a black market: a system of illegal buying and selling of goods

ethical: involving questions of right or wrong behavior

References

Ewen, J., Armstrong, D., Parker, K., & Seddon, P. (2012). *Reintroduction biology: Integrating science and management*. Oxford: Wiley-Blackwell.

Kemmerer, L. (2010). Nooz: Ending zoo exploitation. In R. Acampora (Ed.), *Metamorphoses of the zoo* (pp. 37–56). Lanham, MD: Lexington.

Building Better Vocabulary

ACTIVITY 10 **Practicing Three Kinds of Vocabulary from Context**

Read each important vocabulary word or phrase. Locate it in the essay if you need help remembering the word or phrase. Then circle the best synonym, antonym, or collocation from column A, B, or C.

Type of Vocabulary	Important Vocabulary	A	B	C
Synonyms	**1.** mimic	simulate	species	succeed
	2. roam	attempt	kill	wander
	3. ensure	explain	guarantee	provide
	4. harm	consider	hurt	steal
Antonyms	**5.** indigenous	alien	endanger	hospitable
	6. tame	foreign	prey	wild
	7. extinction	participation	removal	survival
	8. vast	balanced	dependent	tiny
Collocations	**9.** expose an animal ___ a problem	in	on	to
	10. across the ___	future	globe	needs
	11. unforeseen ___	colleagues	dangers	reserves
	12. protect an animal ___ a predator	from	in	to

Grammar for Writing

Comparative Forms (-er, more / less; as ... as, the same ... as)

There are two ways to form the comparative form of adjectives and adverbs.

When one thing is more than another	Examples
If the word is one syllable, add -er to the end of the word.	fast → fast**er** light → light**er**
If the word contains two syllables and ends in -y, change the -y to -i and add -er.	heavy → heav**ier** lazy → laz**ier**
Some words must be preceded by *more*.	comfortable → **more** comfortable dangerous → **more** dangerous
With all adjectives and adverbs, the opposite idea is expressed by the word *less*.	fast → **less** fast heavy → **less** heavy dangerous → **less** dangerous

When two things are similar	Examples
If the word is an adjective or adverb, use *as … as.*	fast → **as** fast **as** heavy → **as** heavy **as** dangerous → **as** dangerous **as**
If the word is a noun, use *the same … as.*	price → **the same** price **as** reason → **the same** reason **as**
The most common usage for these two structures is in a negative sentence.	This year's winter storm was not **as** powerful **as** last year's.

ACTIVITY 11 Working with *more* and *-er*

Write the correct comparative form of the word in parentheses.

1. In this chapter, the author suggests that the creation of the United Nations in 1945 was (difficult) _____ than most history texts admit.

2. In this experiment, the researchers used existing data because they believed it was (reliable) _____ than any new data that they could obtain at the present time.

3. As a society, we have to decide if getting an education or not getting an education is (expensive) _____ in the long run.

4. The valleys in the Himalayas are (deep) _____ than any of those in Europe or South America.

5. Most readers prefer the definitions found in online dictionaries because they tend to be worded (concisely) _____ than those in many traditional dictionaries.

ACTIVITY 12 Working with *not as … as*

Write a sentence using *not as … as* for any fact related to the subject given.

1. geography ___Egypt is not as large as Saudi Arabia.___

2. population _____

_____

3. medicine _____

_____

4. climate _____

_____

5. economy _____

_____

6. history _____

_____

7. education _____

_____

8. personality _____

_____

Grammar for Writing

Parallel Structure

Good writers use **parallel structure** in their writing. Parts of a sentence that have the same function should have the same form. Using parallel structure makes your writing much easier for the reader to understand.

Use parallel structure with *and* (coordinating conjunctions).	
✗ In July, the weather is hot, dry, and it is very windy. ✓ In July, the weather is **hot, dry, and very windy.**	Be sure to use parallel structure with a coordinating conjunction such as **and**.
Use parallel structure for items in a list or series.	
✗ The number of days in January is greater than April. ✓ **The number of days** in January is greater than **the number of days** in April. ✓ **January** is longer than **April.**	The first example is wrong because you are comparing *number* with *April*, which are not similar things.
✗ The smell of fried chicken is not as strong as fried fish. ✓ The **smell of fried chicken** is not as strong as the **smell of fried fish.** ✓ **Fried chicken** does not smell as strong as **fried fish.**	The first example is wrong because it compares a smell with a food, which are not similar things.
To avoid using the same noun twice, it is common to use the pronouns *that* (singular) or *those* (plural).	
OK In some countries, the **cost** of water is higher than the **cost** of oil. *Better* In some countries, the **cost** of water is higher than **that** of oil.	The first example is acceptable, but it is wordy and a little awkward. The *that of* structure results in a more fluent sentence.

ACTIVITY 13 Editing for Parallel Structure

Each sentence contains an error in parallel structure. Rewrite the sentence correctly.

1. According to the most recent data, the population of Spain is larger than Greece.

_____

_____

2. The company's annual report indicates excellent sales in January, March, and in July.

_____

_____

3. With only five days until the deadline, our team's project is not as good as the other team.

_____

_____

4. Many children like watching television and to play computer games.

_____

_____

5. To apply for a loan, you read about our different loan packages on our website, fill out the application completely, and submitted it to the correct loan officer at the bank.

_____

_____

6. According to the report, schools in California spend more money per student than New York.

_____

_____

7. For better heart health, three great forms of exercise involve our legs: jogging, distance running, and to take brisk walks.

_____

_____

8. To relax, I like surfing the Internet, working in the garden, and crossword puzzles.

_____

_____

Twelve of the sixteen words in parentheses contain an error involving one of the grammar topics featured in this unit. If the word or phrase is correct, write *C*. If it is incorrect, fill in the blank with a correction.

Essay 12

Two Extremely Dangerous Reptiles

1   Crocodiles and alligators are large **reptiles** that most people cannot easily **differentiate**. In fact, these two animals are so similar in appearance, **attributes,** and other characteristics that most people **randomly** use one name for the other. Despite these similarities, there are several very **1** (importanter) _____ differences between crocodiles and alligators that allow people to **distinguish** one from the other.

2   Because most humans never get **2** (more close) _____ enough to these animals to examine them carefully, people assume these creatures are physically **analogous**. To start with, alligators and crocodiles differ in color. Alligators are blackish gray, while crocodiles **tend to be** greenish brown. In addition, the heads of alligators and crocodiles are **3** (different) _____. Alligators have a much **4** (more wide) _____ **snout** that is shaped like a U; crocodiles, in contrast, have a **5** (more long) _____ and **6** (more narrow) _____ snout that **resembles** the letter V. Finally, crocodiles and alligators differ in how their teeth are arranged.

a reptile: a cold-blooded animal that lays eggs

to differentiate: to recognize the difference between two or more things

an attribute: a good quality or feature

randomly: without any special reason or guidance

to distinguish: to recognize the difference between two similar things

analogous: alike; comparable

to tend to be: are usually

a snout: the nose of an animal

to resemble: to look like another person

crocodile

alligator

When alligators close their mouths, their teeth are not **visible**. In sharp contrast, when crocodiles close their mouths, their lower teeth are clearly visible. These three external differences are **7** (**substantial**) _____, yet few people are aware of them.

3   Another difference between these two reptiles is that they live in very different areas of the globe. Crocodiles are generally found in tropical areas of Australia, Asia, Africa, and South America. Alligators, on the other hand, have a much **8** (limited) _____ habitat, as they are primarily found in the southeastern United States and in China. In particular, the Everglades National Park in southern Florida in the United States is especially interesting to **zoologists** because it is one of the only places where both alligators and crocodiles **coexist**.

4   Finally, these reptiles differ in their general **demeanor** toward other animals in their territory, especially in regard to their reactions to nearby wildlife—and humans. While both of them can kill a much **9** (more large) _____ animal, crocodiles seem to be much **10** (more aggressive) _____ **11** (that) _____ alligators. For example, if another animal **splashes** in the water near a crocodile, the crocodile will almost immediately attack the animal. Because alligators **inhabit** a **12** (smaller) _____ area of the planet **13** (from) _____ crocodiles, there are far fewer human deaths due to alligators. In contrast, crocodiles, particularly the Nile crocodile, may be responsible for hundreds of human deaths each year. However, it is difficult to **verify** an exact count because many of these deaths happen in very **remote** areas (Woods, 1983).

5   At first glance, alligators and crocodiles certainly look similar in shape, but a **14** (carefuller) _____ examination of their characteristics proves that these animals are not as similar **15** (than)

visible: able to be seen

substantial: quite a lot; a good amount of

a zoologist: a scientist who studies animals

to coexist: to live together

demeanor: behavior

to splash: to cause water to spread or move

to inhabit: to live in an area

to verify: to check for accuracy

remote: an area with very few people and very little activity

_____ most people believe. **Key** differences between these two creatures include physical characteristics, habitat, and **16** (their demeanor is different) _____. Because very few humans ever get to know these differences, it is likely that people will continue to confuse alligators and crocodiles, unless they consult their encyclopedias.

key: important

Reference

Wood, G. (1983). *The guinness book of animal facts and feats.* London: Sterling.

Building Better Vocabulary

ACTIVITY 15 **Practicing Three Kinds of Vocabulary from Context**

Read each important vocabulary word or phrase. Locate it in the essay if you need help remembering the word or phrase. Then circle the best synonym, antonym, or collocation from column A, B, or C.

Type of Vocabulary	Important Vocabulary	A	B	C
Synonyms	**1.** remote	distant	physical	resemble
	2. distinguish	differentiate	inhabit	splash
	3. coexist	live together	run away	work alone
	4. resemble	be together	look like	talk about
Antonyms	**5.** randomly	convincingly	intentionally	successfully
	6. substantial	very bad	very little	very possible
	7. key	unhappy	unnecessary	unverified
	8. wide	glance	narrow	visible
Collocations	**9.** responsible ___	by	for	with
	10. in ___ contrast	good	large	sharp
	11. in ___	glance	particular	reptile
	12. ___ in appearance	dangerous	habitat	similar

Original Student Writing: Comparison Essay

In this section, you will follow the seven steps in the writing process to write a comparison essay. If you need help, refer to Unit 2, pages 34–46.

ACTIVITY 16 **Step 1: Choose a Topic**

Your first step is to choose a topic for your essay. For a comparison essay, you need a topic for which you can develop three solid points comparing or contrasting the two subjects. Your teacher may assign a topic, you may think of one yourself, or you may choose one from the suggestions in the chart. As you consider possible topics, ask yourself, "What do I know about this topic? What do my readers know? What else do I need to know? Do I need to research this topic?"

Humanities	*Literature:* Compare two authors. *History:* Compare two leaders. *Philosophy:* Compare two systems of thought.
Sciences	*Biology:* Compare two diseases. *Geology:* Compare two kinds of rocks. *Astronomy:* Compare two planets.
Business	*Consumer affairs*: Compare two stores that sell similar products.
Personal	Compare two important days in your life. Why was each day so important?

1. What topic did you choose? _____

2. Why did you choose this topic? _____

_____

3. How well do you know this topic? What is your experience with it?

_____

_____

ACTIVITY 17 **Step 2: Brainstorm**

A. Use the chart to brainstorm a list of information about each subject.

TOPIC: _____	
Subject 1: _____	**Subject 2:** _____

B. Now fill in the Venn diagram using the information from the chart you completed.

C. Decide if you are going to focus on the similarities or the differences between the two subjects or on both similarities and differences. Then choose three points of comparison that you will use and list them here.

1. _____

2. _____

3. _____

ACTIVITY 18 **Step 3: Outline**

Prepare a simple outline of your essay. This outline is a point-by-point outline, but you may use the block comparison if your teacher approves.

Title: _____

I. Introduction

  A. Hook: _____

_____

  B. Connecting information: _____

_____

  C. Thesis statement: _____

_____

II. Body Paragraph 1 (Point of Comparison 1): _____

    A. _____

    B. _____

III. Body Paragraph 2 (Point of Comparison 2): _____

    A. _____

    B. _____

IV. Body Paragraph 3 (Point of Comparison 3): _____

    A. _____

    B. _____

V. Conclusion: _____

_____

Peer Editing of Outlines

Exchange books with a partner. Read your partner's outline. Then use the following questions to help you to comment on your partner's outline. Use your partner's feedback to revise your outline.

1. Is there any aspect of the outline that is unclear to you? Give details here.

_____

_____

_____

2. Can you think of an area in the outline that needs more development? Make specific suggestions.

_____

_____

_____

3. If you have any other ideas or suggestions, write them here.

_____

_____

_____

ACTIVITY 19   Step 4: Write the First Draft

Use the information from Steps 1–3 to write the first draft of your comparison essay. Use at least four of the vocabulary words or phrases from the Building Better Vocabulary activities in this unit. Underline these words and phrases in your essay. Try to also use at least two of the words from the Academic Word List in the *Brief Writer's Handbook with Activities* on pages 230–231.

ACTIVITY 20   Step 5: Get Feedback from a Peer

Exchange papers from Step 4 with a partner. Read your partner's first draft. Then use Peer Editing Sheet 5 (available online at NGL.Cengage.com/GW5) to help you to comment on your partner's writing. Be sure to offer positive suggestions and comments that will help your partner improve his or her essay.

ACTIVITY 21   Step 6: Revise the First Draft

Read the comments on Peer Editing Sheet 5 about your essay. Then reread your essay. Can you identify places where you should make revisions? List the improvements you plan to make.

1. _____

   _____

   _____

2. _____

   _____

   _____

3. _____

   _____

   _____

Use all the information from the previous steps to write the final version of your paper. Often, writers will need to write a third or even a fourth draft to express their ideas as clearly as possible. Write as many drafts as necessary to produce a good essay.

ACTIVITY 22   Step 7: Proofread the Final Draft

Be sure to proofread your paper several times before you submit it so you find all the mistakes and correct them.

Additional Topics for Writing

Here are ten more ideas for topics for additional comparison essay writing.

PHOTO
TOPIC: Look at the photograph on pages 102–103. Compare and contrast two places that are popular travel destinations.

TOPIC 2: Compare and/or contrast two of your favorite restaurants.

TOPIC 3: Would you rather live in a house or an apartment? Why?

TOPIC 4: If you were making a movie of your favorite book, who would you cast in the lead role? Compare and/or contrast two actors and discuss which one would be the more appropriate choice.

TOPIC 5: How did you decide to attend the school you are now attending? Describe the process you used to compare and/or contrast the different schools you considered.

TOPIC 6: Compare and/or contrast two explorers. What did they do and how did their discoveries affect history?

TOPIC 7: Compare and/or contrast your hometown to the city you live in now. Which one would you prefer to live in if you had your choice? Why?

TOPIC 8: Compare and/or contrast two candidates for public office.

TOPIC 9: Look at a local ballot issue in an upcoming election and compare and/or contrast the opposing sides. How would you vote and why? Alternatively, you could write about an imaginary election or a current controversial issue with two sides.

TOPIC 10: Compare and/or contrast two sports teams. Which do you think will win the championship this year? Why?

Timed Writing

How quickly can you write in English? There are many times when you must write quickly, such as on a test. It is important to feel comfortable during those times. Timed-writing practice can make you feel better about writing quickly in English.

1. Read the essay guidelines below. Then take out a piece of paper.

2. Read the writing prompt below the guidelines.

3. Write a basic outline including the thesis and your main points of comparison. You should spend no more than five minutes on your outline.

4. Write a five-paragraph essay.

5. You have 40 minutes to write your essay.

Comparison Essay Guidelines

- Use the point-by-point method.

- Remember to give your essay a title.

- Double-space your essay.

- Write as legibly as possible (if you are not using a computer).

- Include a short introduction (with a thesis statement), three body paragraphs, and a conclusion.

- Try to give yourself a few minutes before the end of the activity to review your work. Check for mistakes in spelling, comparative forms, and parallel structure.

Compare good bosses and bad bosses. These can be real or imaginary people. Concentrate on what makes them good or bad bosses.

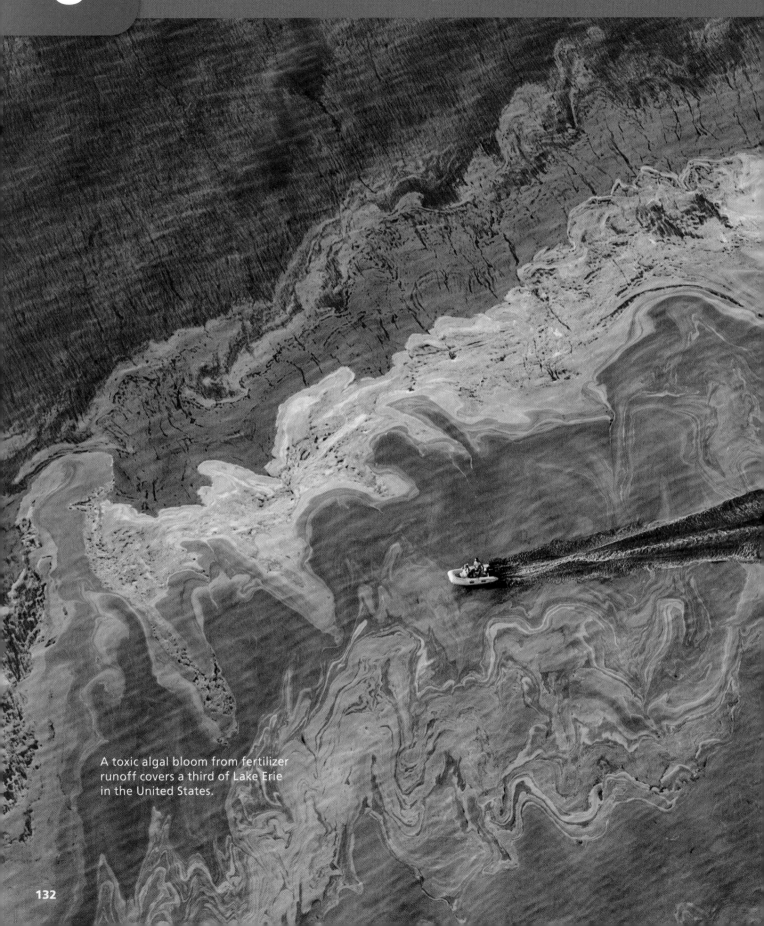

A toxic algal bloom from fertilizer runoff covers a third of Lake Erie in the United States.

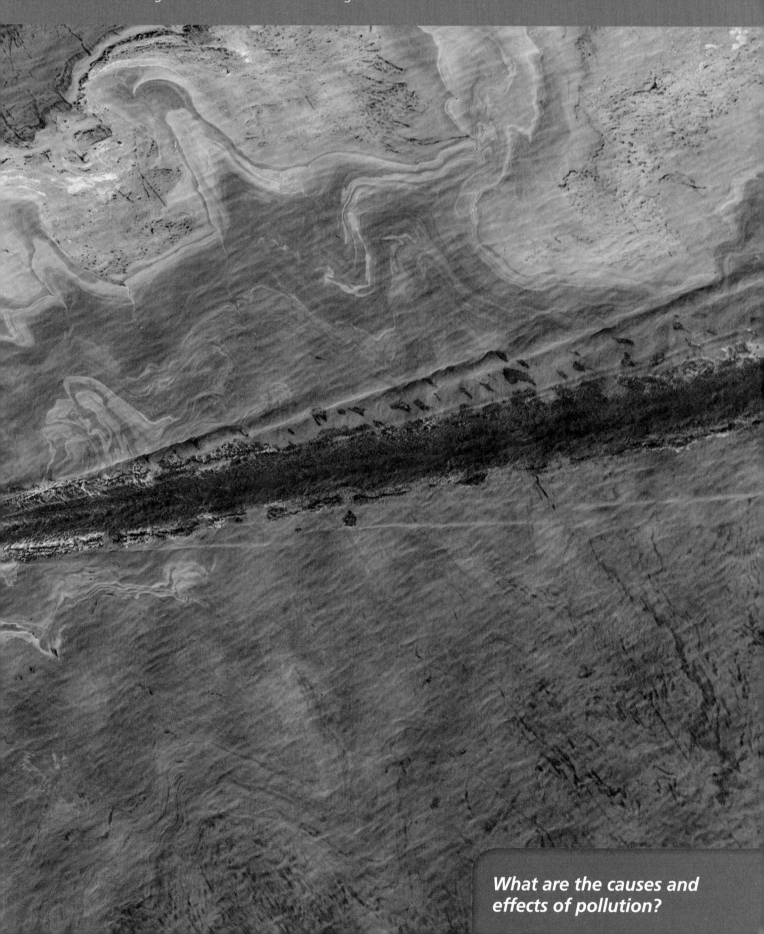

OBJECTIVES To learn how to write a cause-effect essay
To use effective transitions in cause-effect writing
To use verb tenses consistently
To recognize and avoid sentence fragments

What are the causes and effects of pollution?

What Is a Cause-Effect Essay?

We all understand cause-effect relationships; for example, lightning can cause fire. As a student you know that if you stay up late the night before a test to watch a movie and do not study, you may not perform well on the test the following day. A **cause-effect essay** tells how one event (the cause) leads to another event (the effect).

A cause-effect essay can do one of two things:

- It can analyze the ways in which one or more effects result from a particular cause. (Focus-on-Effects Method)
- It can analyze the ways in which one or more causes lead to a particular effect. (Focus-on-Causes Method)

In other words, your essay may focus more on the effects of a cause or more on the causes of one effect. Either approach provides a useful means of discussing the possible relationship between the two events. It is not a good idea to mix several causes and several effects in an essay because your focus may become unclear.

In cause-effect essays, it is easy to suggest that because one event preceded another event, the former event caused the latter. Simply because one event follows another one sequentially does not mean that the two actions are related. For example, people often complain that as soon as they finish washing their car, it starts to rain. Obviously, washing a car does not cause rain. Writers need to be sure that the causes and effects they describe are logically connected.

How Is a Cause-Effect Essay Organized?

There are two basic ways to organize a cause-effect essay: **focus-on-effects** or **focus-on-causes**. If your assignment is to write a cause-effect essay on the topic of global warming, you could write two kinds of essays:

- In a **focus-on-effects essay**, you would write about the threatened habitat of polar bears as a result of global warming and the melting of large parts of the Arctic Circle. Your essay might include five paragraphs and look like this:

INTRODUCTION	Paragraph 1	Hook Connecting information Thesis
BODY	Paragraph 2	Effect 1: dangerous swimming conditions • sea ice platforms farther apart
	Paragraph 3	Effect 2: scarcity of food • fewer hunting opportunities
	Paragraph 4	Effect 3: reduced population • Females with less body weight have lower reproduction rates.
CONCLUSION	Paragraph 5	Restated thesis Suggestion/opinion/prediction

- In a **focus-on-causes essay**, you would write about the causes of global warming, such as excessive carbon dioxide in the atmosphere. In this case, the organization for this essay could have five paragraphs and look like this:

INTRODUCTION	Paragraph 1	Hook Connecting information Thesis
BODY	Paragraph 2	Cause 1: human activities • carbon dioxide from vehicles • not recycling (requires creating more products from scratch)
	Paragraph 3	Cause 2: increased industrial activity • greater carbon dioxide from burning fuels to run factories
	Paragraph 4	Cause 3: deforestation • Increased human population requires more space, so trees are cut down. • Fewer trees mean less oxygen, which causes a higher percentage of carbon dioxide in the atmosphere.
CONCLUSION	Paragraph 5	Restated thesis Suggestion/opinion/prediction

Great Topics for Cause-Effect Essays

What is a great topic for a cause-effect essay? This type of essay may focus more on the causes or more on the effects, but most writers answer this question by thinking of an effect or a final result. The brainstorming stage then requires thinking about one or more causes of that effect.

When selecting topics for this type of essay, a good writer should consider relevant questions such as:

- What is the end effect?
- Is there one primary effect, or are there several effects?
- Is there one primary cause, or are there several causes?

As you read this list of some general topics that lend themselves well to a cause-effect essay, notice that the last two in each group do not use the obvious words *cause* or *effect*:

Focus on Causes	Focus on Effects
the causes of the high divorce rate in some countries	the effects of pollution in my country
the causes of World War I	the effects of high salaries for athletes
the causes of low voter participation in elections	the effects of the Internet on how businesses are run
the reasons new teachers quit	the impact of technology on education
why only a small percentage of people read newspapers today	what happens when a large percentage of adults cannot read well

ACTIVITY 1   Identifying Topics for Cause-Effect Essays

Read these eight topics. Put a check mark (✔) next to the four that could be good topics for cause-effect essays.

_____ 1. The reasons that the earth's weather has changed so much in the last century

_____ 2. Bangkok versus Singapore as a vacation destination

_____ 3. A trip to visit my grandparents

_____ 4. The increasing use of computers in schools

_____ 5. Explaining dietary guidelines for children

_____ 6. How to play the piano

_____ 7. Why a student received a scholarship

_____ 8. Why the birth rate is falling in many countries

Can you think of two additional topics that would be excellent for a cause-effect essay?

9. _____

10. _____

Supporting Details

After you have selected a topic, your task is to determine whether you will focus more on the causes of the issue or the effects of it. This process will also help you to select and develop supporting details for your essay, which is an important step in constructing a solid essay.

When you brainstorm your plan for this essay, a useful technique is to make two lists. One list has as many causes as you can think of. The second list has as many effects or results as you can think of. The list that is bigger—the causes or the effects—should determine the primary focus of your essay.

Here is an example for an essay about the difficulty of learning English:

Causes	Effects
14 vowel sounds	Some people study it for years.
unpredictable spelling system	People spend millions of dollars to learn it.
12 verb tenses	There are many jobs for teaching English.
phrasal verbs	Some people never learn it well.
vocabulary from German and from Latin	Some people have a weak vocabulary.

ACTIVITY 2   Brainstorming for Two Methods

One of the topics that we hear so much about in today's society is stress. In this activity, you will use the space in the boxes on page 138 to brainstorm ideas for an essay on the topic of stress. In the first box, your organization will address the focus-on-effects method. In the second box, your organization will address the focus-on-causes method. After you complete these tasks, work with a partner or a small group to discuss your answers.

Focus-on-Effects Method

Cause:

_____

_____

$\downarrow$

Effects:

_____

_____

_____

_____

_____

Focus-on-Causes Method

Causes:

_____

_____

_____

_____

_____

$\downarrow$

Effect:

_____

_____

This essay discusses some effects that weather has had on events in history. Discuss the Preview Questions with a partner. Then read the essay and answer the questions that follow.

Preview Questions

1. Can you name a time when the weather had an effect on an event that you attended? Was it a positive effect or a negative effect?

2. In the 1200s, the warrior Khubilai Khan tried to invade Japan by sailing from the Asian mainland to Japan. A certain kind of weather event prevented the invasion. Write three guesses in the diagram about what this weather was. Do not consult the Internet, a book, or a person.

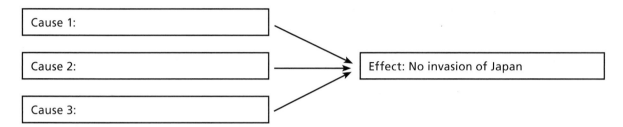

3. Go back in time. Imagine you are a captain of a troop of 500 soldiers and you want to attack your enemy at night. However, it is raining heavily. What are three possible effects of the rain?

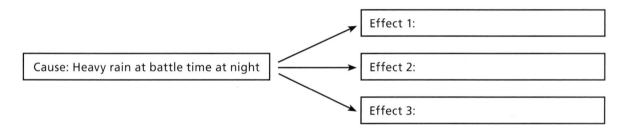

Essay 13

How Weather Has Changed World History

1   It is **tempting**, and often comforting, to think that humans control their **fates**. The decisions that people make in their daily lives can affect many things, and the **course** of their lives **cumulatively** reflects these many small decisions. On the other hand, people cannot control every aspect of their environments, and forces beyond human control frequently **intervene** in human affairs. Notwithstanding many people's opinion that the weather has little influence in their lives besides determining what clothes they wear on a particular day, the weather has in fact caused world history to radically shift in important ways that are still felt today.

2   Numerous examples from world history **document** the long-term effects of weather in the formation of cultures and nations. In the thirteenth century, Khubilai Khan ruled over the vast Mongol empire, which **spanned** from the Pacific Ocean in the east to the Black

tempting: attractive; desirable

fate: the plan for the future that has been decided and that you cannot control

a course: a route or direction

cumulatively: formed over time by many parts or additions

to intervene: to become involved in something in order to influence the final result

Sea in the west, from present-day Siberia in the north to Afghanistan in the south. To expand his **reign** further, Khubilai Khan **mounted** two invasions of Japan. Two **monsoons**, however, caused him to end his attacks. Delgado (2008) describes legendary accounts of this event: "The legend, oft repeated in countless history books, speaks of gigantic ships, numbering into the thousands, crewed by indomitable Mongol warriors, and of **casualties** on a massive scale, with more than 100,000 lives lost in the final invasion attempt of 1281" (p. 4). Because of this unexpected defeat, Khubilai Khan decided to **stage** a third invasion of Japan, but he died before he could fulfill this **ambition**. Without these monsoons, Japan might have been defeated by the Mongols and thus lost its identity as a unique culture, with far-reaching consequences for Asian and world history.

3   In the early years of America's Revolutionary War, which began in 1775, it appeared likely that the British would **crush** the armies of her colonial territory and incorporate it back into the empire. The British troops were a well-trained and disciplined army that was feared worldwide. In contrast, the American troops were newly trained, sometimes poorly organized, and lacked sufficient resources to fight effectively. General George Washington could have easily been defeated in the Battle of Long Island on August 22, 1776. Historical records show that Sir William Howe, the British commander, was clearly defeating Washington on Long Island and was actually winning **handily** (Seymour, 1995). Nonetheless, the weather intervened when a heavy **fog** rolled in, so the American forces were able to **retreat**, regroup, and survive to fight

to document: to maintain a written record of; to write about

to span: to extend from one point to another

a reign: a time of political control, especially for kings, queens, or unelected officials

to mount: to prepare something so that it takes place

a monsoon: a strong rain storm that happens at a certain time of the year

a casualty: an injury or death in a severe event such as an accident or a war

to stage: to plan, organize, and make something happen

ambition: a strong desire for power, wealth, or fame

another day. Because of this fog, the United States was not defeated in its struggle for freedom. Consequently, today's United Kingdom of England, Wales, Scotland, and Northern Ireland does not include the United States. The United States is not a commonwealth of a mother country, as Canada and Australia are, though the United States still has strong **ties** to its colonial past.

4   When Napoleon Bonaparte invaded Russia in the early nineteenth century, he met with early successes that appeared to guarantee that he might eventually rule the world as his personal **domain**. His soldiers **captured** Moscow and destroyed the city, which encouraged him to push farther in his military campaigns. However, because of his dreams of glory, Napoleon **overlooked** the simple fact that Russian winters are extremely cold. When the temperatures fell below freezing, many of his soldiers and their horses died in the **brutal** weather. As Belloc (1926) writes in his classic study of the Napoleonic wars, "The cold *was* the **abominable** thing: The **dreadful** enemy against which men could not fight and which destroyed them" (p. 217). As a result of the failure of Napoleon's Russian campaigns, his own rule ended relatively soon after. His defeat led to a reorganization of power throughout the European nations, as well as to the rise of Russia as a major world power.

5   As these three examples **unambiguously** demonstrate, the weather has caused numerous huge shifts in world history as well as in power balances among cultures and nations. Without the rainy storms of the monsoon season, Japan might be the eastern outpost of Mongolia; without the appearance of **dense** fog, the United States might still be a territory of the United Kingdom; and without winter snow, Muscovites might speak French. Today weather **forecasters** can usually predict with a high degree of accuracy when thunderstorms, hurricanes, tsunamis, and tornadoes will strike, but the course of history cannot be fully isolated from the effects of the weather.

References

Belloc, H. (1926). *Napoleon's campaign of 1812 and the retreat from Moscow*. New York: Harper.

Delgado, J. (2008). *Khubilai Khan's lost fleet: In search of a legendary armada*. Berkeley, CA: University of California Press.

Seymour, W. (1995). *The price of folly: British blunders in the War of American Independence*. London: Brassey's.

to crush: to destroy

handily: easily

fog: a type of weather similar to a cloud very near the ground

to retreat: to go back

a tie: a connection

domain: land that a ruler or government controls

to capture: to catch; to trap

to overlook: to fail to notice or know about

brutal: severe

abominable: disgusting; causing hateful feelings

dreadful: extremely bad; causing fear

unambiguously: not ambiguously; clearly and definitely

dense: thick

a forecaster: a person who predicts something, often the weather

Post-Reading

1. What is the topic of the essay? _____

2. What is the writer's thesis? _____

   _____

3. What is the cause that the writer describes in the essay? _____

   _____

   _____

141

4. What are some of the effects that the writer describes?

_____

_____

5. Write one detail that strongly supports the thesis statement.

_____

_____

6. How is this essay organized?

☐ focus-on-causes method   ☐ focus-on-effects method

7. Can you think of any information that the author should have included to make the message of the essay stronger?

_____

_____

_____

Building Better Sentences: For further practice, go to Practice 3 on pages 239–240 in the Appendix.

Building Better Vocabulary

ACTIVITY 4   Practicing Three Kinds of Vocabulary from Context

Read each important vocabulary word or phrase. Locate it in the essay if you need help remembering the word or phrase. Then circle the best synonym, antonym, or collocation from column A, B, or C.

Type of Vocabulary	Important Vocabulary	A	B	C
Synonyms	**1.** capture	catch	fulfill	prosper
	2. tempting	attractive	inherent	precise
	3. forecast	dread	predict	reign
	4. on account of	due to	prior to	regardless of
Antonyms	**5.** handily	by vehicle	on foot	with difficulty
	6. dense	thin	superior	reluctant
	7. eventually	beyond	cumulatively	immediately
	8. expand	differentiate	proceed	shrink
Collocations	**9.** span ___ Greece	from England to	near England and	with England or
	10. ___ in a dispute	duplicate	intervene	merge
	11. a brutal ___	friendship	lunch	storm
	12. defeat ___	an attack	an enemy	a reptile

ACTIVITY 5 Analyzing the Organization

Use the words from the box to complete the outline of "How Weather Has Changed World History." Reread the essay on pages 139–141 if you need help.

> • the Battle of Long Island in the American Revolutionary War, during which fog helped the American forces to retreat
>
> • The course of history cannot be fully isolated from the effects of weather.
>
> • H. Belloc, who documents the effect of the Russian winter
>
> • The weather has changed world history in important ways still felt today.
>
> • Japan's cultural identity would have changed if Khan had succeeded in his invasion.

Title: How Weather Has Changed World History

I. Introduction

   A. Describe how people think they control their fates.

   B. Suggest, however, that people cannot control every aspect of their environments.

   C. Thesis statement: _____ .

II. Body Paragraph 1

   A. Provide the example of Khubilai Khan and his invasion of Japan.

   B. Cite the study of J. Delgado, who describes Khubilai Khan's failed invasion.

   C. Discuss how _____

      _____ .

III. Body Paragraph 2

   A. Provide the example of _____ .

      _____ .

   B. Cite the study of W. Seymour, who documents the circumstances of the battle.

   C. Discuss how the United States might have remained a member of the British Commonwealth, if not for a heavy fog.

IV. Body Paragraph 3

   A. Provide the example of Napoleon Bonaparte's invasion of Russia.

   B. Cite the study of _____ .

   C. Discuss the consequences of Napoleon's defeat in relation to Russia's rise as a world power.

V. Conclusion

   A. Summarize the three examples from the body paragraphs.

   B. Suggest that, although weather forecasters can predict the weather with more accuracy than in the past, _____ .

Strong Thesis Statements for Cause-Effect Essays

A strong thesis statement for a cause-effect essay indicates whether the essay focuses on causes or on effects. Sometimes the thesis statement uses the words *cause(s)* or *effects(s)*, but this is not necessary if either the cause or the effect is implied in the statement. In addition, a thesis statement sometimes includes a number, such as *three causes* or *two effects*, but this is also optional.

Focus	Example thesis statement
on causes	Many customers prefer to shop online for **three** important reasons.
	The increase in obesity in our country is due to food commercials, cheap fast food, and video games.
on effects	This essay will discuss the **effects** of watching too much TV on children's family life, interpersonal skills, and school life.
	Most people are not aware of the positive **effects** of simply walking for 20 to 30 minutes per day.

ACTIVITY 6   **Writing Strong Thesis Statements for Cause-Effect Essays**

Write a thesis statement for each topic. When you finish, compare your answers with a partner's.

1. the causes of bullying

_____

_____

2. the effects of being an only child

_____

_____

3. the causes of choosing a vegan diet

_____

_____

4. the effects of society's love for computers

_____

_____

Transitions and Connectors in Cause-Effect Essays

Transitions and connectors are important in cause-effect essays because they help indicate causation or effect regarding the topic. Perhaps the most familiar cause-effect transition word is *because*: "X happened **because** Y happened." Precise use of transitions helps the reader to follow the writer's reasoning about cause-effect relationships.

The transitions for both a focus-on-causes essay and a focus-on-effects essay are the same because both kinds of essays discuss one or more causes or one or more effects.

Transitions and Connectors Commonly Used in Cause-Effect Essays		
as a consequence	due to	on account of
as a result	(the) effect (of X)	owing to (for this) reason
(X can be) attributed to (Y)	(a key) factor of (X)	(X is the) reason for (Y)
because	for this reason	(X is a) result of (Y)
because of	furthermore	(X) resulted in (Y)
caused	if (X), then (Y)	since
(X is the) cause of (Y)	in addition (to)	so
(X is) caused by (Y)	in order to	therefore
(one) consequence of this (is that . . .)	(X) influences (Y)	this means that . . .
consequently	(X) leads to (Y)	thus

ACTIVITY 7   Identifying Transitions and Connectors in an Essay

Reread "How Weather Has Changed World History" on pages 139–141. Find seven transitions or connectors. Copy the sentences here, underline the transition or connector, and write the paragraph number in the parentheses.

1. _____

    _____ ( )

2. _____

    _____ ( )

3. _____

    _____ ( )

4. _____

    _____ ( )

5. _____

    _____ ( )

6. _____

    _____ ( )

7. _____

    _____ ( )

Studying Transitions and Connectors in an Example Cause-Effect Essay

ACTIVITY 8 Warming Up to the Topic

Answer the questions on your own. Then discuss them with a partner or in a small group.

1. What was the happiest time in your life? Describe what happened. Why were you so happy?

_____

_____

_____

2. There is a saying that "Money can't buy happiness." Do you agree or disagree with this statement? In 75–100 words, explain your answer.

_____

_____

_____

_____

_____

_____

ACTIVITY 9 Using Transitions and Connectors in an Essay

Read "Happiness" and circle the correct transition words or phrases.

Essay 14

Happiness

1   What makes a person happy? **1** (If / So) people want to be happy—and few people **proclaim** their desire to be sad—should they seek money and professional success? Many experts in fields such as sociology, psychology, and public policy are attempting to answer this **seemingly** simple question of what makes people happy and how communities, social organizations, and employers can **facilitate** happiness by implementing a few simple strategies. In this new field of happiness studies, some **intriguing** answers are beginning to emerge about what makes people happy. Surprisingly, they support the longstanding **hypothesis** that money cannot buy happiness.

2   One of the **chief obstacles** to happiness is referred to as *social comparison*. When people compare themselves to other people, they prefer to see themselves as in some way superior. In an experiment, social

to proclaim: to state loudly or clearly for the record

seemingly: apparently

to facilitate: to make easier or more likely to happen

intriguing: extremely interesting

a hypothesis: an idea or theory that has not been proven

chief: main; principal

an obstacle: something that stops progress or forward movement

scientists asked whether people would prefer earning $50,000 per year while their peers earned $25,000 per year, or whether they would prefer earning $100,000 per year while their peers averaged $250,000 per year. Even though people would earn more in the **latter scenario**, most chose the **former** as a consequence of their desire to see themselves as more successful than others (Layard, 2005). **2** (In addition / Thus), a simple way to increase happiness is for people to reject the urge to compare themselves to others based on their finances and to live within their **means**.

3   **3** (Another / Other) way to increase people's sense of personal happiness is for them to be true to themselves and keep their personal sense of **integrity**. While this advice may seem rather **trite**, people who respect and follow their authentic desires generally report being happier than people who do not. As Martin (2012) explains, "At its core, authenticity implies discovering and **pursuing** what we care about most deeply." He further explains the **reciprocal** relationship between happiness and authenticity: "As much as authenticity contributes to the pursuit of happiness, then, happiness in turn contributes to identifying our authentic selves" (p. 55). When people limit their personal desires **4** (in order / in spite) to obtain certain goals, they may achieve greater financial success but actually **end up** unhappier.

4   **5** (Finally / Therefore), sometimes people benefit from social rules that encourage them to improve their lives, even when these laws cost more money. While few people enjoy paying taxes, some taxes make people happier **6** (although / because) they improve the overall quality of people's lives. In their study of smoking and cigarette taxes, Gruber and Mullainathan (2006) conclude that "taxes may affect the happiness of former smokers (by making

the latter: the second of two presented options

a scenario: an imagined situation

the former: the first of two presented options

means: a person's ability to afford

integrity: the personal quality of being honest and fair

trite: boring, unimportant, or no longer special, especially due to overuse

to pursue: to try hard to obtain

reciprocal: inversely related; mutually agreed upon

to end up: to reach a final condition or place, often without an original intention

it easier to **resist** the temptation to resume smoking) or **prospective** smokers (by making it easier to never start smoking in the first place)" (p. 139). This example demonstrates how a society's rules can ⑦ (cause / lead) to the general happiness of its populations, even through the apparently negative practice of increased taxation. Taxes also contribute to the funds available for other social purposes, which proves further justification for their use.

to resist: to fight against something so that it does not happen

prospective: related to future possibility of happening or coming true

5   These are **merely** three ways that scholars of happiness studies have determined that people can employ to **enhance** their personal happiness. People should avoid comparing themselves to others financially. They should seek to live as their authentic selves in their personal and professional lives. ⑧ (Furthermore / In contrast), they should welcome rules, laws, and even taxes that increase the general happiness of the population. Everyone says they want to be happy, and happiness studies are helping people learn how to lead happier lives rather than to passively expect happiness to find them.

merely: simply; only

to enhance: to improve

References

Gruber, J., & Mullainathan, S. (2006). Do cigarette taxes make smokers happier? In Yew-Kwang Ng & Lok Sang Ho (Eds.), *Happiness and public policy: Theory, case studies, and implications* (pp.109–146). Basingstoke, England: Palgrave Macmillan.

Layard, R. (2005). *Happiness: Lessons from a new science*. New York: Penguin.

Martin, M. (2012). *Happiness and the good life*. Oxford: Oxford University Press.

Building Better Vocabulary

ACTIVITY 10 **Practicing Three Kinds of Vocabulary from Context**

Read each important vocabulary word or phrase. Locate it in the essay if you need help remembering the word or phrase. Then circle the best synonym, antonym, or collocation from column A, B, or C.

Type of Vocabulary	Important Vocabulary	A	B	C
Synonyms	**1.** pursue	chase	mount	overlook
	2. obstacle	difficulty	extinction	forecast
	3. authentic	challenging	likely	real
	4. scenario	demeanor	example	verification
Antonyms	**5.** intriguing	accurate	uninteresting	worthwhile
	6. the former	the incentive	the latter	the organizer
	7. hinder	facilitate	navigate	range
	8. chief	essential, vital	far, remote	minor, lesser
Collocations	**9.** the means ___ something	do	doing	to do
	10. care about something ___	deeply	happily	tritely
	11. my overall ___ of	core	example	impression
	12. obtain a ___	desire	goal	tax

Grammar for Writing

Consistent Verb Tense Usage

Good writers are careful to use the same verb tense throughout an essay. While it is true that an essay may have, for example, some information about the past and some information about the present, most of the information will be about one time, most likely either past or present. Do not change verb tenses without a specific reason for doing so.

Explanation	Examples
When describing an event in the past tense, maintain the past tense throughout your explanation.	In our experiment, we **placed** three live fresh-water plants (each approximately 20 centimeters in length) into a quart jar that **was filled** with fresh water at 70 degrees Fahrenheit. We **left** the top two centimeters of the jar with air. We then carefully **added** a medium goldfish.
When talking about facts that are always true, use present tense in your explanation.	The sun **is** the center of the solar system. The earth and other planets **revolve** around the sun. Most of the planets **have** at least one moon that **circles** the planet, and these moons **vary** tremendously in size, just as the planets **do**.
In writings such as a report, it is possible to have different verb tenses reflecting different times.	According to this report, the police now **believe** that two men **stole** the truck and the money in it.

In the paragraph, correct the verbs where the tense shifts for no reason.

Paragraph 4

The Experiment

In our experiment, we placed three live fresh-water plants (each approximately 20 centimeters in length) into a quart jar that is filled with fresh water at 70 degrees Fahrenheit. We left the top two centimeters of the jar with air. We then carefully added a medium goldfish. Next, we tighten the lid and wrapped tape tightly around the lid. This very last step is done to ensure that no air can enter or exit the bottle. The jar was placed on a shelf where it is exposed to indirect sunlight for approximately eight hours each day. At 1 p.m. every day for a week, we observed the fish swimming in the jar. On several occasions, we notice that the plants emit multiple bubbles of a gas. The fish survived for the entire week. No food or air was provided. Thus, these green plants in the jar produced a gas, and we believed this gas was oxygen.

Grammar for Writing

Sentence Fragments

For many writers, sentence fragments, or incomplete sentences, are difficult to avoid. Writing a fragment instead of a complete sentence is considered a very serious error because it shows a lack of understanding of the basic components of a sentence, namely a subject and a verb that express a complete thought. Because fragments are one of the most serious errors in writing, it is imperative to learn how to avoid them.

Explanation	Examples
A sentence must have a subject and a verb and be able to stand by itself in meaning.	✗ **Because I read and studied the textbook often.** ✓ I scored 97 on the quiz **because I read and studied the textbook often.**
It is possible to begin a sentence with **because, although, if, when,** or **while,** but the sentence needs a second part with another subject-verb combination.	✗ **Because I studied for the final exam a great deal.** ✓ **Because I studied a great deal,** my score on the final exam was 99. ✓ My score on the final exam was 99 **because I studied a great deal.**

ACTIVITY 12 Working with Fragments

Write *C* on the line next to complete sentences. Write *F* if there is a fragment and circle the fragment.

_____ 1. Despite the heavy wind and the torrential rain, the young trees around the lake were able to survive the bad weather. It was a miracle.

_____ 2. The huge, two-story houses all have a very similar design. With no difference except the color of the roofs.

_____ 3. Ireland has a rich and colorful history. One with many stories of fairies and elves.

_____ 4. Shopping malls are a very popular tourist attraction in many cities, but some tourists are not interested in them. Shopping is not for everyone.

_____ 5. Because of the popularity of the film. Producers were anxious to begin work on its sequel.

_____ 6. The chef added so much spice to the stew that only the most daring of his patrons tasted it. The result was that less than half of the food was consumed.

_____ 7. There was a strange tension in the air. After so many years of separation.

_____ 8. My mother is so organized that she uses a color-coding system in her kitchen pantry. My father, on the other hand, is one of the most unorganized people that I know.

_____ 9. What is a dream and why do we dream? Scientists really do not understand dreams, but I wish someone could explain them to me.

_____ 10. Thousands of commuters were late for work this morning. Since the bus workers are on strike over pay and health benefits.

For more work with sentence fragments, see the *Brief Writer's Handbook with Activities,* pages 217–220.

ACTIVITY 13 **Editing an Essay: Review of Grammar**

Ten of the fifteen words or clauses in parentheses contain an error involving one of the grammar topics featured in this unit. If the word or phrase is correct, write *C*. If it is incorrect, fill in the blank with a correction.

Essay 15

How the Light Bulb Changed the World

1   Few inventions have changed the world as **dramatically** as Thomas Alva Edison's light bulb. **1** (With the **flip** of a switch. He turned darkness into light, thus **revolutionizing** people's lives.) _____

_____

_____

While the effects of the light bulb have been **overwhelmingly** positive, scientists have also identified some of its harmful effects, proving that even the greatest achievements often bring with them unexpected side effects that offset their advantages.

2   **2** (One of the most positive of the light bulb's **accomplishments** is that it has allowed people to expand their lives into the dark hours of night.) _____

_____

Human productivity **3** (increases) _____ dramatically after its invention because better lighting **enabled** people

---

dramatically: greatly; exceedingly

a flip: a turn from one position to the opposite

to revolutionize: to change completely (and possibly suddenly)

overwhelmingly: greatly; by a large number or amount

an accomplishment: anything a person has been able to do successfully, especially after some difficulty

to enable: to make able to happen

to read, study, work, play, and socialize into the late hours. **4** (Also, the **prevalence** of affordable lighting. This allowed companies to continue to manufacture their products during the night hours, when necessary.) _____

_____

_____

prevalence: the condition of being widespread or extremely common

Electric lighting also **enhanced** public safety because of city streets being **illuminated** without the **potential** danger of gas. Now that light bulbs **5** (are) _____ everywhere, it is **virtually** impossible to imagine a world without them, for they are a core part of the **infrastructure** of modern society.

to enhance: to improve

to illuminate: to light up

potential: possible

virtually: just about; almost completely

3   **6** (Nonetheless, it is important to **acknowledge** the negative consequences of the light bulb as well, including a phenomenon that scientists term *light pollution*.) _____

_____

_____

infrastructure: basic structures, such as roads and bridges, needed for a region to function properly

to acknowledge: to show recognition of; to admit that something is real

Miranda (2003) **laments** the "changes in the biology of ecosystems, in the life of people due to invasive lighting, and the 'artificialization' of the

to lament: to regret

night" (p. 7). **7** (These problems have been caused by excessive lighting. **Primarily** in **urban** areas.) _____

_____

8 (Animals and humans are biologically prepared for the changing rhythms of night and day, and constant lighting undermines these rhythms.) _____

_____

_____

Light pollution also **9** (clouded) _____ the night skies so that people cannot see the stars, which **10** (**frustrated**) _____ astronomers and anyone who **11** (loved) _____ looking up to the heavens to inspect its wonders.

4   **12** (Another unintended consequence of the light bulb. Is a phenomenon referred to as *switch psychology*, which theorizes that people become conditioned by light switches and other modern conveniences to expect immediate solutions to their problems.) _____

_____

_____

_____

Switch psychology lessens a person's sense of **self-efficacy**, which Hockenbury and Hockenbury (2006) define as "The degree to which you are subjectively **convinced** of your own capabilities and effectiveness in meeting the demands of a particular situation" (p. 486). People are so used to light switches immediately bringing light that some find themselves at a loss for words when a light **13** (did not go) _____ on; they feel that they are incapable of correcting the situation or undertaking any steps to solve the problem.

5   Edison's achievement with the light bulb rightly **14** (**deserves**) _____ celebration for its contributions to human comfort and productivity. At the same time, we must be careful to recognize

primarily: mainly

urban: city; the opposite of *rural*

frustrated: disappointed; unsatisfied

self-efficacy: the power to produce a desired result or effect

convinced: very sure; certain

to deserve: to merit

153

some of its unintended consequences, such as light pollution and switch psychology, that threaten to **tarnish** his shining **legacy**.

15 (Many lasting **innovations** that have contributed dramatically to humanity's advancement. These innovations can also be the cause of unintended results, and we must **strive** to **mitigate** these consequences to take full advantage of their predominant benefits.) _____

_____

_____

_____

_____

to tarnish: to stain; to lessen the image of

a legacy: a personal history or record

an innovation: a new idea, invention, or method

to strive: to try hard to do or achieve something

to mitigate: to make something less harsh or severe

References

Hockenbury, D., & Hockenbury, S. (2006). *Psychology* (4th ed.). New York: Worth.

Miranda, P. (2003). Discurso del representante de CONAMA (Both versions, in English and in Spanish). In H. Schwarz (Ed.), *Light pollution: The global view* (pp. 3–14). Dordrecht, The Netherlands: Kluwer Academic Publishers.

Building Better Vocabulary

ACTIVITY 14 **Practicing Three Kinds of Vocabulary from Context**

Read each important vocabulary word or phrase. Locate it in the essay if you need help remembering the word or phrase. Then circle the best synonym, antonym, or collocation from column A, B, or C.

Type of Vocabulary	Important Vocabulary	A	B	C
Synonyms	**1.** incapable	can not	must not	should not
	2. prevalent	common	intentional	key
	3. revolutionize	anticipate	change	mate
	4. tarnish	make dirty	make happy	make tired
Antonyms	**5.** urban	indigenous	rural	vivid
	6. convinced	doubting	dreading	learning
	7. excessive	dramatic	on account of	very little
	8. mitigate	deserve	increase	mimic
Collocations	**9.** the main cause ___ something	by	of	with
	10. ___ everywhere	dramatically	substantially	virtually
	11. ___ someone's help	acknowledge	denote	merge
	12. unintended ___	consequences	fog	goal

Original Student Writing: Cause-Effect Essay

In this section, you will follow the seven steps in the writing process to write a cause-effect essay. If you need help, refer to Unit 2, pages 34–46.

ACTIVITY 15 Step 1: Choose a Topic

Your first step is to choose a topic for your essay. For a cause-effect essay, you want to choose a topic for which you can develop three causes of one effect or three effects from one cause. Your teacher may assign a topic, you may think of one yourself, or you may choose one from the suggestions in the chart. As you consider possible topics, ask yourself, "What do I know about this topic? What do my readers know? What else do I need to know? Do I need to research this topic?"

Humanities	*Literature:* The effects of writing a novel on a computer
	History: The causes of an important historical event such as World War I
	Philosophy: The effects of Socrates on modern thought
Sciences	*Biology:* The causes of cancer
	Geology: The effects of burning oil and gas
	Meteorology: The causes of climate change
Business	*Economics:* The causes of inflation
Personal	The effects of your attitude toward challenges in life

1. What topic did you choose? _____

2. Why did you choose this topic? _____

   _____

3. How well do you know this topic? What is your experience with it?

   _____

   _____

A. Use the chart to brainstorm a list of possible causes and effects for your topic.

TOPIC: _____	
Causes: _____	Effects: _____
_____	_____
_____	_____
_____	_____
_____	_____
_____	_____
_____	_____
_____	_____
_____	_____
_____	_____
_____	_____
_____	_____

B. Now carefully consider the causes and effects. Which focus do you think would be better for your essay? If you have more causes, then you should write a focus-on-causes essay with one effect. If you have more effects, then you should write a focus-on-effects essay with one cause.

ACTIVITY 17 **Step 3: Outline**

Prepare a simple outline of your essay. Focus either on causes or on effects.

Title: _____

  I. Introduction

    A. Hook: _____

_____

    B. Connecting information: _____

_____

    C. Thesis statement: _____

_____

II. Body Paragraph 1 (Cause 1 or Effect 1): _____

    A. _____

    B. _____

III. Body Paragraph 2 (Cause 2 or Effect 2): _____

    A. _____

    B. _____

IV. Body Paragraph 3 (Cause 3 or Effect 3): _____

    A. _____

    B. _____

V. Conclusion: _____

_____

Peer Editing of Outlines

    Exchange books with a partner. Read your partner's outline. Then use the following questions to help you to comment on your partner's outline. Use your partner's feedback to revise your outline.

1. How is this essay organized?

    ☐ focus-on-causes method   ☐ focus-on-effects method

2. Is there any aspect of the outline that is unclear to you? Give details.

_____

_____

_____

3. Can you think of an area in the outline that needs more development? Make specific suggestions.

_____

_____

_____

4. If you have any other ideas or suggestions, write them here.

_____

_____

_____

ACTIVITY 18 **Step 4: Write the First Draft**

Use the information from Steps 1–3 to write the first draft of your cause-effect essay. Use at least four of the vocabulary words or phrases from the Building Better Vocabulary activities in this unit. Underline these words and phrases in your essay. Try to also use at least two of the words from the Academic Word List in the *Brief Writer's Handbook with Activities* on pages 230–231.

ACTIVITY 19 **Step 5: Get Feedback from a Peer**

Exchange papers from Step 4 with a partner. Read your partner's first draft. Then use Peer Editing Sheet 6 (available online at NGL.Cengage.com/GW5) to help you to comment on your partner's writing. Be sure to offer positive suggestions and comments that will help your partner improve his or her essay.

ACTIVITY 20 **Step 6: Revise the First Draft**

Read the comments on Peer Editing Sheet 6 about your essay. Then reread your essay. Can you identify places where you should make revisions? List the improvements you plan to make.

1. _____

_____

_____

2. _____

_____

_____

3. _____

_____

_____

Use all the information from the previous steps to write the final version of your paper. Often, writers will need to write a third or even a fourth draft to express their ideas as clearly as possible. Write as many drafts as necessary to produce a good essay.

ACTIVITY 21 **Step 7: Proofread the Final Draft**

Be sure to proofread your paper several times before you submit it so you find all the mistakes and correct them.

Additional Topics for Writing

Here are ten more ideas for topics for additional cause-effect essay writing.

PHOTO
TOPIC: Look at the photo on pages 132–133. There are several different types of pollution, for example, water, land, and light pollution. Choose one type of pollution. What are the causes or effects of this type of pollution on the environment?

TOPIC 2: What are the causes of illiteracy?

TOPIC 3: What are the effects of overcrowding in cities?

TOPIC 4: What effects can one person have on the government?

TOPIC 5: Why do many people prefer foreign goods?

TOPIC 6: What are the causes of credit card debt?

TOPIC 7: Discuss how people's childhood experiences influence their lives.

TOPIC 8: What are the effects of sudden wealth (such as when a person wins the lottery)?

TOPIC 9: What are the effects of poverty?

TOPIC 10: What are the causes of a recent political crisis?

Timed Writing

How quickly can you write in English? There are many times when you must write quickly, such as on a test. It is important to feel comfortable during those times. Timed-writing practice can make you feel better about writing quickly in English.

1. Read the essay guidelines below. Then take out a piece of paper.

2. Read the writing prompt below the guidelines.

3. Write a basic outline including either **one cause** and more than one effect or a few causes and **one effect**. You should spend no more than five minutes on your outline.

4. Write a five-paragraph essay.

5. You have 40 minutes to write your essay.

Cause-Effect Essay Guidelines

- Use the focus-on-causes or the focus-on-effects organization for this essay. Do not write about multiple causes and multiple effects.

- Remember to give your essay a title.

- Double-space your essay.

- Write as legibly as possible (if you are not using a computer).

- Include a short introduction (with a thesis statement), three body paragraphs, and a conclusion.

- Try to give yourself a few minutes before the end of the activity to review your work. Check for mistakes in spelling and consistent verb tense, and look for sentence fragments.

We all face personal troubles in our lives. Think about a recent challenging situation in your life at home, at work, at school, or with friends. What were the causes of this situation? What were its effects? Although you will discuss both causes and effects, remember to emphasize either the causes of the situation or the effects of the situation.

A winding highway in New Taipei City
on the island of Taiwan

OBJECTIVES To learn how to write an argument essay
To use effective transitions and connectors in argument writing
To understand the important role of modals in argument essays
To learn how to use -*ly* adverbs of degree in advanced writing

*Should a driver's license
ever be taken away
due to age?*

What Is an Argument Essay?

We frequently attempt to persuade others to agree with our viewpoints, such as which movie to watch or where to go on vacation. In writing an **argument essay**, we use written words to achieve a similar goal. In argument essays, sometimes referred to as persuasive essays, writers attempt to convince their readers to agree with them on a particular issue. By explaining their reasons for holding a particular belief, writers hope to sway others to share their point of view or to take a particular action. For example, in an argument essay about why people should recycle, you might explain two or three reasons that recycling is good for the environment. After giving these reasons for recycling, you should present an opinion that people who do not recycle might say, such as "One person cannot make a difference." Your response to that opposing opinion could then include data showing how much garbage one person produces per year and how much of that could be recycled.

One type of argument essay is a newspaper or magazine editorial where writers choose an issue and explain its relevance to their readers to create a community of like-minded thinkers. For example, an editorial writer might endorse a particular candidate in an election, with the hope of persuading readers to vote for the candidate the writer thinks will do the best job. We strongly recommend reading an editorial in a newspaper of your choice to help you understand what argument writing is. In fact, you should read editorials in a few different newspapers or similar sources to become familiar with the writing style and organization of good argument writing.

Another type of argument essay writing appears in blogs as the blog writer explains his or her reasons for supporting or disagreeing with a certain issue. Of course not all blog entries are persuasive writing, but many are in fact very good examples with well-supported opinions.

Well-written and organized argument essays clearly and logically explain a writer's reasons behind a given viewpoint. However, writers should not exaggerate their claims. It is better to be candid about the limitations of their viewpoint than to overstate the case. If their arguments seem exaggerated or untrue, readers will distrust the writers and not accept their ideas.

How Is an Argument Essay Organized?

Your goal in an argument essay is to convince your readers that your opinion about an issue (your thesis statement) is valid and important. To accomplish this goal, your essay must state your opinion about the issue clearly. However, your essay also needs to be balanced to show that you understand the issue completely. One way to do this is to include an opposing viewpoint, or **counterargument**. Even though you are arguing one side of an issue (either *for* or *against*), you must think about what someone on the other side of the issue would argue. After giving your opponent's point of view, you offer a **refutation**. This means that you refute the other point of view, or show how it is wrong. Discussing only your opinion makes your essay sound biased, and your readers may not be convinced of your viewpoint.

An argument essay is organized in the same general manner as the other essays in this book.

- It begins with an **introductory paragraph** that introduces the topic and thesis of the essay.

- The **body paragraphs** discuss the pros and cons of the thesis statement. As with all types of essays, the body paragraphs have supporting information.

- An argument essay often contains a **counterargument**, which is an opposing opinion, in the body of the essay. This counterargument is presented, explained, and then suggested to be untrue or less important in the **refutation**.

- The **conclusion** summarizes the main points of the argument and restates the writer's thesis.

In a five-paragraph essay, one way to organize the body paragraphs is for paragraphs two and three to provide support for your thesis, and then for paragraph four to introduce and refute a counterargument. However, the number of body paragraphs can be as few as two or as many as necessary to explain your position. For example, if you are writing a five-paragraph essay in which you argue that people should recycle as much as they can, paragraphs two and three could give reasons to support your thesis. Then paragraph four could present the opposing idea that recycling is ineffective, along with a refutation of that opposing idea. Such an essay might look like this

INTRODUCTION	Paragraph 1	Hook Connecting information Thesis
BODY	Paragraph 2	Support 1: Recycling saves energy. • Creating glass from recycled glass uses 50 percent less energy than making new glass. • Recycling one can of soda saves enough energy to run a TV for three hours.
	Paragraph 3	Support 2: Recycling reduces air pollution. • Using recycled products helps reduce the amount of pollution in our air.
	Paragraph 4	Opposing viewpoint(s) • Counterargument: One person cannot make a difference. • Refutation: Each person produces 1,600 pounds of waste each year, but as much as 1,100 pounds of that total could be recycled.
CONCLUSION	Paragraph 5	Restated thesis Suggestion/opinion/prediction

Great Topics for Argument Essays

What is a great topic for an argument essay? Obviously, it should be an issue that you feel strongly about, know something about, and would like to share your opinions on. What is your opinion on the issue? Why do you feel this way? Can you think of some reasons why people might think differently than you do?

When selecting topics for this type of essay, consider relevant questions such as:

- Does the topic have two (or more) viewpoints? A topic without at least two viewpoints is not suitable.

- How much do you know about this topic? You should choose a topic that you know about and feel passionately about.

As you read this list of general topics that lend themselves well to an argument essay, ask yourself what your opinion is about the topic. Can you also think of at least one opposing viewpoint for each topic?

General Topics for Argument	
limiting oil exploration in environmentally sensitive areas	requiring a test for people who want to have children
legalizing capital punishment	raising the driving age
mandating military service	using animals for medical research
requiring school uniforms	getting rid of zoos
banning cigarettes	rating or restricting video games

ACTIVITY 1 Identifying Topics for Argument Essays

Read these eight topics. Put a check mark (✓) next to the four that could be good topics for argument essays.

_____ 1. The first time I flew in a plane

_____ 2. The choice of a specific candidate to vote for in an election

_____ 3. How and why birds migrate south for the winter

_____ 4. Steps in negotiating an international contract

_____ 5. The necessity of higher taxes on gasoline

_____ **6.** Why schools should offer after-school programs for at-risk students

_____ **7.** Reasons that you deserve a raise at your job

_____ **8.** How to play chess well

Can you think of two additional topics that would be excellent for an argument essay?

9. _____

10. _____

Supporting Details

After you have selected a topic, think about what you already know about the issue and what you need to find out. Asking yourself questions about both sides of the issue is a good way to generate details to include in your essay.

When you brainstorm your plan for an argument essay, a useful technique is to fill in a pro-con chart with the pro points in favor of the thesis statement and the con points against the thesis statement. If you cannot generate many ideas for one or both sides, you need to do more research on the issue or choose a different issue.

Here is a pro-con chart for an essay arguing that people over age eighteen should (or should not) be required to vote:

Thesis Statement: Voting should be required by all citizens over eighteen.

Pro	Con
1. In a democracy, everyone should participate.	1. In a democracy, people should have the right to vote as well as not to vote.
2. In our history, many people have died in wars so that we can vote.	2. Some people do not know the candidates and do not want to make a decision.
3. If everyone votes, then the chosen candidate will represent the whole country.	3. Some people know the candidates and do not want to have to vote for any of them.

ACTIVITY 2 **Brainstorming Supporting Ideas**

Read the thesis statements and complete the pro-con charts. Write three ideas to support each statement. Then write three ideas against each statement. Finally, choose another topic and write a thesis statement and pro-con supports for your new topic.

1. _Thesis statement_: Adults should be required to pass a test before they can become parents.

Pro	Con
1.	1.
2.	2.
3.	3.

2. *Thesis statement*: The death penalty helps society to protect innocent people.

Pro	Con
1.	1.
2.	2.
3.	3.

3. *Your thesis statement*: _____

Pro	Con
1.	1.
2.	2.
3.	3.

ACTIVITY 3 **Studying an Example Argument Essay**

This essay suggests that studying abroad is a valuable experience for university students. Discuss the Preview Questions with a partner. Then read the essay and answer the questions that follow.

Preview Questions

1. If you were going to complete a semester abroad, where would you want to go? Explain your answer.

2. Can you think of three reasons that a student should study abroad? Can you think of three reasons that students should not study abroad? Complete the pro-con chart.

Thesis statement: All students should complete at least one semester abroad.

Pro	Con
1.	1.
2.	2.
3.	3.

3. Do you think colleges and universities should modify their graduation requirements to include the mandatory completion of at least one semester in a study-abroad program? Why or why not?

The Best Classroom

1   Because of such factors as the rise of the Internet, the ease of global travel, and a dramatic increase in international trade, the world is more interconnected than ever before. In the past, people could enjoy a successful career without ever moving from their home region, but now many people have jobs that involve some international interactions. **Given** these new conditions, it is essential that all college and university students experience new cultures as part of their education. To achieve this objective and to emphasize the importance of intercultural studies, colleges and universities should require students to study abroad for at least one semester of their undergraduate education.

2   One of the primary reasons that studying abroad contributes so effectively to students' education is that it requires them to live and learn in a new culture that is different from their **upbringing**. In their analysis of the educational benefits of study-abroad programs, Brewer and Cunningham (2009) conclude that real learning is often **triggered** by a serious **dilemma** that causes the individuals involved to question

given: because of; due to

upbringing: the way or manner in which a child is raised by parents or caregivers

to trigger: to cause to happen

a dilemma: a choice between two things that are equally good or bad

167

assumptions they may have held for their entire lives (p. 9). As Brewer and Cunningham demonstrate, students' daily assumptions are challenged by the experience of living abroad, from simple concerns, such as appropriate breakfast foods, to more complex matters, such as how societies should be organized and other cultural conventions. By experiencing a new culture firsthand, students will better appreciate the unique features of both their host and their home countries, as well as better understand the **repercussions** of these cultural differences.

3   Studying abroad also greatly **facilitates** learning a new language. While students should prepare to study abroad by learning this language in the classroom, thereby establishing a **framework** for future success, few experiences **enhance** language learning more than living in a country where it is used. As Kauffmann, Martin, and Weaver (1992) state, "Foreign settings offer many new resources for instruction, practice, and evaluation. Teaching methods that take advantage of the local environments can certainly be expected to improve on classroom methods" (p. 36). For example, when learning a new language in a classroom, students might practice ordering food at a restaurant or asking directions to a museum; when studying abroad, however, they will have to put these skills to the test in real-world situations.

4   Additionally, students benefit from studying their academic **discipline** from a new perspective. At first, this argument may appear illogical: math is math, whether in Peru or Poland, and the **fundamental** principles of chemistry do not change from Ghana to Germany. Still, the ways in which disciplines are organized and taught may vary **considerably** from one region to another, and so students will see their discipline **in a new light** if it is taught in even a slightly different method or order. Learning to see the ways in which knowledge itself is organized can be one of the greatest benefits of studying abroad.

5   Though studying abroad offers many advantages, some may argue that a semester or a year abroad is nothing but a vacation. Yes, it is true that some students choose to treat studying abroad as a vacation rather than the rich academic experience that it can be. The bad actions of a few students should not **invalidate** study abroad programs as a whole or cause colleges to abandon their efforts in this regard. In fact, in a long-term study of 3,400 students, Dwyer and Peters (2004) found that a large number said studying abroad had an impact on their world view (96 percent), increased their self-confidence (96 percent), and gave them the skill sets they needed for the career they chose (76 percent). Clearly, studying abroad is not just a party. Students' home institutions should offer preparatory workshops and orientation seminars so that students will be ready for the requirements of the program and will better understand how it connects with their current academic work. Studying abroad unites academic demands with the **thrill** of discovering a new culture, and students will gain immeasurably more from the experience if they are prepared prior to departure for what they will discover there.

---

an assumption: a belief or an opinion

a repercussion: a negative result that was not expected

to facilitate: to help; to make easier

a framework: a basic structure

to enhance: to make something better, easier, or more effective

a discipline: field of study; subject area

fundamental: basic; most important

considerably: a great amount; to a significant degree

in a new light: in a new way

to invalidate: to prove that something is not true

the thrill: the excitement

6   Given the numerous benefits of studying abroad, colleges and universities should require that their students take advantage of this opportunity, while also doing everything possible to keep these experiences affordable through reduced tuition and **subsidized** fees. It is essential that students learn to negotiate our increasingly interconnected world by exploring new cultures as part of their education. In a world made smaller by technological advances, students who graduate with the experience of living in a foreign culture will also be better prepared to succeed in their careers.

References

Brewer, E., & Cunningham, K. (2009). Capturing study abroad's transformative potential. In E. Brewer & K. Cunningham (Eds.), *Integrating study abroad into the curriculum: Theory and practice across the disciplines* (pp. 1–29). Sterling, VA: Stylus.

Dwyer, M., & Peters, C. (2004). The benefits of study abroad. *Transitions Abroad, 27* (5), 56–57.

Kauffmann, N., Martin, J., & Weaver, H., with J. Weaver. (1992). *Students abroad, strangers at home: Education for a global society.* Yarmouth, ME: Intercultural Press.

to subsidize: to help pay for the cost of something

Post-Reading Questions

1. How many paragraphs does this essay have? _____

2. What is the topic of the essay? _____

3. What is the writer's thesis? _____

   _____

4. What reasons does the writer give for her viewpoint?

   _____

   _____

   _____

5. After reading this student's essay, do you agree with the thesis? Why or why not?

   _____

   _____

   _____

6. If you answered *no* to the previous question, answer a. If you answered *yes*, answer b.

a. If you disagree with the thesis, what could the writer have done to make her point more convincing?

_____

_____

_____

b. If you agree with the thesis, what are some ways in which the writer could have been even more convincing?

_____

_____

_____

7. Does the last sentence in the conclusion offer a suggestion, an opinion, or a prediction?

_____

Building Better Sentences: For further practice, go to Practice 4 on page 240 in the Appendix.

Building Better Vocabulary

ACTIVITY 4 Practicing Three Kinds of Vocabulary from Context

Read each important vocabulary word or phrase. Locate it in the essay if you need help remembering the word or phrase. Then circle the best synonym, antonym, or collocation from column A, B, or C.

Type of Vocabulary	Important Vocabulary	A	B	C
Synonyms	1. trigger	arrange	cause	enter
	2. assess	leave	persuade	test
	3. dilemma	liquid	necessity	problem
	4. impact	effect	knowledge	view
Antonyms	5. abroad	distant	local	weak
	6. repercussion	cause	individual	mastery
	7. complex	frequent	necessary	simple
	8. affordable	believable	expensive	honest
Collocations	9. ___ abroad	hear	mention	study
	10. my current ___	quickness	situation	upbringing
	11. ___ for granted	look	make	take
	12. vary ___	calmly	considerably	well

Use the words from the box to complete the outline of "The Best Classroom." Reread the essay on pages 167–169 if you need help.

- To achieve this objective, colleges and universities should require students to study abroad for at least one semester of their undergraduate education.
- Consider the real-world language situations in which students have to operate every day.
- Demonstrate that study abroad improves students' lives.
- Suggest that seeing new ways to organize knowledge is a major outcome of studying abroad.
- Offer a prediction
- Show how studying abroad teaches students about not only the foreign culture but also their own culture.

Title: The Best Classroom

  I. Introduction

    A. The world is a smaller place.

    B. People's jobs now depend on international connections.

    C. Thesis statement: _____.

 II. Body Paragraph 1

    A. Show how studying abroad makes students experience a foreign culture.

    B. _____.

III. Body Paragraph 2

    A. Discuss how studying abroad contributes to learning a foreign language.

    B. _____.

IV. Body Paragraph 3

    A. Explain how studying abroad allows students to see their academic discipline from a new perspective.

    B. _____.

 V. Body Paragraph 4

    A. Address a common opposing idea that studying abroad is just a vacation.

    B. Prove that A is not accurate here: _____.

    C. Argue that schools need to prepare their students for study abroad so they know the requirements and goals.

VI. Conclusion

    A. Suggest that studying abroad should be required.

    B. _____ about the future lives of students who graduate from a college or university that has a required study abroad component.

Strong Thesis Statements for Argument Essays

A strong thesis statement for an argument essay states a clear position on the issue. The thesis often includes a word or phrase that signals an opinion, such as **should**, **ought to**, **need to**, **have an obligation to**, or even **must** or **had better**.

In addition, a thesis statement sometimes uses general phrases such as **for a number of reasons**, **for a number of important reasons**, or **in many ways**. Sometimes a thesis statement may list the actual reasons for supporting or opposing an idea or say how many reasons will be discussed in the paper.

Finally, a thesis statement can use hedging words such as **some** or **some people** as well as **may**, **might**, **can**, **seem**, or **appear** with the verb to limit or qualify an unsupported statement. These thesis statements often use a contrasting connector such as **although**, **while**, or **despite**.

Type of thesis	Example thesis statement
simple thesis	It is easy to demonstrate that pets help humans **in many ways**.
	School uniforms **should** be required **for three reasons**.
stronger thesis, listing reasons	College students **should** be encouraged to pursue a career in science because of **the large number of job options** and **the higher salaries**.
	Taxes are a necessary part of our society; without them, we could not pay for **our roads and bridges** or **our schools**.
stronger thesis including possible counterargument	**Although some** may object to the death penalty, this punishment is a necessity to **control public order** and **ensure people's safety**.
	While some people think paying taxes is unfair, all of us **should** pay taxes because we all benefit from **what they provide in our daily lives**.

- The thesis statement for an argument essay cannot be a fact. A fact is not a good topic for this kind of essay because a fact cannot be argued. For example, "the number of people in the United States" is not controversial. "The population of the United States is increasing every year" is not a good thesis statement because it is a fact, and there is no way to argue this point.

- A thesis statement should not be a personal opinion that cannot be proved. For example, "Popcorn is more delicious than peanuts" cannot be proved because this is based on one person's opinion.

- The thesis statement must state or imply a position on the issue, and the position should be very clear. For the topic of "cigarette smoking," a possible thesis statement is "The manufacture of cigarettes should be stopped." In contrast, the statement "Cigarette smoking isn't a very good idea" is too vague and general to be a thesis.

ACTIVITY 6 Writing Strong Thesis Statements for Argument Essays

Write a pro thesis statement and a con thesis statement for each topic. When you finish, compare your answers with a partner's.

1. Topic: University education for everyone

Pro thesis statement: _____

_____

Con thesis statement: _____

_____

2. Topic: Paying professional athletes extremely high salaries

Pro thesis statement: _____

_____

Con thesis statement: _____

_____

3. Topic: Using alternative energy sources

Pro thesis statement: _____

_____

Con thesis statement: _____

_____

Strong Counterargument and Refutation Statements for Argument Essays

The most important technique in persuading readers that your viewpoint is valid is to support it in every paragraph, but another strong technique is to write a good **counterargument** that goes against your thesis statement. Introducing this counterargument adds credibility to your essay. It shows that you understand more than one point of view about your topic.

After you provide a counterargument, you must give a **refutation**, or a response to the counterargument, that either disproves it or shows it to be weaker or less important than your point.

In simple terms, imagine that you are having an argument with a friend about your topic. She disagrees with your opinion. What do you think will be her strongest argument against your point of view? That is your counterargument. How will you respond to her counterargument? Your answer is your refutation.

Look at the following excerpt from "The Best Classroom" on pages 167–169. The counterargument is in italics and the refutation is underlined.

> Though studying abroad offers many advantages, *some may argue that a semester or a year abroad is nothing but a vacation.* Yes, it is true that some students choose to treat studying abroad as a vacation rather than the rich academic experience that it can be. The bad actions of a few students should not invalidate study-abroad programs as a whole. In fact, in a long-term study of 3,400 students, Dwyer and Peters (2004) found that a large number said studying abroad had an impact on their world view (96 percent), increased their self-confidence (96 percent), and gave them the skill sets they needed for the career they chose (76 percent). Clearly, studying abroad is not just a party.

As you can see, what begins as a counterargument ends up as another reason in support of the writer's opinion.

ACTIVITY 7 **Writing Refutations for Counterarguments**

For each counterargument, write a one-sentence refutation. Remember to use a contrasting connection word (*although, while, despite*) to begin your refutation.

1. Topic: Mandatory retirement for pilots

   Thesis statement: Pilots should be required to retire at age 60 to ensure the safety of passengers.

   Counterargument: Some people may believe that older pilots' experience can contribute to flight safety.

   Refutation: *While this may be true for a handful of pilots, the vast majority of people report weaker eyesight, hearing, and motor skills as they age.*

2. Topic: National identity cards

   Thesis statement: A national identity card would make life better for everyone, especially when voting, applying for a job, or paying taxes.

   Counterargument: Some people might oppose national identity cards because they are afraid of the government having too much control in their daily lives.

   Refutation: _____

   _____

3. Topic: Teachers' salaries

   Thesis statement: Teachers' salaries should be tied to their students' test scores.

   Counterargument: Some people may believe that a teacher's role in a student's test score is not that important.

   Refutation: _____

   _____

Transitions and Connectors in Argument Essays

Transitional phrases and connectors in argument essays help the reader to follow the logical development of the argument. These transitions can be used to connect sentences, ideas, and paragraphs. Here are some common transitions and connectors for developing support in your argument and for addressing a counterargument.

Transitions and Connectors That Develop a Point Further			
additionally	correspondingly	furthermore	moreover
also	for example	in a similar manner	similarly
besides	for instance	likewise	what is more

Transitions and Connectors That Address a Counterargument			
although	even though	nevertheless	still
but	however	nonetheless	though
conversely	in contrast	on the other hand	while
despite	in spite of	some people might say	yet

ACTIVITY 8 **Identifying Transitions and Connectors in an Argument Essay**

Reread "The Best Classroom" on pages 167–169. Find seven transitions or connectors. Copy the sentences here, underline the transition or connector, and write the paragraph number in the parentheses.

Transitions/Connectors That Develop a Point Further

1. _____
   _____ ( )

2. _____
   _____ ( )

3. _____
   _____ ( )

Transitions/Connectors That Address a Counterargument

1. _____
   _____ ( )

2. _____
   _____ ( )

3. _____
   _____ ( )

4. _____
   _____ ( )

Studying Transitions and Connectors in an Example Argument Essay

ACTIVITY 9 **Warming Up to the Topic**

Answer the questions on your own. Then discuss them with a partner or in a small group.

1. What does the term *overfishing* mean? _____

   _____

2. Do a quick Internet search for the term *overfishing*. Write three facts that you learn.

   _____

   _____

3. What are some possible solutions to the problem of overfishing?

_____

_____

_____

4. What is a fish farm? Are there any fish farms located near where you live?

_____

_____

_____

ACTIVITY 10 **Using Transitions and Connectors in an Essay**

Read "Empty Oceans" and circle the correct transition words or phrases.

Essay 17

Empty Oceans

1   Imagine going to a sushi restaurant that could no longer serve fish.
Such a scenario may seem very difficult to believe, but the fish populations
of the earth's oceans face severe threats. Like land animals that have been
hunted to near extinction, such as buffalo, elephants, and tigers, marine

animals also need to be protected if they are to survive into future generations. Governments **1** (encourage / must encourage) **sustainable** fishing practices and other regulatory guidelines to ensure that the oceans preserve their variety of animal and plant life as well as sufficient fish populations.

2   The oceans are being **depleted** primarily due to consumer demand for seafood, which creates a financial **incentive** for marine businesses to overfish. As National Geographic documents, "Demand for seafood and advances in technology have led to fishing practices that are depleting fish and shellfish populations around the world. Fishers remove more than 77 billion kilograms (170 billion pounds) of wildlife from the sea each year." Similarly, Pichegru and her colleagues (2012) researched the challenges facing fish populations due to industrial fishing, concluding that "the development of industrial fishing in the twentieth century has reduced the total number of predatory fish globally to less than ten-percent of pre-industrial levels . . . and profoundly altered marine environments" (p. 117). Because of this enormous reduction, many species of fish and shellfish cannot reproduce quickly enough to **compensate for** the numbers that have been removed, which further **compounds** the problem.

3   **2** (Despite / What is more), shifting ocean environments have made it very difficult for many fish to find enough prey to feed upon, and without a sufficient food supply, their population growth can be severely limited. Overfishing causes many other problems in the oceans. Changing the oceanic environment drastically multiplies the challenges that sea creatures face, as evidenced by such factors as the **collapse** of coral reefs in oceans throughout the world and other such worrisome trends.

4   **3** (As a result / While) some people may **downplay** the problem of overfishing of our oceans, the statistics confirm its **gravity**. The number of fish is decreasing, and fishermen have to go farther and farther to find fish to catch. Stronger government controls of the fishing industry would help limit overfishing. **4** (Additionally / On one hand), tax breaks could be given to companies that operate fish

sustainable: able to continue to use longer; continuing for future generations

to deplete: to use up; to finish all of something

an incentive: a reason or motivation to do something

to compensate for: to make up for; to substitute for

to compound: to make something worse

collapse: destruction; breakdown

to downplay: to minimize the importance of something

gravity: a very serious quality or condition

farms, which are perhaps one of the simplest solutions to this problem. Rather than taking fish and shellfish from the ocean, fish farmers build unique facilities, such as tanks, aquariums, and other **marine enclosures**, to raise these animals. **5** (Before / While) fish farming may be unfamiliar to many people, the practice dates back to 2000 B.C.E. in China, and its training manuals include a 475 B.C.E. essay on raising carp by Fan Lai (Shepherd and Bromage, 1992, p. 2). With modern advancements in technology, fish farming promises to **revolutionize** how humans fish.

marine: having to do with the ocean

an enclosure: an area or container for keeping animals

to revolutionize: to change in a significant way

5   Because the oceans are huge, most people have not thought about oceans without fish. **6** (Because / Nevertheless), the fish in our oceans are in real trouble. In 1992, the United Nations Conference on Environment and Development defined the goal of sustainable development as meeting the "needs of the present without limiting the ability of future generations to meet their own needs" (Caulfield, 1997, p. 167). Without practical responses to the issue of sustainable fishing, including the necessity of **suspending** certain fishing practices and monitoring the health of the oceans, the planet risks losing many species of marine wildlife. By limiting fishing in the oceans and developing commercial fish farms, we can succeed in both raising fish for human consumption and preserving fish for the future.

to suspend: to stop something, usually for a short time

References

Caulfield, R. (1997). *Greenlanders, whales, and whaling: Sustainability and self-determination in the Arctic.* Hanover, NH: University Press of New England.

Pichegru, L., Ryan, P., van Eeden, R., Reid, T., Grémillet, D., & Wanless, R. (2012). Industrial fishing, no-take zones and endangered penguins. *Biological Conservation, 156,* 117–125.

Shepherd, J., & Bromage, N. (1992). *Intensive fish farming.* Oxford: Blackwell Science.

Sustainable fishing. National Geographic Education. (n.d.) Retrieved from http://education.nationalgeographic.com/education/encyclopedia /sustainable-fishing/?ar_a=1

Building Better Vocabulary

Practicing Three Kinds of Vocabulary from Context

Read each important vocabulary word or phrase. Locate it in the essay if you need help remembering the word or phrase. Then circle the best synonym, antonym, or collocation from column A, B, or C.

Type of Vocabulary	Important Vocabulary	A	B	C
Synonyms	**1.** a colleague	a co-worker	a friend	an incident
	2. enormous	fancy	gloomy	huge
	3. alter	change	imagine	vanish
	4. preserve	join	protect	serve
Antonyms	**5.** a solution	an answer	an opinion	a problem
	6. unique	common	purchase	respond
	7. deplete	need	increase	omit
	8. downplay	emphasize	revolutionize	suggest
Collocations	**9.** ___ limited	happily	next	severely
	10. a vast ___	entry	family	number
	11. ___ than	essential	given	rather
	12. a ___ incentive	financial	kind	population

Grammar for Writing

Modals

Modals are words that are used together with verbs. Modals express ability, possibility, or obligation, and are very important in writing because they change the tone of a sentence. For example, modals such as **must** and **had better** make a verb sound stronger, while modals such as **may**, **might**, **should**, **can**, and **could** make a verb softer, weaker, or less certain.

Modals play a special role in argument essays because writers need to state a clear opinion about the topic. In this case, strong modals such as *must* and *had better* help writers assert their main point and tell readers that something has to happen. Another very useful modal is *should*. Although *should* is not quite as strong as *must* or *had better*, it gives a clear recommendation or assertion and is therefore often used in argument essays:

Clear assertion: The sale of cigarettes **should** be banned immediately.

In addition, writers of argument essays need to acknowledge opposing opinions and then provide a refutation of that opinion. Modals such as *may, might, could,* and *can* help writers make an opposing opinion sound weak. In particular, the use of *may* and *might* weakens the opposing viewpoint. The use of key modals is essential in constructing a well-written counterargument and refutation.

Clear opposing opinion: Although the new law banning smoking in restaurants **may** have been passed with good intentions, citizens **have to** realize that the government has overstepped its powers here.

Meaning	Examples
advisability	The sale of cigarettes **should** be banned immediately. Companies **ought to** supply health insurance to all employees. People **had better** realize that the plan to increase taxes will cause problems in their daily lives.
possibility	Students' test scores **may** increase if students spend at least thirty minutes per day writing. The effect of global warming **might** be reduced if pollution controls are passed. Doubling the price of fatty foods **could** reduce public consumption of these unhealthy foods.
certainty	Implementing the proposed changes in health care **will** result in a much healthier population.
necessity	For these reasons, the minimum age to obtain a driver's license **must** be raised immediately. Although the new law banning smoking in restaurants may have been passed with good intentions, citizens **have to** realize that the government has overstepped its powers here.

The verb after a modal is always in the base, or simple, form with no inflected ending (*-ing, -ed, -en, -s*). In addition, do not put the word *to* between the modal and the verb (unless *to* is part of the modal).

✗ The solution **might lies** in obtaining better raw materials.

✗ The solution **might to lie** in obtaining better raw materials.

✓ The solution **might lie** in obtaining better raw materials.

ACTIVITY 12 Working with Modals

Circle the six modals in this paragraph. Find the two errors and write the corrections above the errors.

A Trick for Remembering New Words

The task of learning and remembering new vocabulary words can be difficult. However, one technique that works very well for many students is the "key-word method." In this technique, learners must first to select a word in their native language that looks or sounds like the target English word. Then they should form a mental association or picture between the English word and the native-language word. For example, an English speaker learning the Malay word for door, *pintu*, might associating this target word with the English words *pin* and *into*. The learner would then visualize someone putting a "pin into a door" to open it. This could help the learner to remember *pintu* for door. Research on second-language learning shows that this technique consistently results in a very high level of learning.

Grammar for Writing

-ly Adverbs of Degree

One way to make your writing more precise, more formal, and more advanced is to use **adverbs of degree** before adjectives (and other adverbs). Some common examples include **very**, **really**, **so**, and **too**; however, *-ly* **adverbs of degree** are more common in writing. The form of these adverbs of degree is easy to learn: they end in *-ly*.

Adverbs of degree give information about the extent of something. They occur most often before adjectives, especially past participles used as adjectives. Instead of using common words *very* and *really* in your essays, make your writing more original and more advanced by using other adverbs of degree.

Common *-ly* Adverbs of Degree			
absolutely	especially	internationally	simply
adequately	extremely	partially	strongly
completely	fully	particularly	thoroughly
decidedly	greatly	perfectly	totally
deeply	hardly	practically	tremendously
enormously	highly	profoundly	utterly
entirely	immensely	scarcely	virtually

-ly Adverbs of Degree + _____	Examples
adverb of degree + adjective	Online courses are **immensely** popular.
adverb of degree + past participle as adjective	Tracy Jenks is an **internationally** recognized expert in antiterrorism.
adverb of degree + adverb of manner	Teachers today are under pressure to cover material in certain courses **extremely** quickly.

ACTIVITY 13 **Working with *-ly* Adverbs of Degree**

Unscramble the words and write each sentence correctly.

1. thoroughly / the speaker's remarks / was / by / the audience / disgusted

_____

2. no longer / accurate / the medical tests / are / completely / used for heart disease

_____

3. is that it is / about the weather / that we know / unpredictable / utterly / the sole fact

_____

4. recognized as / was widely / the doctor / cancer research / an expert in

_____

5. it was proven / dish was / although the / to be unhealthy / immensely popular,

_____

6. to persuade / it can be / higher taxes / to vote for / difficult / citizens / extremely

_____

ACTIVITY 14   Working with Adverbs

Circle the correct word in each set of parentheses.

Reporting Bad News

In a company, how should bad news be reported to employees? The **1** (bad / badly) news should be communicated up front in **2** (direct / directly) written messages. Even in an **3** (indirect / indirectly) written message, if you have done a **4** (convincing / convincingly) job of explaining the reasons, the bad news itself will **5** (natural / naturally) come as no surprise; the decision will appear **6** (logical / logically) and reasonable—indeed the only logical and **7** (reasonable / reasonably) decision that could have been made under the circumstances. Readers should not be **8** (tremendous / tremendously) shocked by any sudden news. To keep the reader's goodwill, state the bad news in **9** (positive / positively) or **10** (neutral / neutrally) language, stressing what you are able to do rather than what you are not able to do. In addition, put the bad news in the middle of a paragraph and include additional discussion of reasons in the same sentence or **11** (immediate / immediately) afterward. People may **12** (great / greatly) appreciate news that is delivered in this direct way, no matter how bad the news is.

ACTIVITY 15   Editing an Essay: Review of Grammar

Twelve of the sixteen words or phrases in parentheses contain an error involving one of the grammar topics featured in this unit. If the word or phrase is correct, write *C*. If it is incorrect, fill in the blank with a correction.

No More Spam

1   Spam, which Flynn and Kahn (2003) define as " **1** (unsolicited e-mail) _____ that is neither wanted nor needed" (p. 179) by anyone, **threatens** the entire e-mail system. E-mail is a **vital** method of communication today, but the **2** (annoyingly mountain) _____ of spam threatens to destroy this important **means** of modern communication. If e-mail is to continue to be useful, laws against

to threaten: to promise to harm somebody or something

vital: essential; very important

a means: a method; a way

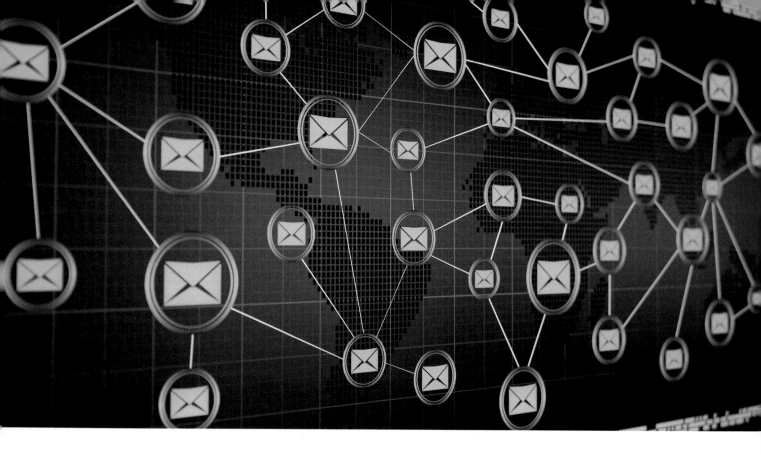

spam **3** (may) _____ be strengthened and **4** (strictly **enforced**) _____ to avoid the **exploitation** of e-mail.

2   If the government does not act quickly to prevent the further increase of spam, the problem **5** (will certainly to get) _____ much worse. Computer programs allow spammers to send hundreds of millions of e-mails **6** (virtual **instantly**) _____ . As more and more advertisers turn to spam to sell their products, the e-mail that people want to receive **7** (could to be) _____ greatly **outnumbered** by junk e-mail. Will people continue to use e-mail if **8** (they had to delete) _____ 100 pieces of spam for each personal e-mail they receive, and if the proportion of important e-mails becomes insignificant? It is estimated that "85 to 95 percent of all e-mail sent is spam," a problem that costs consumers and companies billions of dollars annually (Freeman, 2009, p. 120).

3   Although this problem with e-mail is **troubling** for private individuals, it is even worse for large businesses, which cannot ignore its harmful effects. Many spam e-mails contain computer viruses that

to enforce: to force someone to obey something

exploitation: the use of something unfairly for profit

instantly: immediately

to outnumber: to have a larger number than

troubling: worrying; disturbing

9 (can shut down) _____ the entire network of a business. Companies rely on e-mail for their employees to communicate with one another. Spamming **corrupts** their internal communications, and can even cause equipment to **malfunction**, so that a company's employees are **10** (thus complete unable) _____ to communicate effectively. Such a situation results in a loss of productivity for the company and sometimes requires the company to redesign its communication network. These computer problems raise the company's costs, **11** (which must) _____ then be passed on to the consumer.

to corrupt: to cause to become bad or to not work

to malfunction: to not work properly

4   Despite these problems for individuals and businesses, some people **12** (should argue) _____ that criminalizing spam limits spammers' right to free speech. However, how free is speech that **drowns out** other voices that people want to hear? Commercial speech that is designed to encourage people to spend money is **13** (legal differently) _____ from people's right to voice their personal opinions. The right to free speech does not allow companies to flood computer inboxes with e-mail garbage. Yes, free speech is an **14** (essentially component) _____ of the exchange of ideas necessary for any society and should not be restricted by unnecessary regulations. Unwanted e-mails, however, threaten to harm effective communication, not **nurture** it.

to drown out: to make it impossible to hear something

to nurture: to encourage to grow

5   Because of these important reasons, lawmakers **15** (may legislate) _____ increased penalties or **levy** other types of fines or taxes against spam. Spammers **16** (should fined) _____, and perhaps jailed, if they continue to disturb people with their **constant** calls for attention and money. E-mail was designed to be a helpful tool to allow people all over the world to communicate quickly and efficiently, but spam threatens to destroy this amazing advance in human communication.

to levy: to collect by legal authority

constant: nonstop; continuous

References

Flynn, N., & Kahn, R. (2003) *E-mail rules: A business guide to managing policies, security, and legal issues for e-mail and digital communications.* New York: American Management Association.

Freeman, J. (2009). *The tyranny of e-mail: The four-thousand-year journey to your inbox.* New York: Scribner.

Building Better Vocabulary

ACTIVITY 16 Practicing Three Kinds of Vocabulary from Context

Read each important vocabulary word or phrase. Locate it in the essay if you need help remembering the word or phrase. Then circle the best synonym, antonym, or collocation from column A, B, or C.

Type of Vocabulary	Important Vocabulary	A	B	C
Synonyms	**1.** nurture	encourage	happen	injure
	2. entire	friendly	numerous	whole
	3. a component	an essay	a part	a reason
	4. vital	necessary	personal	slow
Antonyms	**5.** shut down	deliver	start	tolerate
	6. delete	add	explain	taste
	7. constant	always	once	totally
	8. allow	flood	prohibit	waste
Collocations	**9.** a ___ employees	disaster's	company's	method's
	10. even ___	delicious	poor	worse
	11. ___ instantly	internal	private	virtually
	12. a means of ___	communication	millions	trouble

Original Student Writing: Argument Essay

In this section, you will follow the seven steps in the writing process to write an argument essay. If you need help, refer to Unit 2, pages 34–46.

ACTIVITY 17 Step 1: Choose a Topic

Your first step is to choose a topic for your essay that you understand well, including both sides of the issue. Your teacher may assign a topic, you may think of one yourself, or you may choose one from the suggestions below. As you consider possible topics, ask yourself, "What do I know about this topic? What do my readers know? Even though I know this topic well, do I need additional information in order to explain the topic better to my readers?"

Humanities	Present an argument about the quality of a movie. Should your readers see the movie or not?
Sciences	Is it right to use animals to test the safety of medicines and health products for humans?
Business	Should the government eliminate the national minimum wage?
Personal	When should you disagree with your parents?

1. What topic did you choose? _____

2. Why did you choose this topic? _____

   _____

3. How well do you know this topic? What is your experience with it?

   _____

   _____

ACTIVITY 18 **Step 2: Brainstorm**

Write a thesis statement that expresses your opinion about the issue. Keep in mind that a thesis statement cannot be a question. Then jot down at least three pro ideas and three con ideas for the thesis statement.

Thesis statement: _____

Pro	Con
1.	1.
2.	2.
3.	3.

ACTIVITY 19 **Step 3: Outline**

Prepare a simple outline of your essay. This outline is for five paragraphs, but you may have more or fewer paragraphs if your teacher approves.

Title: _____

   I. Introduction

   A. Hook: _____

   _____

   B. Connecting information: _____

   _____

   C. Thesis statement: _____

   _____

II. Body Paragraph 1 (Supporting Point 1): _____

    A. _____

    _____

    B. _____

    _____

III. Body Paragraph 2 (Supporting Point 2): _____

    A. _____

    _____

    B. _____

    _____

IV. Body Paragraph 3: _____

    A. Concession: _____

    _____

    B. Refutation: _____

    _____

V. Conclusion:_____

    _____

Peer Editing of Outlines

Exchange books with a partner. Read your partner's outline. Then use the following questions to help you to comment on your partner's outline. Use your partner's feedback to revise your outline.

1. Is there any aspect of the outline that is unclear to you? Give details here.

_____

_____

_____

2. Can you think of an area in the outline that needs more development? Make specific suggestions.

_____

_____

_____

3. If you have any other ideas or suggestions, write them here.

_____

_____

_____

ACTIVITY 20   **Step 4: Write the First Draft**

Use the information from Steps 1–3 to write the first draft of your argument essay. Use at least four of the vocabulary words or phrases from the Building Better Vocabulary activities in this unit. Underline these words and phrases in your essay. Try to also use at least two of the words from the Academic Word List in the _Brief Writer's Handbook with Activities_ on pages 230–231.

ACTIVITY 21   **Step 5: Get Feedback from a Peer**

Exchange papers from Step 4 with a partner. Read your partner's first draft. Then use Peer Editing Sheet 7 (available online at NGL.Cengage.com/GW5) to help you to comment on your partner's writing. Be sure to offer positive suggestions and comments that will help your partner improve his or her essay.

ACTIVITY 22   **Step 6: Revise the First Draft**

Read the comments on Peer Editing Sheet 7 about your essay. Then reread your essay. Can you identify places where you should make revisions? List the improvements you plan to make.

1. _____

_____

_____

2. _____

_____

_____

3. _____

_____

_____

     Use all the information from the previous steps to write the final version of your paper. Often, writers will need to write a third or even a fourth draft to express their ideas as clearly as possible. Write as many drafts as necessary to produce a good essay.

Be sure to proofread your paper several times before you submit it so you find all the mistakes and correct them.

Additional Topics for Writing

Here are ten more ideas for topics for additional argument essay writing.

PHOTO TOPIC: Look at the photograph on pages 160–161. In most places, the minimum driving age is between 16 and 18, and drivers can keep their licenses as long as they are good drivers. Do you think there should be a maximum age after which a person can no longer keep a driver's license?

TOPIC 2: Should lawyers work hard to defend a client they think is guilty?

TOPIC 3: Should public libraries have filters on computers that limit the kinds of Internet sites that patrons can access?

TOPIC 4: Most countries offer free education through high school. Should university education also be free?

TOPIC 5: Should television shows be allowed to use adult language?

TOPIC 6: Should the requirements for your college major be changed?

TOPIC 7: Should women be allowed to serve in combat positions in the military?

TOPIC 8: Should parents send their children to a school that gives instruction in more than one language?

TOPIC 9: Should junk food manufacturers be allowed to advertise their products to children?

TOPIC 10: Should health care be provided by the government?

Timed Writing

How quickly can you write in English? There are many times when you must write quickly, such as on a test. It is important to feel comfortable during those times. Timed-writing practice can make you feel better about writing quickly in English.

1. Read the essay guidelines below. Then take out a piece of paper.

2. Read the writing prompt below the guidelines.

3. Write a basic outline, including the thesis and the main points of support for your argument. You should spend no more than five minutes on your outline.

4. Write a five-paragraph essay.

5. You have 40 minutes to write your essay.

Argument Essay Guidelines

- Be sure to present and refute a counterargument in the body of your essay.

- Remember to give your essay a title.

- Double-space your essay.

- Write as legibly as possible (if you are not using a computer).

- Include a short introduction (with a thesis statement), three body paragraphs, and a conclusion.

- Try to give yourself a few minutes before the end of the activity to review your work. Check for spelling and the correct use of modals and -*ly* adverbs.

Should people eat a vegetarian diet? Write an argument essay for or against vegetarianism.

Louis Dodd's depiction of a United States
frigate and a British frigate during the
War of 1812.

How did one person influence the outcome of a U.S. war?

Writing a Research Paper

RESEARCH PAPER	a longer essay in which writers present their perspective on a topic using research from a variety of sources such as books, magazines, journals, and the Internet

In research papers, writers demonstrate their knowledge of and unique interpretation of a topic. Because a research paper is longer than an essay, writers can develop the topic in greater depth.

Research papers and essays share many of the same features. Both types of writing begin with an introductory paragraph that includes a thesis statement. They both have supporting paragraphs that develop and explore the thesis and a concluding paragraph that summarizes the major points of the argument.

One difference between an essay and a research paper is that a research paper, as its title suggests, includes research from other sources and is therefore longer than an essay. Writers must cite the work of various scholars to support the research writer's interpretation of the topic.

Preparation for Writing

Writing a research paper includes several steps, but by far the most important step is researching or investigating the topic. You cannot write a research paper without doing research. Therefore, one of the most important strategies to prepare to write a successful research paper is to read about the topic.

It is essential that you understand what other experts have written about your topic, which will then allow you to form your own unique interpretation of the topic based on the multiple sources you have read. The more information you gather about your topic before you start planning and writing, the better your paper, and the writing process, will be.

Steps in Writing a Research Paper

In writing an essay, you have to choose a topic, brainstorm, make an outline, write the first draft, get feedback, revise the first draft, and proofread the final draft. The steps in writing a research paper are similar to those in writing an essay. One very important difference, however, is that there is much more emphasis on including research from other experts in a research paper.

Step 1: Narrow Your Topic

Getting your topic right is essential. If your topic is too general, it will be difficult to focus your writing on specific details. On the other hand, a topic that is too specific will produce a short paper that does not have enough depth.

For example, if your research paper is about science, your topic cannot be chemistry or chemical experiments; these topics are too broad. Similarly, if you are taking a history class, you cannot write a paper on the topic of American history because it is too general. Instead, you should focus on a smaller section of the larger field that you can manage in one paper.

Here are some examples of how you can narrow general topics so they have more potential for a research paper.

Too general	Better, but still too general	Good topic
Health	Allergies	The Recent Increase in Human Allergies
World History	Famous World Wars	The Causes of World War I
Families with Several Children	Birth Order	Birth Order and Economic Success
Wars Involving the United States	The War of 1812	The Role of the Pirate Jean Lafitte in the War of 1812
Sports	Basketball	James Naismith: The Inventor of Basketball

ACTIVITY 1 Practice with Research Paper Topics

Your assignment is to write a research paper that is five to seven double-spaced pages long (approximately 1,500 words) with at least three cited sources. Read each pair of possible topics and place a check mark (✔) by the better choice. In some cases, neither example may be perfect for this assignment, so be prepared to explain your answer choice. (Hint: Some of these are not easy to decide.)

1. ＿＿＿ a. Astronomy

＿＿＿ b. The naming of our planets

2. ＿＿＿ a. How to achieve world peace

＿＿＿ b. How Europe shaped the map of Africa

3. ＿＿＿ a. The meaning of O. Henry's short story "The Gift of the Magi"

＿＿＿ b. A comparison of works by O. Henry, William Shakespeare, and Stephen King

4. ＿＿＿ a. Women's job opportunities in Europe in 1815, 1915, and 2015

＿＿＿ b. The greatest achievements of Prime Minister Indira Gandhi

5. ＿＿＿ a. The salaries of current professional basketball players

＿＿＿ b. The rules of basketball

Step 2: Find Information from Sources

When locating sources for your research, you might begin by searching **Google** or **Wikipedia** for some general background information for yourself. However, you will have to move from this initial search to one that will lead you to **scholarly sources** because Google and Wikipedia are not acceptable for an academic research paper. They can provide you with general overviews of topics, but the point of a research paper is to move beyond the surface of a subject and to study it in greater depth.

One possible source to begin locating good material is Google Scholar at **scholar.google.com**. Unlike the regular google.com site, this one specializes in scholarly works. If you can identify one or two good scholarly articles, you can read through their bibliographies for other potential articles. This kind of search is one of the most underrated and least discussed tools that can help you find more helpful research articles.

Researchers contribute knowledge on a topic; they do not merely repeat what others have already said. Therefore, after you have reviewed the results of a Google or Wikipedia search to have a better idea of the general information about a topic, proceed to your school's library website. This website will typically include a number of highly specified **databases** that will allow you to focus exclusively on your subject matter.

ACTIVITY 2 **Identifying Sources for a Research Paper from Google Scholar**

Using a topic you chose in Activity 1, conduct an Internet search to find five possible articles that you might consider reading. Write down the titles of the articles, the source (journal, website, etc.), the year, and the page numbers for APA style documentation. See the example below.

Topic: The War of 1812

Title	Source	Year	Pages
1. American Trade Restrictions during the War of 1812	*The Journal of American History* (Volume 68, Number 3)	1981	517–538

Your topic: _____

Title	Source	Year	Pages
1.			
2.			
3.			
4.			
5.			

Step 3: Evaluate Sources

How do you know which sources you can trust and which you should avoid? Most of all, consider the **professional reputation of the author**. Is he or she a respected authority in the field, or a completely unknown person or someone with ideas that are very different from those of the majority of scholars? You may not recognize every author's name, but it is a good idea to try to find out a little about their backgrounds before you use them in your paper. In general, a scholar is associated with a university or college, so see if you can determine the author's academic home.

Second, you should consider the **publisher** or **journal** that publishes the work. University and academic presses publish high-quality material that has been peer-reviewed before publication. For a source to be peer-reviewed, experts in the field assess the merits of the paper before it is published, which ensures that it is of high quality. The Internet has many "expert sources," but a peer-reviewed journal is always preferred for reputable sources. Many other sources, however, are collections of individual people's ideas and have not been reviewed by others. Remember that it is very easy for any individual, whether qualified or unqualified, to create a website and post information. You must consider the credibility of this information based on the type of source.

Finally, be sure to consider whether the material you are analyzing remains a **timely** source. Many research papers require you to use current sources, which often means they have been published within the last ten or twenty years. However, if you are writing a paper on a historical event that happened in 1800, it is probably acceptable to use sources from 1970 or 1980 (or earlier) because the information about this event may be similar to more current information. In this case, you should follow the assignment instructions. Whether the date of publication is 1980 or 2015, it is your responsibility as a researcher to be sure that all the sources you use contain information that is up to date and relevant.

ACTIVITY 3 **Evaluating Sources for a Research Paper**

As you answer the questions, consider the five sources you identified in Activity 2, not the titles of the works.

1. What is the best source? _____

    Explain your reasons: _____

    _____

    _____

2. What is the weakest source? _____

    Explain your reasons: _____

    _____

    _____

Step 4: Document Sources

You need to document your sources in two different places in your paper. The first place is inside the paper, and the second is at the end.

Citation methods vary according to academic professions and fields, so ask your teacher about the citation method that is required in your coursework. Two of the most common styles are **APA** (American Psychology Association) and **MLA** (Modern Language Association). In general, APA is used in the sciences, while MLA is used in the humanities.

Citations Inside the Paper

When you give information that is not your original work, you must cite it. This means that you identify the source where you found the information.

In APA style, you mention the author of the work and the year of publication. Notice the citation in this example:

> Regardless of his reasons behind it, Lafitte's decision to assist the United States played a crucial role in the Battle of New Orleans. The British would have likely won the battle with his assistance because the city would have been isolated from the interior (de Grummond, 1968).

If the material is a direct quotation, you should also provide the page number where the original material is located.

> Many historians debate Lafitte's reasons for not siding with the more powerful force of the war, and Latimer (2007) proposes: "The gang threw in their lot with the Americans only because they realized that the offer the British were making was, in fact, an ultimatum: The British were finally enforcing Spanish authority in the area on behalf of their ally" (p. 371).

There are three basic ways to include the author's name that you are citing.

1. Use the author's name and a reporting verb such as *says*, *explains*, or *reports*.

   Johnson (2011) says that the war began because one country needed money.

2. Use the preposition *according to*.

   According to Johnson (2011), the war began because one country needed money.

3. Cite the author's name after the information.

   The war began because one country needed money (Johnson, 2011).

Citations in the References (APA) or Works Cited (MLA)

In addition to providing information on sources where they are used in your writing, you should also list all the works, or sources, of the words and ideas you used in the **References** (APA) or **Works Cited** list (MLA) at the end of your paper.

Study the following example of references using APA format that lists five works. The second and fifth entries are books. The others are from journals.

References

Carter, R. (1987). Vocabulary and second/foreign language teaching. *Language Teaching, 20,* 3–16.

Folse, K. (2004). *Vocabulary myths: Applying second language research to classroom teaching.* Ann Arbor, MI: University of Michigan Press.

Lotto, L., & de Groot, A. (1998). Effects of learning method and word type on acquiring vocabulary in an unfamiliar language. *Language Learning, 48* (1), 31–69.

Martin, M. (1984). Advanced vocabulary teaching: The problem of synonyms. *The Modern Language Journal, 68* (2), 130–137.

Wilkins, D. (1972). *Linguistics in language teaching.* London: Edward Arnold.

ACTIVITY 4 Discovering the Parts of a References List

Answer the questions about the reference list above.

1. How many entries are there? _____

2. How are the entries sequenced in the list? _____

3. Does the year of publication have any effect on sequencing? Why does the 1972 article come last?

   _____

   _____

4. Which ones are books? _____ How do you know? _____

   _____

5. Which ones are journals? _____ How do you know? _____

   _____

6. What do book entries have that journal entries do not have? _____

   _____

7. What is capitalized? _____

   What is not capitalized? _____

   Does any of this information surprise you? Explain. _____

   _____

8. Two of the titles have a colon (:). What do you think this means? _____

   _____

Answer the questions about the References list for a research paper titled "Evidence of How We Learn Foreign Language Vocabulary."

References

Carrell, P. (1991). Second language reading: Reading ability or language proficiency. *Applied Linguistics, 12* (2), 159–179.

Chaudron, C. (1982). Vocabulary elaboration in teachers' speech to L2 learners. *Studies in Second Language Acquisition, 4* (2), 170–180.

Chun, D., & Plass, J. (1996). Effects of multimedia annotations on vocabulary acquisition. *The Modern Language Journal, 80* (2), 183–199.

Chun, D., & Plass, J. (1997). Research on text comprehension in multimedia environments. *Language Learning & Technology, 1* (1), 60–81.

Clipperton, R. (1994). Explicit vocabulary instruction in French immersion. *The Canadian Modern Language Review/La Revue Canadienne des Langues Vivantes, 50,* 736–749.

Daneman, M., & Green, I. (1986). Individual differences in comprehending and producing words in context. *Journal of Memory and Language, 25,* 1–18.

Elley, W. (1989). Vocabulary acquisition from listening to stories. *Reading Research Quarterly, 24* (2), 174–187.

Elley, W., & Mangubhai, F. (1983). The impact of reading on second language learning. *Reading Research Quarterly, 19* (1), 53–67.

Gipe, J. (1979). Investigating techniques for teaching word meanings. *Reading Research Quarterly, 14* (4), 625–644.

Henriksen, B. (1999). Three dimensions of vocabulary development. *Studies in Second Language Acquisition, 21,* 303–317.

Huckin, T., & Coady, J. (1999). Incidental vocabulary acquisition in a second language. *Studies in Second Language Acquisition, 21,* 181–193.

Hulstijn, J. (1993). When do foreign-language readers look up the meaning of unfamiliar words? The influence of task and learner variables. *The Modern Language Journal, 77* (2), 139–147.

Jenkins, J., Matlock, B., & Slocum, T. (1989). Two approaches to vocabulary instruction: The teaching of individual word meanings and practice in deriving word meaning from context. *Reading Research Quarterly, 24* (2), 215–235.

Joe, A. (1998). What effect do text-based tasks promoting generation have on incidental vocabulary acquisition? *Applied Linguistics, 19* (3), 357–377.

Koda, K. (1996). L2 word recognition research: A critical review. *The Modern Language Journal, 80* (4), 450–460.

Laufer, B. (1990). Why are some words more difficult than others? *International Review of Applied Linguistics in Language Teaching, 28* (4), 293–307.

Laufer, B. (1998). The development of passive and active vocabulary in a second language: Same or different? *Applied Linguistics, 19* (2), 255–271.

Luppescu, S., & Day, R. (1993). Reading, dictionaries, and vocabulary learning. *Language Learning, 43* (2), 263–287.

Minton, M. (1980). The effect of sustained silent reading upon comprehension and attitudes among ninth graders. *Journal of Reading, 23* (6), 498–502.

Nagata, N. (1996). Computer vs. workbook instruction in second language acquisition. *CALICO Journal, 14* (1), 53–75.

Newton, J. (1995). Task-based interaction and incidental vocabulary learning: A case study. *Second Language Research, 11* (2), 159–177.

Ott, C., Butler, D., Blake, R., & Ball, J. (1973). The effect of interactive-image elaboration on the acquisition of foreign language vocabulary. *Language Learning, 23* (2), 197–206.

1. How many entries are there? _____

2. How are they arranged? _____

3. How many are journal articles? _____

4. Which journals have more than one listing in this bibliography? _____

_____

5. What is the oldest article? What is the most recent article? _____

_____

_____

6. How are multiple sources with the same author sequenced?

_____

_____

_____

An Example Research Paper

The following is an example research paper titled, "The Pirate's Unnecessary Battle: Jean Lafitte and the War of 1812." As you study the research paper, notice the annotations in the left-hand column.

Essay 19

Student/class information according to the teacher's requirements

William White
History 367
September 30, 2014

Title of paper on page 1 only, centered

The Pirate's Unnecessary Battle: Jean Lafitte and the War of 1812

1   Most battles are fought to win wars, and most wars are fought between armies, but the role of the pirate Jean Lafitte in the War of 1812 is an exception. The War of 1812 was between the United States of America and Great Britain, and it took place only a few decades after the United States declared its independence in 1776. Lafitte was a **notorious pirate** and smuggler in the Gulf of Mexico, a man on the **margins** of society who played a critical role in the Battle of New Orleans. Oddly enough, that battle began after the United States and Great Britain had signed a treaty to end the war. Lafitte's efforts in the War of 1812 certainly helped to establish the United States as a world power, but history should neither **downplay** his criminality nor minimize his accomplishments.

Background information

Jean Lafitte: Life of a Pirate

Headers are not required, but they can help readers navigate a paper better. Follow the guidelines that your teacher gives you.

Authors' names introduce a citation. Quotation marks surround a direct quotation and page number appears in parentheses.

The writer reconciles sources with conflicting information.

2   Basic biographical details concerning Lafitte's early life are difficult to learn. Indeed, Hart and Penman (2012) call him a "man of **legend** more than fact" (p. 199) because, although numerous stories tell about his career as a pirate and a soldier, most of these accounts cannot be clearly documented. Even his name invites debate, with most sources using the English spelling (Lafitte) rather than the French spelling (Laffite). Most historians agree that Lafitte was born around 1780, but historians disagree on his birthplace. For example, Davis (2005) suggests that Lafitte's birthplace was Pauillac, France (p. 2), while Ramsay (1996) proposes he was likely born in the French colony of Saint-Domingue, which today comprises parts of the Dominican Republican and Haiti.

Depiction of a sentry guarding Jean LaFitte's hideout.

Chronological transition

3   It is clear that Lafitte and his brother Pierre were engaged in piracy and smuggling in the late 1700s and early 1800s. Their father worked as a merchant, so it is likely that they spent their adolescent years near the sea and learned much about trade routes, international ports, and the economic potential of criminal activity. They arrived in New Orleans in the early 1800s and began trading with local merchants. A few years later, as tensions with Great Britain rose, the United States passed the **Embargo** Act of 1807, which prohibited American merchants from trading with unfriendly European nations. The embargo caused financial hardship for numerous businesses, both legitimate and criminal enterprises, and so the Lafitte brothers turned other people's adversity into their economic gain.

4   Having established their base on Barataria, a small island located south of New Orleans in Barataria Bay, the Lafitte brothers positioned themselves as the dominant pirates and smugglers of the region, including the profitable trade in New Orleans, which has long been one of the United States' busiest ports. With Pierre running their enterprise in New Orleans and Jean taking care of the daily operations in Barataria, the Lafittes quickly became quite rich and powerful while living under the shadow of the law and pursuing their criminal schemes. The brothers controlled several ships and crews, which robbed other vessels, and they then traded the stolen goods in New Orleans. Governors of Louisiana occasionally attempted to shut down the Lafittes' criminal operations, but without success, and many of the people of New Orleans supported the brothers' activities because they brought goods into the city that were forbidden by the embargo. Given Jean Lafitte's illegal actions, it is rather surprising that he became a leading figure in the Battle of New Orleans and, for some, an American hero.

Lafitte's Role in the War of 1812

Headers help readers understand the organization of the paper.

5   The War of 1812 began on June 18, 1812, after U.S. President James Madison and Congress declared war on Great Britain in **retaliation** against a series of **hostile** actions, including **harassment** of American ships on the seas and minor battles fought over the Canadian border. Great Britain's navy was the strongest military force in the world at the time, so many people assumed that the American forces would be quickly crushed. Much of the War of 1812 was fought in the Atlantic Ocean and on the Canadian border in the Great Lakes region, but command of the Mississippi River was seen as critical for the United States to maintain its territories. In addition, whichever side controlled the Mississippi River and its numerous channels would also control its largest port, New Orleans, which was of incredible importance for sending supplies to troops. Given these strategic conditions, both American and British forces turned their attention to the Gulf of Mexico toward the end of the conflict. Both sides in the conflict also realized that if they desired to capture New Orleans, the pirate Jean Lafitte would be a very valuable **ally**, and they sought to ensure that he would not remain neutral in the conflict.

6   The British attempted to gain the cooperation of Lafitte first, offering him assurances of their goodwill. According to Owsley (1981), "The first suggestion by the British that the Baratarians might join forces with them and allow use of the base at Barataria as a point of attack against New Orleans is found in Pigot's report to Admiral Cochrane dated June 8, 1814" (p. 108). Surely this offer must have been very tempting to Lafitte, for in the early 1800s the United Kingdom was by far the more powerful nation. Of French background by birth, Lafitte likely would not have felt much loyalty to the United States, and it is important to remember that Louisiana did not join the union until April 30, 1812, only a few months before the war began. Many historians debate Lafitte's reasons for not siding with the more powerful force of the war, and Latimer (2007) proposes: "The gang threw in their lot with the Americans only because they realized that the offer the British were making was, in fact, an **ultimatum**: The British were finally enforcing Spanish authority in the area on behalf of their ally" (p. 371). Also, while Louisiana had only recently joined the United States of America, this state has a rich French legacy, which might have influenced Lafitte's loyalties. Regardless of his reasons behind it, Lafitte's decision to assist the United States played a crucial role in the Battle of New Orleans. The British would have likely won the battle with his assistance because the city would have been isolated from the interior (de Grummond, 1968). Given his knowledge of sea routes and Louisiana's marshy waterways, Lafitte would have been an invaluable ally for the British regime, and if New Orleans fell to the British, the war would likely have lasted much longer.

Transition word

7   Nonetheless, the fact that Lafitte refused to cooperate with the British forces did not mean that he would join with the United States, nor that the United States would desire to work with a pirate. Stagg (2012) describes how Andrew Jackson, who led the U.S. forces in the campaign, hesitated to enter into an alliance with Lafitte because doing so "went against his personal **inclinations**" (p. 152). Upon arriving in New Orleans, however, Jackson realized that the city lacked sufficient defenses to protect itself against a British invasion, and so drastic measures needed to be taken. To this end, Jackson realized that Lafitte's experience with ships, his knowledge of the region's geography, and the many men under his command would be great advantages for the United States in the coming battle. Lafitte negotiated with Jackson for the pardon of his men following the battle, and this **fragile** alliance between the U.S. military and a group of pirates began. The British fleet reached the Mississippi River on December 23, 1814, and began hostilities soon after.

Transition word

8   With Lafitte's assistance and technical advice, particularly concerning the placement of American defenses, the United States had a decisive victory over the British—with the British reporting over 2000 dead, whereas the Americans lost less than one hundred. However, it turned out that the Battle of New Orleans need not have been fought, and many soldiers lost their lives without reason. The Treaty of Ghent, which ended the war, was signed on December 24, 1814, with the Battle of New Orleans occurring on January 8, 1815. If communication had traveled more quickly in the early 1800s, the Battle of New Orleans would never have **commenced**, and thus Lafitte would not hold his place in American history. Moreover, neither the United States nor Great Britain gained any lasting advances through the war: "In strict military and diplomatic terms, the War of 1812 accomplished almost nothing. All that the United States had managed was to convince the British to return all territorial boundaries and diplomatic disputes to their prewar status" (Eustace, 2012, p. xi).

9   After his participation in the War of 1812, Lafitte again devoted his ambitions to piracy and, once again living in the criminal underworld, soon faded from public view. Wall (1997) documents that "federal officials forced Lafitte to move from Barataria Bay" and that he then "established a new headquarters on Galveston Island and continued his illegal slave business" (p. 97). With his brother Pierre, Lafitte sided with Spain in the Mexican War of Independence, acting as **spies** from their base in Galveston. However, in the following decades, governmental authorities largely freed the Gulf of Mexico from piracy, and Jean and Pierre Lafitte found themselves in an environment no longer friendly to their criminality: "The world they had known and in which they could hope to **flourish** had left them behind, and the new world of the Gulf simply had no room for their kind" (Davis, 2005, p. 467). Even pirates have families, and Lafitte married Madeline Regaud around 1820, with whom he had a child who died at a young age. Some historians think Lafitte changed his name and began a new life freed from his past, while others think he died in a battle at sea, possibly at the hands of his men who revolted against him.

Conclusion

Not all conclusions are marked
with headers, but this header is
common for this purpose.

10   So much remains unknown about Jean Lafitte's life, yet it is clear that he played a critical role in this unnecessary battle. He remains a man of legend, such as the longstanding belief, which lacks any evidence, that he rescued the exiled French emperor Napoleon Bonaparte and brought him safely to freedom in Louisiana. Indeed, he is a particularly celebrated figure in Louisiana, with the Jean Lafitte National Historical Park and Preserve named in his honor. Without strong support in history, however, the stories about such men as Lafitte are appealing but make it hard to distinguish fact from fiction. Considered a hero for his contributions to an unnecessary war, one cannot deny that Lafitte was also a criminal throughout much of his life.

In APA format, this is the bibliography title.

Titles of sources such as books or journals are in italics.

The city of the book publisher is separated from the publisher by a colon.

References

Davis, W. (2005). *The pirates Laffite: The treacherous world of the corsairs of the Gulf*. Orlando, FL: Harcourt.

De Grummond, J. *The Baratarians and the Battle of New Orleans*. (1968). Baton Rouge, LA: Louisiana State University Press.

Eustace, N. (2012). *1812: War and the passions of patriotism*. Philadelphia, PA: University of Pennsylvania Press.

Hart, S., & Penman, R. (2012). *1812: A nation emerges*. Washington, DC: Smithsonian Institution.

Latimer, J. (2007). *1812: War with America*. Cambridge, MA: Belknap.

Owsley, F., Jr. (1981). *Struggle for the Gulf borderlands: The Creek War and the Battle of New Orleans, 1812–1815*. Gainesville, FL: University of Florida Press.

Ramsay, J. (1996). *Jean Laffite: Prince of pirates*. Austin, TX: Eakin.

Stagg, J. C. A. (2012). *The War of 1812: Conflict for a continent*. Cambridge: Cambridge University Press.

Wall, B., Ed. (1997). *Louisiana: A history* (3rd ed.). Wheeling, IL: Harlan Davidson.

notorious: well-known or famous due to bad deeds

a pirate: a person who robs at sea

a margin: an edge or outside limit

to downplay: to speak of something or someone in such as way so as to reduce its importance

a legend: a story that has been repeated many times but cannot be verified

an embargo: a government order to prohibit the movement of ships into or out of a port

retaliation: the act of repaying in kind, usually for revenge

hostile: extremely unfriendly or aggressive

harassment: the act of disturbing or annoying someone repeatedly

an ally: a person, group, or country associated with another for a common purpose

an ultimatum: a final demand from one person or group that the other side must agree to in order to avoid a heavy penalty

an inclination: a belief

fragile: weak; delicate

to commence: to begin

a spy: a person who works for a government to discover secrets of the other side

to flourish: to succeed

Original Student Writing: Research Paper

ACTIVITY 6 Write a Research Paper

Follow the guidelines you have practiced in this book to write an essay that is suitable for a research paper. Your teacher will give you specific requirements for your paper. For a review of the steps in the writing process, see Unit 2, pages 34–46.

Brief Writer's Handbook
with Activities

Sentence Types

Many people do not write well because they do not use a variety of types of sentences. In this section, we offer ideas for writing correct sentences of several kinds. This section reviews three sentence types: **simple**, **compound**, and **complex**. Good writers use all three types of sentences for a variety of styles.

The Two Basic Parts of a Sentence

A sentence in English consists of two parts: **subject** and **predicate.** The subject is the part of the sentence that contains who or what the sentence is about. The predicate contains the verb that tells something about the subject.

subject	predicate
Students from that high school	earned the best math scores in our state.

subject	predicate
New medicines	are stopping the spread of many dangerous diseases.

The most important part of the predicate is the **verb**, and the most important part of the subject is the **simple subject**. It is often much easier to find the verb first and then find the subject. In the first example, the verb is *earned*. The complete subject is *students from that high school*. Can you find one word that is the central idea of the complete subject? In this case, the simple subject is *students*.

In the second example, the verb is *are stopping*. The complete subject is *new medicines*. The simple subject is *medicines*.

ACTIVITY 1 **Subjects and Predicates**

Read each sentence. Then draw a line between the complete subject and the complete predicate. The first one has been done for you.

1. Many inventions and discoveries / have changed human life forever.

2. In 1875, Alexander Graham Bell made the first telephone, a revolutionary invention for communication.

3. At the young age of 29, Alexander Graham Bell invented the telephone.

4. In the late nineteenth century, Karl Benz designed the first practical automobile with an internal combustion engine.

5. Barthelemy Thimonnier, a French tailor, invented the world's first sewing machine in 1830.

6. In 1809, Humphry Davy, an English chemist, developed the first electric light.

7. Less than a century ago, Alexander Fleming discovered penicillin.

8. It is impossible to imagine life without these tremendous developments.

Clauses

A **clause** is a subject-verb combination. Study the following examples. The subjects are underlined, and the verbs are **boldfaced**.

Each of the following sentences has one subject-verb combination and therefore one clause:

The <u>girls</u> **played** tennis.

The <u>girls and boys</u> **played** tennis.

The <u>girls and boys</u> **played** tennis and then **went** to the mall.

Each of the following sentences has two subject-verb combinations and therefore two clauses:

The <u>girls</u> **played** tennis, and the <u>boys</u> **went** to the mall.

The <u>girls and boys</u> **played** tennis, and then <u>they</u> **went** to the mall.

There are two kinds of clauses: **independent** and **dependent.**

Independent Clauses

An **independent clause** is easy to recognize because it can stand alone. It has meaning all by itself. Study the following examples. The subjects are <u>underlined</u>, and the verbs are **boldfaced.**

Each of the following sentences has one independent clause:

The <u>girls</u> **played** tennis.

The <u>girls and boys</u> **played** tennis.

The <u>girls and boys</u> **played** tennis and then went to the mall.

Each of the following sentences has two independent clauses:

The <u>girls</u> **played** tennis, and the <u>boys</u> **went** to the mall.

The <u>girls and boys</u> **played** tennis, and then <u>they</u> **went** to the mall.

Dependent Clauses

In the sentence below, there are also two clauses, but only one is an independent clause:

The <u>girls</u> {<u>who</u> **played** tennis} **went** to the mall later.

In this sentence, *The girls … went to the mall later* is an independent clause. The words *who played tennis* also make up a clause but cannot stand alone. This clause has no meaning without the rest of the sentence. We call this second kind of clause a **dependent clause** because it depends on the rest of the sentence to have meaning.

The dependent clauses in these sentences have been <u>underlined</u>:

The book <u>that I bought</u> is extremely interesting.

A bilingual dictionary is ideal for learners <u>whose English is not good yet</u>.

ACTIVITY 2 **Independent and Dependent Clauses**

Read these six sentences about reality television programs. Identify the underlined clauses as either independent (*I*) or dependent (*D*).

_____ 1. Reality television programs, <u>which are quite popular</u>, drive my mother crazy.

_____ 2. *Survivor*, <u>which is broadcast on CBS</u>, places castaways in a remote location and makes them fend for themselves.

_____ 3. <u>*American Idol* is a singing competition</u> that looks for the next vocal superstar.

_____ 4. Many of the singers <u>who audition for *American Idol*</u> are not very talented.

_____ 5. <u>Donald Trump's show *The Apprentice*</u>, in which he hires an intern, <u>is known for its trademark phrase "You're fired!"</u>

_____ 6. Jasper is a producer for *Big Brother*, <u>which is much more popular in Britain than in the United States</u>.

Read these six sentences about Mark Twain. Identify the underlined clauses as either independent (*I*) or dependent (*D*).

_____ **1.** When Mark Twain was a boy, <u>his family moved to Hannibal, Missouri</u>, where he spent many hours playing on the Mississippi River.

_____ **2.** *A Connecticut Yankee in King Arthur's Court*, <u>which is one of Twain's most popular books</u>, was made into a movie.

_____ **3.** One of Mark Twain's most famous books is *The Adventures of Huckleberry Finn*, <u>which is a story about a young boy and a slave.</u>

_____ **4.** <u>Tom Sawyer</u>, whose adventures have delighted many readers, <u>is known for his pluck and determination.</u>

_____ **5.** <u>Twain's *Life on the Mississippi* describes adventures</u> that befell him as a riverboat pilot.

_____ **6.** Mark Twain was born in 1835 and died in 1910, <u>which were both years when Halley's Comet was in view.</u>

Sentence Type 1: Simple Sentences

A **simple sentence** has one subject-verb combination.

<u>I</u> **have** a cat.

<u>My cat</u> **is** gray.

<u>The name of my cat</u> **begins** with the letter *B*.

A simple sentence can have two or more subjects.

<u>France</u> and <u>Germany</u> **are** located in Europe.

Because of the heavy rains yesterday, <u>Highway 50</u>, <u>Eisenhower Boulevard</u>, and <u>Temple Avenue</u> **were** impassable.

A simple sentence can have two or more verbs.

The <u>cat</u> **curled up** into a ball and **went** to sleep.

The <u>cat</u> **yawned**, **curled up** into a ball, and **went** to sleep.

Read these sentences about *Saturday Night Live* (*SNL*). Underline the subject and circle the verb.

1. A weekly late-night TV show, *Saturday Night Live* made its debut on October 11, 1975.

2. Extremely popular in the United States, *Saturday Night Live* has launched the careers of many famous comedians, including John Belushi, Eddie Murphy, and Mike Myers.

3. Lorne Michaels, a Canadian, has produced and managed *SNL* for more than 35 years.

4. The weekly guest host of *SNL* plays an active role in picking the skits for the show.

5. At the precocious age of seven, actress Drew Barrymore hosted *SNL*.

Sentence Type 2: Compound Sentences

A **compound sentence** has two or more subject-verb combinations.

The <u>rain</u> **began** to fall, so <u>we</u> **stopped** playing tennis.

The <u>store</u> **had** a special sale on children's clothes, and <u>hundreds</u> of parents **flocked** there to shop for bargains.

In a compound sentence, the subject-verb combinations are connected by a **coordinating conjunction**. To remember coordinating conjunctions, you can use the mnemonic *FANBOYS* (*for, and, nor, but, or, yet, so*). Of these seven coordinating conjunctions, the most commonly used are *and, but,* and *so. For* is not very common in modern English.

for: <u>I</u> **will not tell** a lie, *for* <u>it</u> **would not be** honest.

and: <u>Helen</u> **takes** the car, *and* <u>she</u> **picks up** Larry on the way to work.

nor: <u>I</u> **would not like** to join you for lunch, *nor* **would** <u>I</u> **like** to join you for dinner.

but: <u>Carrie</u> **wanted** to go to the café, *but* <u>Francis</u> **refused** to join her there.

or: **Do** <u>I</u> **want** to go now, *or* **do** <u>I</u> **want** to go later?

yet: University <u>students</u> often **take** an overload of courses, *yet* <u>they</u> **should know** not to overtax themselves.

so: The <u>teacher</u> **prepared** her courses the night before, *so* <u>she</u> **was** ready for everything that happened the following day.

ACTIVITY 5   Simple and Compound Sentences

Read these eight sentences about the Super Bowl. Identify each sentence as simple (*S*) or compound (*C*). In the compound sentences, circle the coordinating conjunction.

_____ 1. The Super Bowl is one of the biggest sporting events of the year, so it is always one of the most watched television shows.

_____ 2. The Pittsburgh Steelers, the Dallas Cowboys, and the San Francisco Forty-Niners have each won four or more Super Bowls.

_____ 3. Many millions of people watch the Super Bowl on television, and therefore many companies spend millions of dollars advertising their products during the show.

_____ 4. One of the most famous commercials ever shown during the Super Bowl was a commercial modeled on George Orwell's book *1984.*

_____ 5. The Buffalo Bills lost four Super Bowls in a row, and this fact makes them one of the saddest footnotes in Super Bowl history.

_____ 6. New Orleans, Jacksonville, and Houston have all hosted the Super Bowl, which brings in millions of dollars to the economies of these locales.

_____ 7. Other major sporting events include the Stanley Cup for hockey, Wimbledon for tennis, and the World Series for baseball.

_____ 8. Many people would like to attend the championship games of major sporting teams, but the tickets are quite expensive.

ACTIVITY 6 Identifying Compound Sentences

Read this paragraph about multilingualism. Underline the two compound sentences.

Paragraph 7

Coming from a multilingual family sparked many difficulties in communication for me. For example, when my maternal grandparents would fly from North America to South America to visit us, my mother had to translate among the different family members. We spoke Spanish in our house, but my American grandparents spoke only English. Since they did not speak a word of Spanish, my mother was constantly interpreting questions and answers. Rather than enjoying their visit, my mother had to work as a translator. With my mom's help, I could understand my grandparents, but I wanted to be able to speak to them by myself.

ACTIVITY 7 Original Compound Sentences

Write four compound sentences. Use a different coordinating conjunction in each one.

1. _____

_____

2. _____

_____

3. _____

_____

4. _____

_____

Sentence Type 3: Complex Sentences

A **complex sentence** has at least one independent clause and one dependent clause. Dependent clauses may begin with a variety of connector words. Adverb clauses often begin with words such as *after, because,* or *although.* Noun clauses may begin with *who, what, why,* or *that.* Adjective clauses frequently begin with *that, which,* or *who.*

independent clause	dependent clause
The professor returned the examination	**that** we took last Wednesday.

independent clause	dependent clause
The house sustained some damage	**because** the wind was very strong in this area.

Sentence Types **213**

dependent clause

After the house sustained some damage,

independent clause

we planned some repairs.

independent clause

The dictionary

dependent clause

that you bought for me yesterday

independent clause

is excellent.

ACTIVITY 8 **Identifying Independent and Dependent Clauses**

Read the following sentences about inventions. Each one is a complex sentence. Underline the independent clause and circle the dependent clause. The first one has been done for you.

1. The electric light bulb (that we depend on every night for light) was invented in 1900.

2. Because the Internet is useful and practical, it has caught on rapidly with all ages.

3. Although people complain about high gas prices, no one has invented a fuel-free vehicle yet.

4. Do you know the name of the person who invented the radio?

5. One of the most important inventions that we use every day without thinking has to be the ink pen.

6. When electricity was invented, many people were afraid to have it in their houses.

7. How did people in warm climates survive before air conditioning was invented?

8. When portable media players were introduced, they quickly revolutionized the music industry.

Sentence Variety: Adding Adjectives

Adding adjectives is one of the best ways to improve sentences. Adjectives can add color and vigor to otherwise dull sentences. Adjectives are usually placed in front of nouns.

Good: The wind blew across the lake.

Better: The **cold** wind blew across the **frozen** lake.

ACTIVITY 9 **Original Writing with Adjectives**

Add adjectives to the paragraph to improve this story.

Paragraph 8

Once upon a time, there was a/an _____

monster that lived in a/an _____ forest. The

monster was _____. One day, the monster met

a/an _____ frog. When the monster asked the

frog whether he was ugly, the frog replied, "You are not ugly. You are

_____." The monster and frog then became friends

and soon met a/an _____ princess. Since the princess

was _____, she immediately told them that they were

both _____. The _____ monster,

_____ frog, and _____ princess soon

became _____ friends.

ACTIVITY 10 Order of Adjectives

Read the paragraph about persuasive writing. Fill in the blanks with the phrases from the box. Be sure to put the words in the correct order in each phrase.

effective writing persuasive people other	view our point unique of set exercises next the of	brief a essay given a subject

Much of the writing that we do is persuasive. In

1 _____, we encourage **2** _____

to see **3** _____. In the sample essay, the writer wants

to convince the reader that spam should be outlawed. Through

4 _____, you will go through the process of writing

5 _____ in which you try to persuade your reader

to agree with you on **6** _____.

ACTIVITY 11 Adjectives in Real-World Sentences

Copy four sentences from a novel, a magazine, a newspaper, or the Internet. Circle all the adjectives.

1. _____

_____

2. _____

_____

3. _____

_____

4. _____

_____

ACTIVITY 12 Adding Adjectives to Improve Sentences

Write three sentences without descriptive adjectives. Then improve the same sentences by writing them with at least two adjectives in each sentence.

1. Original Sentence: _____

_____

Improved Sentence: _____

_____

2. Original Sentence: _____

_____

Improved Sentence: _____

_____

3. Original Sentence: _____

_____

Improved Sentence: _____

_____

Prepositional Phrases

Another easy way to add variety to your sentences is to add **prepositional phrases**. A prepositional phrase consists of a preposition and an object (a noun or a pronoun). Study these examples:

A new ambassador **to a foreign country** must learn the customs **of this country** quite quickly.

When I first got an e-mail account ten years ago, I received communications only **from friends, family, and professional acquaintances.**

Notice that the next example sentence has 18 words, but only four of the words are not part of a prepositional phrase:

With the advent **of electricity** **in the late nineteenth century**, thousands **of people** advanced their quality **of life**.

Prepositional phrases can serve all sorts of purposes. For example, prepositional phrases can tell *where* (in the kitchen), *when* (in the late nineteenth century), and *why* (for a better life).

Perhaps the most commonly used prepositions are *at, on, in, for, before, after, with,* and *without.* Here is a larger list:

Prepositions			
about	besides	in lieu of	regarding
above	between	in spite of	since
according to	beyond	including	through
across	by	inside	throughout
after	concerning	instead of	till
against	contrary to	into	to
ahead of	despite	like	toward
along	down	near	under
among	due to	next to	underneath
around	during	of	until
at	except	off	up
because of	for	on	upon
before	from	on account of	versus
behind	in	out	via
below	in addition to	outside	with
beneath	in back of	over	within
beside	in front of	past	without

Read these paragraphs about a famous landmark in California. Underline the prepositional phrases and draw a circle around the prepositions.

Millions of people all over the world have seen the Golden Gate Bridge in San Francisco, so people now equate the Golden Gate Bridge with the city of San Francisco. Although they know that the Golden Gate Bridge is in San Francisco, what they do not know is that the nickname of this structure was "the bridge that couldn't be built." The idea of the construction of a bridge across San Francisco Bay had been discussed for years before the construction of the Golden Gate Bridge was actually started in 1933. For a variety of reasons, this bridge was long considered impossible to build.

First of all, the weather in the area—with high winds, rain, and fog—was rarely good. Second, engineers thought that the strong ocean currents in the bay meant that the bridge could not be built. Furthermore, they were worried about how the strong winds in the area would affect any large structure. Finally, it was the Great Depression. The poor economy was causing people to experience incredible difficulties, so many people thought that it would be foolish to spend such a large amount of money on such an impossible project.

Sentence Problems: Fragments, Run-ons, and Comma Splices

Three common sentence problems are **fragments**, **run-ons**, and **comma splices**.

What Is a Fragment?

A **fragment** is an incomplete sentence.

Running as fast as he can.

The house at the end of the block.

To make a medical breakthrough.

All complete sentences must contain a **subject** and a **verb**. The fragments above can be turned into complete sentences rather easily.

<u>He</u> **is running** as fast as he can.

The <u>house</u> at the end of the block **belongs** to the Meyers.

The <u>research teams</u> **hope** to make a medical breakthrough.

Sometimes fragments contain a **subject** and a **verb,** but they are dependent clauses. When a fragment is incorrectly separated from an independent clause, either the dependent clause must be made into a complete sentence or the dependent clause must be attached to an independent clause.

Fragment (dependent clause):	Because I studied so hard last night.
Independent clause:	I studied so hard last night.
Combined clauses:	Because I studied so hard last night, I easily passed my exam.

Fragment (dependent clause):	After the rain started.
Independent clause:	The rain started.
Combined clauses:	After the rain started, the roads became slippery.

ACTIVITY 14   Identifying Fragments

Identify each item below as a sentence (*S*) or a fragment (*F*).

_____ **1.** Jason went to the store and bought onions.

_____ Not realizing at the time that he needed ginger as well.

_____ **2.** Making her decision carefully.

_____ Pamela ordered two cups of coffee.

_____ Hoping her friend would arrive on time.

_____ **3.** We will first take the children to the zoo, and then we will go to dinner.

_____ **4.** As summer vacation comes closer, I find myself planning a trip to the Caribbean.

_____ To think about this makes me happy.

_____ **5.** I cannot believe what Sheila did, and I am not happy about it!

_____ **6.** I still love my old pony.

_____ Although it does not run that fast.

_____ **7.** With my father nearby, I reached for the broom.

_____ Leaning over too far caused me to fall.

_____ **8.** They were all having a good time.

_____ Even the grown-ups.

ACTIVITY 15   Correcting Fragments

Rewrite four of the fragments from Activity 14 so that they are complete sentences.

a. _____

_____

b. _____

_____

c. _____

_____

d. _____

_____

ACTIVITY 16 Identifying and Correcting Fragments

Read this paragraph. Underline the one fragment. On the lines below the paragraph, rewrite the fragment to make it a complete sentence.

Paragraph 12

The café plays an important role in the daily life of French people. Students go there at any time of day not only to have something to eat or drink but also to relax, to read the paper, or to listen to music. Since many students live quite a distance from the university and since the existing libraries are often overcrowded. The café also offers a place to study. For many young people, the café is the ideal spot to meet one's friends or to strike up a casual conversation with other students. Most French cafés are divided into two parts: the inside section and the terrace, which extends onto the sidewalk. In spring and summer, most customers prefer the terrace, where they can enjoy the good weather and observe the people walking by.

_____

_____

ACTIVITY 17 Identifying and Correcting Fragments

Read this paragraph. Underline the two fragments. On the lines below the paragraph, rewrite the fragments to make them complete sentences.

Paragraph 13

I read two books on business communication. The first book, *Effective Business Communication,* is an essential resource on business correspondence for the modern office. In today's business climate, revolutionized by electronic mail and overnight package delivery. It is important to communicate clearly and precisely in writing. *Effective Business Communication* offers sound advice for business writers; it is comprehensive yet concise. The second book is *Business Writing for Today.* Also claims to be an essential source on business correspondence for today's business world. However, this book is not as well written or as comprehensive. *Business Writing for Today* discusses a few aspects of e-mail that are not covered in *Effective Business Communication.* The authors then move on to samples of business correspondence, but these samples lack any information about the senders' reasons for writing these letters. Therefore, it is my opinion that *Effective Business Communication* would certainly be a more valuable resource guide to have in the office than *Business Writing for Today.*

1. _____

_____

2. _____

_____

Read this paragraph. Underline the two fragments. On the lines below the paragraph, rewrite the fragments to make them complete sentences.

Paragraph 14

> French is widely spoken in Africa. The use of French as a common language is a factor of national integration and cohesion. Where different ethnic groups have traditionally spoken different languages. Twenty African countries use French as their official language. Among the most important French-speaking countries in Africa are Madagascar, Zaire, Senegal, Mali, and Ivory Coast. Formerly French or Belgian colonies. These countries became independent nations in the early 1960s. French is also spoken by large segments of the population in the northern African countries of Morocco, Algeria, and Tunisia.

1. _____

   _____

2. _____

   _____

What Is a Run-on?

A **run-on sentence** is an error in which a sentence lacks the necessary structure to link its ideas together. Typically, a run-on sentence contains two independent clauses incorrectly linked to each another. You might think of a run-on sentence as a wreck in which two sentences have crashed together.

ACTIVITY 19 Identifying Run-on Problems

Identify each of these sentences as a run-on sentence (*RO*) or a complete sentence (*CS*).

_____ **1.** Sheryl always told me not to trust a salesperson like that if only I had listened to her everything would have been fine.

_____ **2.** It takes a long time to knit someone a sweater, but it is a wonderful feeling to give someone a gift that is truly a labor of love.

_____ **3.** The Roman troops in England faced many almost insurmountable difficulties, including disease, hunger, and learning about the new environment.

_____ **4.** The cat gets hungry around 3 p.m. make sure you are there to feed it.

_____ **5.** It is amazing to me that I still watch such childish TV shows as I did when I was a kid, but I really do enjoy them.

_____ **6.** Chaucer is known as the "Father of the English Language" he wrote *The Canterbury Tales*.

_____ **7.** The capital city of Malaysia is Kuala Lumpur, but the seat of the nation's government is in Putrajaya.

_____ **8.** We cannot get a taxi because of the rain if we cannot get a taxi we will miss our plane.

ACTIVITY 20 · Correcting Run-on Problems

Rewrite the four run-on sentences from Activity 19 so that they are correct sentences.

a. _____

_____

b. _____

_____

c. _____

_____

d. _____

_____

ACTIVITY 21 · Identifying and Correcting Run-on Problems

Read this paragraph about a well-known author. Underline the two run-ons. On the lines below the paragraph, rewrite the run-on sentences so that they are correct sentences.

Paragraph 15

Carson McCullers left behind an impressive literary legacy, she died at the age of 50 in 1967. Her work included five novels, two plays, 20 short stories, some two dozen nonfiction pieces, a book of children's verse, and a handful of distinguished poems. Her most acclaimed fiction appeared in the 1940s. McCullers was taken for an exceptional writer at the age of just 23. That was when she published *The Heart Is a Lonely Hunter* (1940), which is set in a small Southern mill town resembling Columbus, Georgia, where she was born on February 19, 1917. People loved this novel, the novel accurately reflects the author's culture and is her most autobiographical tale.

1. _____

_____

2. _____

_____

What Is a Comma Splice?

A **comma splice** is a special kind of run-on sentence in which two independent clauses are joined by a comma. Unfortunately, a comma is not strong enough for this task. Independent clauses must be joined by a semicolon or by a comma and a conjunction.

ACTIVITY 22 Identifying Comma Splice Problems

Identify each as a sentence (*S*) or a comma splice (*CS*).

_____ 1. It is really hot outside today, let's go swimming.

_____ 2. Patsy asked me to join her, and I said that I would.

_____ 3. The jury returned a guilty verdict; the defendant sobbed.

_____ 4. On that TV program, Jack Wallace is Chuck Smith's next door neighbor, this show is about how Jack annoys Chuck all the time.

_____ 5. Cell phones are becoming increasingly popular, and land lines will likely become less and less popular.

_____ 6. My little sister is always cajoling me to help her with her homework, but I encourage her to do it on her own.

_____ 7. My friend Harry will never go to a movie by himself, I go to movies by myself all the time.

_____ 8. I enjoy cooking a lot, seafood is my favorite cuisine.

ACTIVITY 23 Correcting Comma Splice Problems

Rewrite the four comma splices from Activity 22 so that they are correct sentences.

a. _____

_____

b. _____

_____

c. _____

_____

d. _____

_____

Preposition Combinations

Verb + Preposition Combinations

Verb + Preposition			
account for	complain about	hope for	stop from
agree on	comply with	listen to	substitute for
agree with	consist of	look at	talk to
apply for	count on	look for	think about
approve of	depend on	pay for	think of
belong to	hear about	rely on	wait for
care about	hear from	stare at	work on

Adjective + Preposition Combinations

Adjective + Preposition			
accustomed to	connected to / with	famous for	responsible for
acquainted with	delighted at / about	frustrated with	satisfied with
afraid of	dependent on	guilty of	serious about
answerable to	different from	interested in	similar to
attached to	disappointed with / in / by	opposed to	suitable for
aware of	doubtful about	pleased with	suspicious of
bad at	enthusiastic about	popular with	typical of
bored with	envious of	proud of	used to (= accustomed to)
capable of	excited about	related to	

Noun + Preposition Combinations

Noun + Preposition			
advantage of	demand for	invitation to	price of
application for	difference between	lack of	reason for
benefit of	difficulty with	matter with	reply to
cause of	example of	need for	request for
cost of	increase / decrease in, of	opinion of	solution to
decision to	interest in	order for	trouble with

Word Parts (Suffixes)

Studying word parts will help you figure out the meaning of new words and increase your academic vocabulary.

Adjective Endings

Ending	Meaning	Examples
-able / -ible	able to	lik<u>able</u>, flex<u>ible</u>
-al	having the quality of	option<u>al</u>, origin<u>al</u>
-ant	having the quality of	pleas<u>ant</u>, result<u>ant</u>
-ar / -ary	related to	muscul<u>ar</u>, culin<u>ary</u>
-ed	past participle	delight<u>ed</u>, surpris<u>ed</u>
-en	made of	gold<u>en</u>, wood<u>en</u>
-ent	having the quality of	appar<u>ent</u>, insist<u>ent</u>
-esque	in the style of	grot<u>esque</u>, pictur<u>esque</u>
-ful	full of	care<u>ful</u>, mind<u>ful</u>
-ing	present participle	amaz<u>ing</u>, distress<u>ing</u>
-ive	tending to	creat<u>ive</u>, destruct<u>ive</u>
-less	without	aim<u>less</u>, hope<u>less</u>
-like	like, similar to	child<u>like</u>, lady<u>like</u>
-ly	having the quality of	friend<u>ly</u>, man<u>ly</u>
-ory	related to	obligat<u>ory</u>, sens<u>ory</u>
-ous / -ious	full of	fam<u>ous</u>, relig<u>ious</u>
-proof	protected from	fire<u>proof</u>, water<u>proof</u>
-ward	in the direction of	back<u>ward</u>, down<u>ward</u>
-y	related to	laz<u>y</u>, wind<u>y</u>

Noun Endings

Ending	Meaning	Examples
-an / -ian	person related to	Americ<u>an</u>, guard<u>ian</u>
-ance / -ence	condition, state	relev<u>ance</u>, exist<u>ence</u>
-ant / -ent	person who	entr<u>ant</u>, stud<u>ent</u>
-ation	action, state	imagin<u>ation</u>, explan<u>ation</u>
-ee	person who receives something	less<u>ee</u>, trust<u>ee</u>
-er / -or	person who does	bak<u>er</u>, sail<u>or</u>
-ese	person related to	Japan<u>ese</u>, Taiwan<u>ese</u>
-hood	state of	neighbor<u>hood</u>, child<u>hood</u>

Ending	Meaning	Examples
-ics	science, art, or practice	physics, statistics
-ing	gerund (action)	dancing, reading
-ion / -sion / -tion	action, state, result	union, conclusion, reaction
-ist	person who believes or does	communist, typist
-ment	result of action	document, placement
-ness	quality, state	friendliness, trustworthiness
-ship	condition, quality	friendship, leadership
-ty / -ity	quality, condition	density, equality

Verb Endings

Ending	Meaning	Examples
-ate	cause, make	calculate, demonstrate
-en	cause to become	fatten, shorten
-ify	make	clarify, terrify
-ize	make	demonize, plagiarize

Adverb Endings

Ending	Meaning	Examples
-ly	manner of	carefully, unequivocally

Examples of Word Forms across Parts of Speech

Noun	Verb	Adjective	Adverb
benefit	benefit	beneficial	beneficially
care	care	careful, caring	carefully, caringly
difference	differ	different	differently
education	educate	educational	educationally
imagination	imagine	imaginative	imaginatively
persuasion	persuade	persuasive	persuasively
temptation	tempt	tempting	temptingly

Additional Grammar Activities

ACTIVITY 24 Prepositions

Circle the correct preposition in each set of parentheses.

Paragraph 16

1 (In / On) 1812, a collection of fairy tales, or folktales, was published. These stories became very popular not only 2 (at / in) Germany but also throughout Europe and America. The brothers Jacob and Wilhelm Grimm collected the stories during a period that was characterized 3 (by / for) a great interest 4 (for / in) German folklore. Whatever the historical background of the stories, they have long been a part 5 (in / of) childhood experience. Children identify 6 (for / with) the hero, suffer through the inevitable trials and tribulations, and experience relief and triumph when virtue is finally rewarded. Fairy tales are not only 7 (for / to) children, however. Today, a fairy-tale society, founded 8 (at / in) 1956 in Germany, has more than 600 members from all over Europe. Scholars publish books 9 (on / through) fairy-tale motifs and use fairy tales as a source 10 (of / on) information 11 (about / for) life and values 12 (in / on) different times and cultures.

ACTIVITY 25 Verb Tenses

Circle the correct verb tense in each set of parentheses.

Paragraph 17

Carson McCullers left behind an impressive literary legacy when she 1 (has died / died) at the age of 50 in 1967: five novels, two plays, 20 short stories, two dozen nonfiction pieces, a book of children's verse, and a handful of distinguished poems. Her most acclaimed fiction 2 (appears / appeared) in the 1940s. McCullers was taken for an exceptional writer when she 3 (publishes / published) *The Heart Is a Lonely Hunter* (1940) at age 23. This work 4 (is / has) set in a small Southern mill town resembling Columbus, Georgia, where she was born Lula Carson Smith on February 19, 1917. The novel 5 (reflects / reflected) the author's culture and 6 (is / will be) her most autobiographical tale.

ACTIVITY 26 Editing for Specific Errors

Find these 12 errors and underline them: word form (4), verb tense (3), subject-verb agreement (1), preposition (2), and article (2). Then write the corrections above the errors.

Paragraph 18

Johann Wolfgang von Goethe (1749–1832) was universal genius. He was a poem, novelist, dramatist, public administrator, and scientist. He had made significant contributions for the fields of optics, comparative anatomy, and plant morphology. The collected works of this prolific writer appear in 60 volumes before his death. Goethe is one of the greatest lyric poets, and his poetry are read and studied today. Modern theaters present his dramatic. His most famous single work is *Faust*, on which he works his entire lifetime; he published the Part 1 in 1808 and Part 2 in 1832. Early in his career, Goethe was already recognition both in Germany and abroad as one of the great figures of world literary. He can confidently hold his place with the select group from Homer, Dante, and Shakespeare.

ACTIVITY 27 Editing for Specific Errors

Find these five errors and underline them: subject-verb agreement (2), articles (2), and word form (1). Then write the corrections above the errors.

Paragraph 19

What is the story behind the origin of the word *asparagus*? This vegetable name have a very bizarre history. The word *asparagus* means "sparrow grass." What possibility connection could there be between a sparrow, which is name of a beautiful little brown bird, and this vegetable? In former times, the people were served asparagus accompanied by cooked sparrows! Because this green, grasslike vegetable were served with little sparrows, it became known as "sparrow grass" or asparagus.

ACTIVITY 28 **Prepositions**

Circle the correct preposition in each set of parentheses.

Paragraph 20

Chaucer is quite possibly the greatest writer **1** (at / of / on) English literature. Relatively little is known **2** (about / by / to) his early life. He came **3** (by / from / at) a well-to-do merchant family that had lived **4** (at / for / without) several generations in Ipswich, some 70 miles northeast of London. No school records **5** (at / by / of) Chaucer have survived. The earliest known document that names Geoffrey Chaucer is a fragmentary household account book dated between 1356 and 1359. Chaucer is best known **6** (for / like / since) his collection of stories called *The Canterbury Tales*, but this collection **7** (at / of / with) stories is unfinished.

ACTIVITY 29 **Editing Specific Errors**

Five of the eight underlined sections contain errors. Write the corrections above the errors or write *C* (correct) in the space provided.

Paragraph 21

You put ketchup on french fries and other foods all the time, but did you ever stop to ask yourself **1** where this word did come ____ from? Our English word *ketchup* is from the Chinese word *ke-tsiap*. The Chinese created this great food product in the late seventeenth century. Soon afterward, British explorers **2** come ____ across ketchup in nearby Malaysia and brought it back to the Western world. Fifty years later, this sauce became popular in the American colonies. Around this time, people realized that tomatoes enhanced **3** flavor ____ of this sauce, so tomatoes were **4** routinely added ____ to ketchup, and red became the **5** normally ____ color for this sauce. Oddly enough, ketchup did not **6** contains ____ any tomatoes until the 1790s **7** because there was a mistaken presumption that tomatoes were poisonous! ____ Thus, our English word *ketchup* comes from the Chinese name for their original sauce, which was neither red **8** nor ____ tomato-based.

ACTIVITY 30 Editing Specific Errors

Find these five errors and underline them: number (1), verb tense (1), comma splice (1), and preposition (2). Then write the corrections above the errors.

One of the most brilliant composer that the world has ever seen, Franz Schubert (1797–1828), was born in Vienna and lived there until his death. He wrote his first composition in the age of 13 and writes his first symphony at the age of 16. Like Mozart, Schubert was a prolific composer. His list of 998 extant works includes seven masses, nine symphonies, numerous piano pieces, and 606 songs, in a single year, 1815, at the age of 18, he wrote 140 songs. Only a few of Schubert's works were published in his lifetime. He did not profit much from those that he did sell. Like Mozart, he suffered for periods of poverty.

ACTIVITY 31 Editing Specific Errors

Five of the eight underlined selections contain errors. Write the corrections above the errors or write C (correct) in the space provided.

For centuries, **1** the French universities ____ catered only to the educational needs of the students, and their buildings were exclusively academic ones. As the number of university students increased— **2** more than ____ sevenfold between 1950 and 1989—student residences were added. **3** In many part of France, ____ the newer city universities were built **4** in the suburbs, ____ where land **5** were less expensive, ____ while the academic buildings remained in the center of town. In Paris, **6** for the example, ____ the city university **7** is location ____ several miles from the academic Latin Quarter. This creates a serious transportation problem **8** for the students, ____ who must commute long distances.

Academic Word List

Averil Coxhead (2000)

The following words are on the Academic Word List (AWL). The AWL is a list of the 570 highest-frequency academic word families that regularly appear in academic texts. The AWL was compiled by researcher Averil Coxhead based on her analysis of a 3.5 million-word corpus. A form of the 345 words that are blue appear in the essays in *Great Writing 5: From Great Essays to Research*.

abandon	attitude	comprise	cycle	energy	foundation
abstract	attribute	compute	data	enforce	framework
academy	author	conceive	debate	enhance	function
access	authority	concentrate	decade	enormous	fund
accommodate	automate	concept	decline	ensure	fundamental
accompany	available	conclude	deduce	entity	furthermore
accumulate	aware	concurrent	define	environment	gender
accurate	behalf	conduct	definite	equate	generate
achieve	benefit	confer	demonstrate	equip	generation
acknowledge	bias	confine	denote	equivalent	globe
acquire	bond	confirm	deny	erode	goal
adapt	brief	conflict	depress	error	grade
adequate	bulk	conform	derive	establish	grant
adjacent	capable	consent	design	estate	guarantee
adjust	capacity	consequent	despite	estimate	guideline
administrate	category	considerable	detect	ethic	hence
adult	cease	consist	deviate	ethnic	hierarchy
advocate	challenge	constant	device	evaluate	highlight
affect	channel	constitute	devote	eventual	hypothesis
aggregate	chapter	constrain	differentiate	evident	identical
aid	chart	construct	dimension	evolve	identify
albeit	chemical	consult	diminish	exceed	ideology
allocate	circumstance	consume	discrete	exclude	ignorant
alter	cite	contact	discriminate	exhibit	illustrate
alternative	civil	contemporary	displace	expand	image
ambiguous	clarify	context	display	expert	immigrate
amend	classic	contract	dispose	explicit	impact
analogy	clause	contradict	distinct	exploit	implement
analyze	code	contrary	distort	export	implicate
annual	coherent	contrast	distribute	expose	implicit
anticipate	coincide	contribute	diverse	external	imply
apparent	collapse	controversy	document	extract	impose
append	colleague	convene	domain	facilitate	incentive
appreciate	commence	converse	domestic	factor	incidence
approach	comment	convert	dominate	feature	incline
appropriate	commission	convince	draft	federal	income
approximate	commit	cooperate	drama	fee	incorporate
arbitrary	commodity	coordinate	duration	file	index
area	communicate	core	dynamic	final	indicate
aspect	community	corporate	economy	finance	individual
assemble	compatible	correspond	edit	finite	induce
assess	compensate	couple	element	flexible	inevitable
assign	compile	create	eliminate	fluctuate	infer
assist	complement	credit	emerge	focus	infrastructure
assume	complex	criteria	emphasis	format	inherent
assure	component	crucial	empirical	formula	inhibit
attach	compound	culture	enable	forthcoming	initial
attain	comprehensive	currency	encounter	found	initiate

injure	margin	panel	publish	sector	technology
innovate	mature	paradigm	purchase	secure	temporary
input	maximize	paragraph	pursue	seek	tense
insert	mechanism	parallel	qualitative	select	terminate
insight	media	parameter	quote	sequence	text
inspect	mediate	participate	radical	series	theme
instance	medical	partner	random	sex	theory
institute	medium	passive	range	shift	thereby
instruct	mental	perceive	ratio	significant	thesis
integral	method	percent	rational	similar	topic
integrate	migrate	period	react	simulate	trace
integrity	military	persist	recover	site	tradition
intelligent	minimal	perspective	refine	so-called	transfer
intense	minimize	phase	regime	sole	transform
interact	minimum	phenomenon	region	somewhat	transit
intermediate	ministry	philosophy	register	source	transmit
internal	minor	physical	regulate	specific	transport
interpret	mode	plus	reinforce	specify	trend
interval	modify	policy	reject	sphere	trigger
intervene	monitor	portion	relax	stable	ultimate
intrinsic	motive	pose	release	statistic	undergo
invest	mutual	positive	relevant	status	underlie
investigate	negate	potential	reluctance	straightforward	undertake
invoke	network	practitioner	rely	strategy	uniform
involve	neutral	precede	remove	stress	unify
isolate	nevertheless	precise	require	structure	unique
issue	nonetheless	predict	research	style	utilize
item	norm	predominant	reside	submit	valid
job	normal	preliminary	resolve	subordinate	vary
journal	notion	presume	resource	subsequent	vehicle
justify	notwithstand-	previous	respond	subsidy	version
label	ing	primary	restore	substitute	via
labor	nuclear	prime	restrain	successor	violate
layer	objective	principal	restrict	sufficient	virtual
lecture	obtain	principle	retain	sum	visible
legal	obvious	prior	reveal	summary	vision
legislate	occupy	priority	revenue	supplement	visual
levy	occur	proceed	reverse	survey	volume
liberal	odd	process	revise	survive	voluntary
license	offset	professional	revolution	suspend	welfare
likewise	ongoing	prohibit	rigid	sustain	whereas
link	option	project	role	symbol	whereby
locate	orient	promote	route	tape	widespread
logic	outcome	proportion	scenario	target	
maintain	output	prospect	schedule	task	
major	overall	protocol	scheme	team	
manipulate	overlap	psychology	scope	technical	
manual	overseas	publication	section	technique	

Useful Vocabulary for Better Writing

Try these useful words and phrases as you write your essays. Many of these are found in the models in *Great Writing 5: From Great Essays to Research*, and they can make your writing sound more academic, natural, and fluent.

Comparing

Words and Phrases	Examples
NOUN *is* COMPARATIVE ADJECTIVE *than* NOUN.	New York *is* larger *than* Rhode Island.
S + V + COMPARATIVE ADVERB *than* NOUN.	The cats ran faster *than* the dogs.
S + V. *In comparison,* S + V.	Canada has provinces. *In comparison,* Brazil has states.
Although NOUN *and* NOUN *are similar in* NOUN, …	*Although* France *and* Spain *are similar in* size, they are different in many ways.
Upon close inspection, S + V.	*Upon close inspection,* teachers in both schools discovered their students progressed faster when using games.
NOUN *and* NOUN *are surprisingly similar.*	Brazil *and* the United States *are surprisingly similar.*
The same…	Brazil has states. *The same* can be said about Mexico.
Like NOUN, NOUN *also…*	*Like* Brazil, Mexico *also* has states.
Compared to…	*Compared to* U.S. history, Chinese history is complicated.
Both NOUN *and* NOUN…	*Both* dictatorships *and* oligarchies exemplify non-democratic ideologies.
Also, S + V. / *Likewise,* S + V.	The economies in South America seem to be thriving. *Likewise,* some Asian markets are doing very well these days.
Similarly, S + V. / *Similar to* S + V.	The economies in South America seem to be thriving. *Similarly,* some Asian markets are doing very well these days.

Contrasting

Words and Phrases	Examples
S + V. *In contrast,* S + V.	Algeria is a very large country. *In contrast,* the U.A.E. is very small.
Contrasted with / *In contrast to* NOUN	*In contrast to* soda, water is a better alternative.
Although / *Even though* / *Though…*	*Although* Spain and France are similar in size, they are different in many other ways.
Unlike NOUN, NOUN…	*Unlike* Spain, France borders eight countries.
However, S + V.	Canada has provinces. *However,* Brazil has states.
On the one hand, S + V. *On the other hand,* S + V.	*On the one hand,* Maggie loved to travel. *On the other hand,* she hated to be away from her home.
S + V, *yet* S + V.	People know that eating sweets is not good for their health, *yet* they continue to eat more sugar and fat than ever before.
NOUN *and* NOUN *are surprisingly different.*	Finland *and* Iceland *are surprisingly different.*

Showing Cause and Effect

Words and Phrases	Examples
Because S + V / *Because of* S + V	*Because of* the traffic problems, it is easy to see why the city is building a new tunnel.
NOUN *can trigger* NOUN NOUN *can cause* NOUN	An earthquake *can trigger* tidal waves and *can cause* massive destruction.
Due to NOUN	*Due to* the economic sanctions, the unemployment rate skyrocketed.
On account of NOUN / *As a result of* NOUN / *Because of* NOUN	*On account of* the economic sanctions, the unemployment rate skyrocketed.
Therefore, S + V. / *As a result,* S + V. / *For this reason,* S + V. / *Consequently,* S + V.	Markets fell. *Therefore,* millions of people lost their life savings.
NOUN *will bring about* NOUN.	The use of the Internet *will bring about* a change in education.
NOUN *has had a positive / negative effect on* NOUN.	Computer technology *has had both positive and negative effects on* society.
The correlation… is clear / evident.	*The correlation* between junk food and obesity *is clear.*

Stating an Opinion

Words and Phrases	Examples
Without a doubt, doing NOUN *is* ADJECTIVE *idea / method / decision / way.*	*Without a doubt,* walking to work each day *is* an excellent *way* to lose weight.
Personally, I believe / think / feel / agree / disagree / suppose that NOUN . . .	*Personally, I believe that* using electronic devices on a plane should be allowed.
Doing NOUN *should not be allowed.*	Texting in class *should not be allowed.*
In my opinion / view / experience, S + V.	*In my opinion,* talking on a cell phone in a movie theater is extremely rude.
For this reason, S + V. / *That is why I think* S + V.	*For this reason,* voters should not pass this law.
There are many benefits / advantages to NOUN.	*There are many benefits to* swimming every day.
There are many drawbacks / disadvantages to NOUN.	*There are many drawbacks to* eating meals at a restaurant.
I am convinced that S + V.	*I am convinced that* nuclear energy is safe and energy efficient.
NOUN *should be required / mandatory.*	Art education *should be required* of all high school students.
I prefer NOUN *to* NOUN.	*I prefer* rugby *to* football.
To me, banning / prohibiting NOUN *makes sense.*	*To me, banning* cell phones while driving *makes sense.*
For all of these important reasons, S + V.	*For all of these important reasons,* cell phones in schools should be banned.
Based on NOUN, S + V.	*Based on* the facts presented, high-fat foods should be banned from the cafeteria.

Arguing and Persuading

Words and Phrases	Examples
It is important to remember that S + V.	*It is important to remember that* school uniforms would only be worn during school hours.
According to a recent survey, S + V.	*According to a recent survey,* 85 percent of high school students felt they had too much homework.
Even more important, S + V.	*Even more important,* statistics show the positive effects that school uniforms have on behavior.
Despite this, S + V.	*Despite this,* many people remain opposed to school uniforms.
S *must / should / ought to* V.	Researchers *must* stop unethical animal testing.
For these reasons, S + V.	*For these reasons,* public schools should require uniforms.
Obviously, S + V.	*Obviously,* citizens will get used to this new law.
Without a doubt, S + V.	*Without a doubt,* students ought to learn a foreign language.
I agree that S + V; *however,* S + V.	*I agree that* a college degree is important; *however,* getting a practical technical license can also be very useful.

Giving a Counterargument

Words and Phrases	Examples
Proponents / Opponents may say S + V.	*Opponents* of uniforms *may say* that students who wear uniforms cannot express their individuality.
On the surface this might seem logical / smart / correct; however, S + V.	*On the surface this might seem logical; however,* it is not an affordable solution.
S + V; *however, this is not the case.*	The students could attend classes in the evening; *however, this is not the case.*
One could argue that S + V, *but* S + V.	*One could argue that* working for a small company is very exciting, *but* it can also be more stressful than a job in a large company.
It would be wrong to say that S + V.	*It would be wrong to say that* nuclear energy is 100 percent safe.
Some people believe that S + V.	*Some people believe that* nuclear energy is the way of the future.
Upon further investigation, S + V.	*Upon further investigation,* one begins to see problems with this line of thinking.
However, I cannot agree with this idea.	Some people think logging should be banned. *However, I cannot agree with this idea.*
Some people may say (one opinion), *but I* (opposite opinion).	*Some people may say* that working from home is lonely, *but I* believe that working from home is easy, productive, and rewarding.
While NOUN *has its merits,* NOUN…	*While* working outside the home *has its merits,* working from home has many more benefits.
Although it is true that…, S + V.	*Although it is true that* taking online classes can be convenient, it is difficult for many students to stay on task.

Reacting/Responding

Words and Phrases	Examples
TITLE *by* AUTHOR *is a / an …*	*Harry Potter and the Goblet of Fire by* J.K. Rowling *is an* entertaining book to read.
My first reaction to the prompt / news / article was / is NOUN.	*My first reaction to the article was* fear.
When I read / look at / think about NOUN, *I was amazed / shocked / surprised …*	*When I read* the article, *I was surprised* to learn of his athletic ability.

Telling a Story/Narrating

Words and Phrases	Examples
When I was NOUN / ADJ, *I would* VERB.	*When I was* a child, *I would* go fishing every weekend.
I had never felt so ADJ *in my life.*	*I had never felt so* anxious *in my life.*
I never would have thought that …	*I never would have thought that* I could win the competition.
Then the most amazing thing happened.	I thought my bag was gone forever. *Then the most amazing thing happened.*
Whenever I think back to that time, …	*Whenever I think back to that time,* I am moved by my grandparents' love for me.
I will never forget NOUN.	*I will never forget* my wedding day.
I can still remember NOUN. / *I will always remember* NOUN.	*I can still remember* the day I started my first job.
NOUN *was the best / worst day of my life.*	The day I caught that fish *was the best day of my life.*
Every time S + V, S + V.	*Every time* I used that computer, I had a problem.
This was my first NOUN.	*This was my first* time traveling alone.

Appendix

Appendix

Building Better Sentences

Being a good writer involves many skills, such as being able to use correct grammar, vary vocabulary usage, and state ideas concisely. Some student writers like to keep their sentences simple because they feel that if they create longer and more complicated sentences, they are more likely to make mistakes. However, writing short, choppy sentences one after the other is not considered appropriate in academic writing. Study these examples:

The time was yesterday.

It was afternoon.

There was a storm.

The storm was strong.

The movement of the storm was quick.

The storm moved towards the coast.

The coast was in North Carolina.

Notice that every sentence has an important piece of information. A good writer would not write all these sentences separately. Instead, the most important information from each sentence can be used to create one longer, coherent sentence.

Read the sentences again below and notice that the important information has been circled.

The time was (yesterday.)

It was (afternoon.)

There was a (storm.)

The storm was (strong.)

The (movement) of the storm was (quick.)

The storm moved towards the (coast.)

The coast was in (North Carolina.)

Here are some strategies for taking the circled information and creating a new sentence.

1. Create time phrases to introduce or end a sentence: yesterday + afternoon
2. Find the key noun: storm
3. Find key adjectives: strong
4. Create noun phrases: a strong + storm
5. Change word forms: movement = move; quick = quickly; moved = quickly
6. Create prepositional phrases: towards the coast

> towards the coast (of North Carolina)
>
> or
>
> towards the North Carolina coast

Now read this improved, longer sentence:

Yesterday afternoon, a strong storm moved quickly towards the North Carolina coast.

Here are some more strategies for building better sentences:

7. Use coordinating conjunctions (*and, but, or, nor, yet, for, so*) to connect two sets of ideas.

8. Use subordinating conjunctions, such as *after, while, since,* and *because,* to connect related ideas.

9. Use clauses with relative pronouns, such as *who, which, that,* and *whose,* to describe or define a noun or noun phrase.

10. Use pronouns to refer to previously mentioned information.

11. Use possessive adjectives and pronouns, such as *my, her, his, ours,* and *theirs.*

   Study the following example with the important information circled.

   (Susan) (went) somewhere. That place was (the mall.) Susan wanted to (buy new shoes.) The shoes were for (Susan's mother.)

   Now read the improved, longer sentence:

   Susan went to the mall because she wanted to buy new shoes for her mother.

Practices

This section contains practices for essays in Units 4–7. Follow these steps for each practice:

1. Read the sentences. Circle the most important information in each sentence.

2. Write an original sentence from the information you circled. Use the strategies listed on page 237 and this page.

3. Compare your sentences with a partner's to see how the sentences you have built are alike and different.

Practice 1, Unit 4, "How to Succeed in a Job Interview"

A. 1. (Applicants should research the company.)

  2. Applicants should (learn) about the company.

  3. Applicants learn (as much as possible.)

    Applicants should research the company and learn as much about it as possible.

_____

B. 1. Applicants must recognize that the interviewer wants to learn about them.

  2. Applicants should give answers to the questions.

  3. These answers are full.

  4. These answers are detailed.

  5. These answers are unique.

_____

_____

C. 1. In the end, an interview can improve a person's prospects.

   2. These prospects are for the future.

   3. The interview is successful.

   4. The interview is for a job.

   5. This improvement can happen by promoting opportunities.

   6. These opportunities are for employment and future advancement.

_____

_____

Practice 2, Unit 5, "Online and Face-to-Face Learning in the Digital Age"

A. 1. It is often impossible for many students to say anything.

   2. This happens in large classrooms.

   3. These classrooms have fifty or more students.

   4. This happens because the room is big.

   5. This happens because not everyone can hear other students well.

_____

_____

B. 1. Many classes require laboratories.

   2. In these laboratories students conduct experiments.

   3. Drama classes allow students to perform.

   4. These students perform plays.

_____

_____

C. 1. Teachers cannot comment on a student's punctuality.

   2. Teachers cannot comment on a student's presentations before a group.

   3. Teachers cannot comment on a student's interpersonal skills.

   4. These teachers teach online courses.

   5. Teachers' inability to comment on these three areas is due to the online environment.

_____

_____

Practice 3, Unit 6, "How Weather Has Changed World History"

A. 1. It is tempting to think that humans control their fates.

   2. It is often comforting to think that humans control their fates.

_____

_____

B. 1. It appeared likely that the British would crush the armies.

    2. These armies were of her territory.

    3. The territory was colonial.

    4. This happened in the early years of America's Revolutionary War.

    5. This war began in 1775.

_____

_____

C. 1. Napoleon Bonaparte met with early successes.

    2. These successes appeared to guarantee that Napoleon Bonaparte might eventually rule the world.

    3. These successes happened when Napoleon Bonaparte invaded Russia.

    4. This invasion took place in the early nineteenth century.

_____

_____

Practice 4, Unit 7, "The Best Classroom"

A. 1. Additionally, students benefit from studying.

    2. They are studying their academic discipline.

    3. They study their academic discipline from a perspective.

    4. This perspective is new.

_____

_____

B. 1. Studying abroad offers many advantages.

    2. Though studying abroad offers many advantages, some disagree.

    3. These people may argue that a semester abroad is nothing but a vacation.

    4. These people may argue that a year abroad is nothing but a vacation.

_____

_____

C. 1. Studying abroad contributes to students' education.

    2. It does this so effectively.

    3. One of the primary reasons for this is that studying abroad requires students to live and learn in a new culture.

    4. This culture is different from students' upbringing.

_____

_____

Index